Aeroplanes of The Royal Aircraft Factory

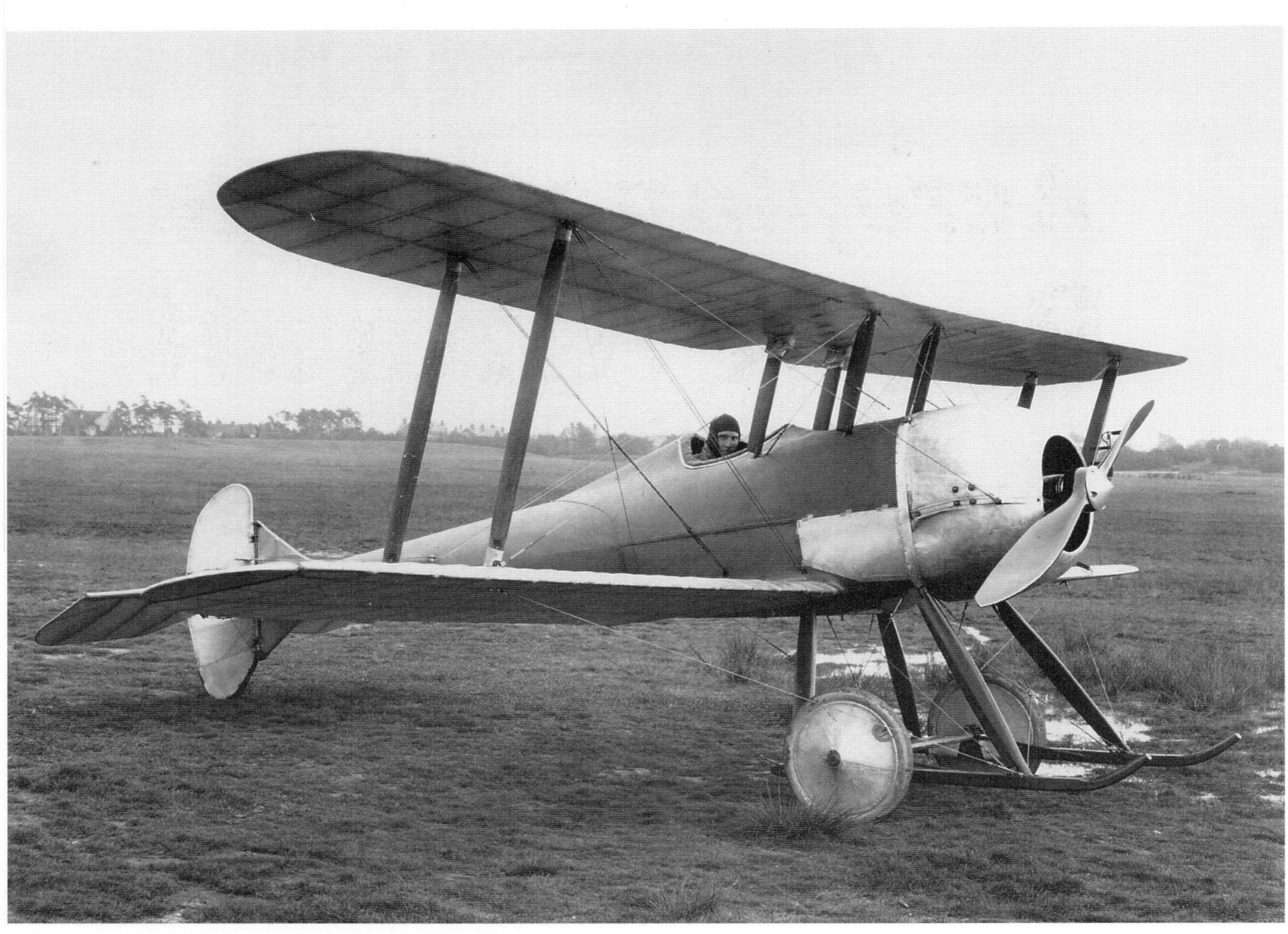

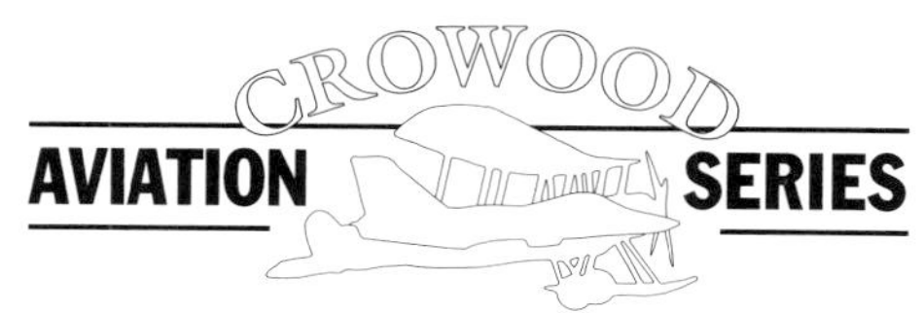

Aeroplanes of the Royal Aircraft Factory

Paul R. Hare

The Crowood Press

First published in 1999 by
The Crowood Press Ltd
Ramsbury, Marlborough
Wiltshire SN8 2HR

British Library Cataloguing-in-Publication Data
A catalogue record for this book is available from the British Library.

ISBN 1 86126 209 4

Photograph previous page: The Royal Aircraft Factory's S.E.2, built in 1913.

Dedication
This book is dedicated to my wife, Linda, for her patience and support.

Typefaces used: Goudy (*text*), Cheltenham (*headings*)

Typeset and designed by
D & N Publishing
Membury Business Park, Lambourn Woodlands
Hungerford, Berkshire.

Printed and bound by Redwood Books, Trowbridge

Contents

Introduction

Were you to ask a group of World War I aviation enthusiasts to name the best British fighter of that war, opinion would probably be divided. Some would, undoubtedly, say the Sopwith Camel, while others would cite the S.E.5a. Ask those same experts to name the worst aeroplane of World War I and the answer would, almost invariably, be unanimous, with all of them choosing the B.E.2c.

Both of these latter aeroplanes, allegedly the best and the worst, as well as several more of the most widely used types which served in that war, were products of the same design facility, the Royal Aircraft Factory at Farnborough, ancestor of the Royal Aircraft Establishment and of today's Defence Evaluation and Research Agency, which is justly renowned worldwide. However, the Royal Aircraft Factory never enjoyed its successor's good reputation, due to the work of a small group of opponents.

Private aircraft manufacturers saw it as a threat to their business; some campaigned against its existence, while a few Members of Parliament, together with the editor of a leading aviation magazine, never missed an opportunity to attack it, and so prejudice opinion against it and its designs. Yet, by gathering together a group of clever scientists, gifted engineers and talented designers it produced numerous ideas that were both original and innovative, and introduced a number of design 'firsts' that were copied worldwide. For example, the Royal Aircraft Factory team produced the first tractor 'scout', the B.S.1, with single bay bracing to its wings; the first 'fighter' specifically designed to be armed with a machine-gun, and invented the streamlined bracing wire. However, it was the subject of several government enquiries and, following the allegation made against it, a judicial review, each of which redefined its role, decimated its staff, and further tarnished its reputation. Thus it has gone down in history with derision and doubt masking its true achievements, and has been remembered for its few failures rather than its many successes. That from it should develop the widely recognized and internationally renowned Royal Aircraft Establishment at Farnborough, today succeeded by the equally well regarded DERA, is similarly demonstrative of its firm foundation in engineering excellence. Without the Royal Aircraft Factory the evolution of the Royal Flying Corps would, inevitably, have been greatly retarded.

CHAPTER ONE

Early History

The establishment which later became the Royal Aircraft Factory started out as a small, almost unofficial, unit set up to manufacture and operate hydrogen-filled balloons for the British Army, and only came into being after the military value of aerial observation had been demonstrated by other nations.

The successful deployment of observation balloons by the Union forces during the American Civil War (1861–65) prompted the British Army in 1863 to carry out a few experimental ascents using a coal-gas balloon hired from a civilian aeronaut, Henry Coxwell. Although these clearly demonstrated the military value of this kind of aerial reconnaissance, it was eventually decided that the British Army had no need of such equipment in times of peace. The Franco-Prussian war of 1870, in which balloons were employed by the besieged Parisians both for message carrying and observation, once again focused attention upon aerial warfare.

Finally, in 1878, authority was given for the construction of an experimental military observation balloon, under the direction of Maj James. L.B. Templer of the Middlesex Militia who was a keen amateur balloonist. This balloon, aptly named 'Pioneer', was an immediate success, and further funding was made available so that additional balloons could be built, and trials conducted with them.

In 1885 balloon detachments accompanied expeditionary forces to both Bechuanaland and the Sudan, thereby placing a severe strain upon the limited resources of the Balloon Equipment Store, as the unit was then known, and so the following year a School of Ballooning was established at Lidsing to train more soldiers in balloon handling. In 1887 Maj Templer was officially appointed 'Instructor in Ballooning' at a salary of £600 per annum, for as a member of the Militia, rather than the regular Army, he could be treated as either a soldier or a civilian, to suit the needs of the moment.

The 1889 summer manoeuvres again demonstrated the balloon's advantages, and led to the proposal that the Balloon Establishment should move to Aldershot so that it would be closer to the Army's main training area. The War Office eventually agreed to the move, and in 1890 the Balloon Section was formally recognized as a unit of the Corps of Royal Engineers. This unit continued to expand, so that by 1897 a further reorganization became necessary and the Balloon School and Balloon Factory were separated, with Templer being appointed to the newly created post of 'Superintendent of the Balloon Factory'. As such, his duties were concerned not only with the manufacture of balloons and their ancillary equipment, but with the development of military aeronautics generally.

In June 1903 a Committee was set up to enquire into the future of 'Military Ballooning' (as Army aviation was then generally known) and to decide where its future lay. The committee comprised three Army officers of field rank, (one of whom, Lt Col H.H. Wilson later became Field Marshal Sir Henry Wilson, Chief of the Imperial General Staff), a civilian from the War Office finance department, and, as secretary, Lt Col John E. Capper, Officer in Charge of the Balloon School.

Evidence was taken from officers who had served with the balloon sections during the recent war in South Africa, as well as two infantry generals, all of whom spoke favourably of aerial observation. In addition, comparisons were made between aeronautical progress in Britain and that in other countries, particularly France, Germany, the USA, Austria, Russia and Switzerland.

The committee's report, published in January 1904, recommended that the Army should have an airship, that the balloon sections should be re-formed into a more integrated unit, and that the Balloon Factory should be moved to a new, less constricted site where balloons could ascend more safely. However, the report was also rather critical of the Balloon Factory's management, and stated that the Factory should restrict its activities to those directly associated with aeronautics rather than carrying out odd jobs for the whole Army. The site eventually chosen for the relocation of the Balloon Factory was, of course, at Farnborough, where it and its successors were to remain for ninety years. The actual move, and the erection of a shed large enough to accommodate the proposed airship, took until early in 1906.

In the Autumn of 1904, Col J.E. Capper, Commandant of the Balloon School, visited the USA so that he could attend the St Louis 'World's Fair', held to celebrate the centenary of the Louisiana purchase, at which there was expected to be a large aeronautical exhibition. He also called upon a number of people who were then eminent in aviation, including Octave Chanute, Professor Langley and the Wright Brothers, who had, by then, made the World's first aeroplane flights. Capper's report on this visit spoke very favourably of the aeroplane's potential for military reconnaissance.

Also at this time the expatriate American showman, Samuel Franklin Cody, who had devised a new and highly stable man-lifting kite system, offered his kites to both the British Army and Navy. Separate trials were held by each Service, with Cody eventually being engaged by the Army and attached to the Balloon School at Aldershot. In April 1906, his position was formalized when he was appointed 'Chief Kite Instructor' to the British Army at a salary of £1,000 per annum.

Col Templer, who retired in 1906, was first and foremost, a balloonist, but his successor, Col Capper, had an equal enthusiasm for all forms of aviation and so, with him as Superintendent, the Balloon Factory started to take an interest in aeroplanes too. In 1904, Capper had returned from America filled with enthusiasm for the purchase of a Wright 'Flyer', but, as the negotiations dragged on year after year, he seems to have decided that the Farnborough staff might just as well design their

Samuel Franklin Cody (1861–1913)

Born in Davenport, Iowa, on 6 march 1861 as S.F. Cowdrey, he worked variously as a cattle drover, buffalo hunter and bronco-buster before joining a Wild West show, touring the Eastern States under the title 'Captain Cody, King of the Cowboys'. The change of surname was possibly an attempt to imply a relationship with the already famous William 'Buffalo Bill' Cody.

He came to Europe in 1889, touring the Music Halls with a shooting act, before staging a blood-curdling melodrama of his own devising entitled 'The Klondyke Nugget'. This successful show-business career afforded him both the time and the money with which to follow his interest in kite flying, a skill he had allegedly learned from a Chinese cook he met on a cattle drive.

From this hobby grew an obsession with the idea of a kite which would be able to carry a man into the air, and in 1901 he had patented a system whereby winged box kites were flown in a train, controlled by a winch. By 1905 he had sold his kites to the Army, and secured an appointment as Chief Kite Instructor, attached to the Balloon Sections.

Once at Farnborough his interests expanded and he first built a 50ft (15m) wingspan glider kite, then the unmanned 'Power Kite' before becoming involved with the airship 'Nulli Secundus' for which he designed much of the propulsion system. On 5 October 1907 he acted as engineer on its flight from Farnborough to London, circling St Paul's Cathedral, and finally landing in the grounds of the Crystal Palace, thus establishing a new record for non-rigid airships.

On 16 October 1908 he made the first sustained, powered flight in Britain in 'British Aeroplane No.1', which he had designed. He later won several major prizes including two Michelin Trophies, one in December 1910 for a flight of 185 miles, (298km) the longest of that year.

The monoplane he designed for the 1912 Military Trials was wrecked when it collided with a cow on landing, but his replacement machine, built in under three weeks, won the competition by a comfortable margin, netting Cody £5,000 in prize money and a production order for two of his aeroplanes for the recently formed RFC.

He was killed on 7 August 1913 when an aeroplane which he had built for the Circuit of Britain race broke up in the air. His passenger, the cricketer W.H.B. Evans, was also killed. Such was his popularity that a crowd of 50,000 people turned out for his funeral, at which every regiment of the British Army was represented. Cody was the first civilian to be buried in Aldershot Military Cemetery.

own aeroplane. In this he was blessed with two strings to his bow: on the one hand he had the indefatigable S.F. Cody who was keen to develop his huge kites into an aeroplane, and on the other he had Lt John W. Dunne of the Wiltshire Regiment, who had joined the Factory early in 1906 with a proposal to develop a stable aeroplane equipped with swept-back wings based upon those of the zanonia seed. These two totally different approaches were followed in parallel, and each produced their first results during 1907.

Cody's design, the 'Power Kite', was, as its name suggested, a modification of his basic kite design, powered by a 12hp Buchet engine driving a pusher propeller. It was not intended to carry a man, but was flown along a wire suspended between two poles within the factory compound.

On the other hand, Dunne's design was considered too revolutionary for such public exhibition, and its trials were held at a remote location in the Scottish highlands. Flown first as a glider, it comprised a pair

The stable Dunne D1 glider. The wheeled trolley was not only used for transport to the chosen test site, but was intended to be used as a launch vehicle too, a path of planks being laid down to give a smooth run.
J.M. Bruce/G.S. Leslie Collection

S.F. Cody piloting British Army Aeroplane No. 1 for its first, 1,340ft (408m), flight on 16 October 1908.
Author's collection

of biplane wings formed into a 'vee' shape with a pronounced 'wash-out' at the tips to ensure stability, and with a canvas seat for the pilot fixed to the centre interplane struts. Its best flight as a glider, with Col Capper at the controls, lasted eight seconds, after which it was decided to carry out the planned conversion to a powered aeroplane by installing two 12hp Buchet engines driving propellers mounted on outriggers behind the wings. However, an accident during the first take-off run caused sufficient damage to bring that year's experiments to a close.

It was not until late summer the following year that Dunne and his party were able to return to Scotland with his newest design, assembly of which was hampered by damaged components and faulty tools. When eventually completed, the machine was able to make a number of glides, each averaging around 60ft (18m), following which Dunne proceeded to assemble the powered machine. The chosen power plant, a 25hp REP, proved unusually troublesome, even for those days, and appears never to have given its rated power. Even though trials were continued right up to the onset of winter, the longest flight achieved was only about 40yd (36m).

Meanwhile, back at Farnborough, construction of Cody's latest design, 'British Army Aeroplane No.1', a huge pusher biplane powered by a 50hp Antoinette engine, was completed by the beginning of September 1908 and was ready for testing. Engine runs and taxi trials on 19 September were followed by some fast ground runs two days later in order that the controls could be tested. On 16 October, after a few initial ground runs, Cody took off and flew across Farnborough Common at a height of around 30ft (9m), covering a distance of almost a quarter of a mile (400m) in 27 seconds, before a wing-tip struck the ground as Cody was obliged to turn sharply to avoid a clump of trees, extensively damaging the machine. The first true powered flight in England had taken place.

Yet by this time Wilbur Wright had amazed the world with his demonstration flights in France and Henri Farman had begun making cross-country flights. The British Press was eager to point out how far Britain had fallen behind.

It was clearly time for the British Government to consider its position on military aviation and so, at the request of the prime minister, a sub-committee of the Committee of Imperial Defence was appointed on 23 October to report on the matter. The members of this committee were:

Lord Esher (Chairman)
Mr David Lloyd George, MP, Chancellor of the Exchequer
Mr R.B. Haldane, MP, Secretary of State for War
Mr R. McKenna, MP, First Lord of the Admiralty
Gen Sir William Nicholson, Chief of the General Staff
Maj Gen J.S. Ewart, Director of Military Operations
Maj Gen Sir Charles Hadden, Master-General of Ordnance
Capt R.H.S. Bacon, RN, Director of Naval Ordnance
Rear-Adm Sir C.L. Ottley (Secretary).

Four meetings were held, and a number of experts consulted. These included: Col Capper; The Hon. C.S. Rolls (co-founder of Rolls-Royce and a noted balloonist and pioneer aviator); Maj B.F.S. Baden-Powell; and Sir Hiram Maxim.

The committee's final report, dated 28 January 1909, is marked 'secret' and begins with the committee's view of the current position in the development of military aviation. It goes on to describe captive balloons and man-lifting kites as being of limited value both for reconnaissance and artillery observation, and it was expected that both would eventually be superseded by airships.

The report suggests that the rigid airship might prove of use in naval warfare, particularly for reconnaissance, since it could carry out many of the scouting duties of a warship at a fraction of the capital cost. The non-rigid type was thought better for use by the Army as it was capable of being deflated and brought home by road.

The report concludes that aeroplanes were still very much in the experimental stage, were limited by their need for prepared take-off facilities, and had yet to demonstrate any ability to climb to a height sufficient to make them safe from small arms fire, and so presented, in the immediate future, neither a serious danger to the safety of Great Britain, nor any practical value to its armed forces. It was also noted that they were being developed commercially, which airships were not, and could already be purchased for as little as £1,000 each.

The committee therefore recommended that the experiments carried out at the military ballooning establishment should be discontinued, but advantage should be taken of private enterprise in this form of aviation.

Thus both Cody and Dunne were discharged, the latter taking up an offer of private financial backing to exploit his design ideas commercially. Cody, on the other hand, requested permission to erect a shed on Laffan's Plain, near to the Balloon Factory's Farnborough site, so that he could continue his experiments at his own expense. 'British Army Aeroplane No. 1', in which he had made his 400yd flight, being deemed of no military value, was given to him outright, although its Antoinette engine, which was required for airship use, was to be returned to the Balloon Factory.

By October 1909 Col Capper had returned to his previous role as Commandant of the Balloon School, although this was now very much an aeronautical backwater, totally divorced from the Factory. He was replaced as Superintendent of the Balloon Factory by Mervyn O'Gorman, a civilian consulting engineer, who was appointed by Lord Haldane, Secretary of State for War. O'Gorman's appointment quickly brought an end to the empirical methods of his predecessors, and instead introduced a new scientific approach, transforming the Balloon Factory into a true research establishment and setting standards for others to follow. He created specialized departments dedicated to the study of Aerodynamics, Metallurgy, Instruments, Physics, Chemistry, Photography and Wireless, and recruited the best men he could find to staff them. It was, for example, his habit to visit Cambridge University with a view to selecting the most outstanding graduates to join the Farnborough team, as well as attracting experienced men from industry. Thus, in January 1910, Frederick M. Green left the Daimler Company to join the Factory staff as 'Engineer in Charge of Design'.

Although the factory's work was, at this time, largely concerned with the development of non-rigid airships, O'Gorman's enthusiasm for aeroplanes as the future of aviation proved infectious, and on 17 October 1910 the War Office announced that the scope of the Balloon Factory was to be enlarged to include work with aeroplanes. There was, however, no suggestion that the Factory should be allowed to design or build aeroplanes; it was to content itself with conducting experiments upon machines obtained from private industry.

A chance meeting the following December between Green and Geoffrey de Havilland, who had just completed building an aeroplane of his own design and who was a little uncertain of what to do next, brought both de Havilland and his aeroplane to Farnborough. The aeroplane, a pusher biplane of fairly conventional design, was purchased outright for £400, and de Havilland was engaged to fulfil the dual roles of designer, working under Green, and test pilot.

The Balloon School, the scope of which had also been increased to include working with aeroplanes, had already begun to acquire an assortment of mismatched machines, including an out-of-date Wright biplane, an experimental Bleriot monoplane and a Paulhan biplane of unconventional design, with which to practise. But O'Gorman had other ideas for the Factory,

Mervyn O'Gorman C.B., D.Sc., M.Inst.C.E., M.I.Mech.E., M.I.E.E., F.R.Ae.S.

The Factory's first civilian Superintendent (although he thought the title 'Director' would have been more appropriate) was Mervyn Joseph Pius O'Gorman, who was appointed on 19 October 1909. His appointment was made, initially on a part-time basis, at a salary of £950 per year, following a recommendation by Lord Rayleigh, Chairman of the Advisory Committee for Aeronautics.

O'Gorman, who had obtained degrees in classics and science at Trinity College, Dublin, followed by postgraduate study at the City and Guilds Institute in London, was by then a well-respected consulting engineer working mostly in the automobile field, and was a partner in the firm of Swinburne, O'Gorman & Baillee.

He was a rather flamboyant character who wore a gold-rimmed monocle and smoked cigarettes through a short holder, the aroma of his Turkish tobacco clearly indicating his whereabouts in the factory.

He brought with him a new scientific approach to aeronautical development, and saw the Factory's role as being to experiment, research and test; to analyse the results of tests upon experimental designs; to prepare specifications; and to reply to scientific queries. In order to achieve this, he sought out and recruited the best scientists, engineers and craftsmen he could find and under his direction the Factory staff grew from around 100 to a wartime peak of over 5,000.

After he left Farnborough in 1916 he became a consultant to the Director General of Military Aeronautics before joining the Aircraft Manufacturing Co. at Hendon.

Geoffrey de Havilland

Geoffrey de Havilland, designer of many of the aeroplanes which bore his name, and of some that did not, was born on 27 July 1882, the second son of a country parson. From the start, he showed a considerable aptitude for technical matters and completed his education with a course at the Crystal Palace School of Engineering.

He first embarked upon a career in the fast-developing motor industry, before realizing that his real interest lay in aviation. He therefore borrowed £1,000 from his maternal grandfather, engaged an assistant, and set about building an aeroplane of his own design. This first aeroplane was wrecked during its initial take-off attempt, fortunately without injury to either de Havilland or to its engine, which he had also designed. A second machine, of a more conventional layout, proved more successful, making its first flight on 10 September 1910. Like many aviation pioneers, de Havilland then had not only to test and develop his machine, but to teach himself to fly it too. With this accomplished he installed a second seat and gave rides first to Frank Hearle, his assistant, and then to his wife.

This machine was sold to the Balloon Factory in December 1910 for £400, its creator taking up employment there as a designer and test pilot. Whilst at Farnborough he designed a number of successful aeroplanes, including the original F.E.2 and many of the B.E. series.

On 1 January 1914 he was appointed Inspector of Aeroplanes with the newly formed Aeronautical Inspection Department (AID) but found that the work was not to his liking, and so in May he joined the Aircraft Manufacturing Company Ltd (Airco) at Hendon as Chief Designer. Here he began the series of aeroplanes which bore his initials. In 1920 he started his own aeroplane company and in 1925 designed what was perhaps his most famous machine, the D.H.60 Moth. The company's later designs included the WW2 Mosquito, and the first jet airliner, the Comet.

He maintained his interest in flying even after retirement, making his last flight as pilot in command in 1952, when he was 70. He died on 21 May 1965.

planning instead to investigate the relative advantages of standard configurations, and so see which were best suited to military use. On 8 March 1911 he presented a paper entitled 'Problems Related to Aircraft' to the Institute of Automobile Engineers, in which he defined the three broad classifications into which the majority of contemporary designs fell. These were as follows:

Class S – Those of which the main wings are preceded by a small plane which is more intensely loaded and succeeded by the propeller (for example, the current Santos-Dumont and Valkyrie designs).

Class B – Those of which the main wings are preceded by the propeller and followed by a smaller plane which is more lightly loaded (for example the Avro, Antoinette, Bleriot and Breguet machines).

Class F – Those which have the main wings followed by a smaller plane more lightly loaded but with the propeller between the main wings and the tailplane (for example, the Bristol Boxkite, Farman or de Havilland types).

These classifications were later expanded, and in November 1911 were published by The Advisory Committee for Aeronautics in 'Research and Memorandum No. 59'.

O'Gorman's paper included a great deal of discussion on the relative aerodynamic properties of each type, and suggested that, although Class B appeared superior overall, S Class might have the edge in safety, principally because it would automatically take up the proper glide path should the engine stop. O'Gorman was therefore of the opinion that the Factory's research should begin with trials of an S-class machine. Of course the Factory, being purely a research and repair facility, lacked the authority to design and build such a machine, and so a clever subterfuge was adopted. The Balloon School's Bleriot XII had been wrecked, and although generally thought to be beyond repair, the remains had nonetheless been taken to the Factory. In December 1910 O'Gorman therefore sought, and was granted, the War Office's permission to 'reconstruct' the machine, by carrying out some modifications at the same time as undertaking the repairs, thereby disguising his intention to build an entirely new machine.

In the meantime, de Havilland's aeroplane (now named F.E.1, or 'F' class Experimental No.1.) would provide data on the handling of that type of machine. Once it had passed its acceptance test, a flight of one hour without repair or adjustment (during which de Havilland was allowed to land twice to warm up, the January day being bitterly cold), numerous experiments were conducted, the machine being flown both as built, and with wing extensions designed to increase its lift.

On 26 April 1911, following the incorporation of the Balloon School into the newly created Air Battalion, Royal Engineers, the Balloon Factory was renamed 'The Army Aircraft Factory', the new name having been chosen by O'Gorman as more fully embracing its true role. That same month the wreckage of a Voisin pusher biplane which had been presented to the Army by the Duke of Westminster arrived at the factory for repair. In due time this too would enjoy 'reconstruction', emerging from the workshops towards the end of the year as the Factory's first example of a B-class aeroplane, the B.E.1.

Advisory Committee for Aeronautics

Formed on 5 May 1909 by the Prime Minister, H.H. Asquith, in order to place aeronautical research on a scientific footing, the committee comprised:

Lord Rayleigh O.M. F.R.S. (President): the co-discoverer of the element Argon, and winner of the Nobel prize for Physics.

Dr R.T. Glazebroke F.R.S.: Director of the National Physical Laboratory.

Mr Horace Darwin.

Sir A.G. Greenhill.

Mr F.W. Lanchester: the prominent physicist.

Mr H.R.A. Mallock.

Prof J.E. Petavel: Head of Mechanical Engineering at Manchester University.

Dr W.N. Shaw.

Capt R.H. Bacon R.N.: Director of Naval Ordnance and Torpedoes.

Maj Gen Sir Charles Hadden: Master General of Ordnance.

Mr F.J. Selby (Secretary).

Based at the National Physical Laboratory at Teddington, it was not intended that the Committee should carry out or initiate research, but that it should investigate and appraise what had been done by others.

In June, the wrecked Bleriot tractor monoplane emerged from the Factory's workshops as a canard biplane, the S.E.1, the only component of the original machine being the engine, a 60hp water-cooled E.N.V. If development of the F.E.1 had been straightforward, that of the canard S.E.1 proved quite the reverse. Its first outing, on 7 June, proved abortive, and the wheels had to be repositioned so as to adjust the balance before it would take off, which it did at 5.30am the following day, with de Havilland at the controls. Two days later the wheels were moved again, and a front skid fitted. Throughout June and July it was constantly modified: the dihedral was reduced, the fuselage striped of fabric, the rear rudders moved back and a front rudder fitted, all in an effort to improve its turning. The elevators were reduced in area and the drive shaft changed. The carburettors were a constant source of trouble, and the undercarriage was never really satisfactory despite constant modification.

At the beginning of August, before going on holiday, de Havilland took Lt Theodore Ridge, the Factory's Assistant Superintendent, who had recently learned to fly, out in the F.E.1, allowing him first to

Research and Memorandum No.59

Type classification of aeroplane design adopted by the Army (later Royal) Aircraft Factory:

S.E. – Santos Experimental, after Santos Dumont, the originator of the 'canard' or tail-first type of aeroplane. The S.E.1 was the only one of this type, the subsequent designs being of the single-seat tractor scout formula. This designation was therefore modified to 'Scout Experimental'.

F.E. – Farman Experimental: pusher biplanes.

B.E. – Bleriot Experimental: general purpose two-seat tractor biplanes.

R.E. – Reconnaissance Experimental: two-seat tractor biplanes specifically designed for reconnaissance purposes.

T.E. – Tatin Experimental: monoplanes with pusher propeller mounted behind the tail.

B.S. – Bleriot Scout: a single-seat variant of the B.E. formula.

In practice the T.E. category was never used, and two more were later added. These were:

C.E. - Coastal Experimental: flying boats.

N.E. - Night Experimental: pusher night fighters.

The canard S.E.1 early in its development, before the provision of an additional rudder above the forward elevator, in an effort to correct its lack of directional stability. Author's collection

taxi, then to make short hops before flying the machine. On 15 August Ridge had a minor crash whilst landing the F.E.1, damaging the undercarriage and one wing. Three days later he insisted on taking up the S.E.1 up, ignoring advice that it was still a tricky machine. In attempting a turn he sideslipped, then spun into the ground, wrecking the machine and receiving injuries from which he died later the same day. The coroner's inquest returned a verdict of 'death by misadventure'.

The machine was not rebuilt (although a list of aeroplanes dated 2 November 1911 refers to the B.E.2 then being built as a 'reconstruction' of the S.E.1, this is almost certainly a clerical error) and the canard layout was abandoned completely. After a suitable interval, Mr S. Heckstall-Smith was appointed as the Factory's new Assistant Superintendent.

On 11 April 1912, following the formation of the Royal Flying Corps, a Government White Paper entitled 'A Memorandum on Naval and Military Aviation' laid down the function of the Factory as being: the higher training of mechanics for the Royal Flying Corps; tests with British and foreign engines and aeroplanes; experimental work; the manufacture of hydrogen (for filling balloons and airships); and general maintenance. It also changed its name yet again, this time to that under which it has become best known, the Royal Aircraft Factory.

A view across Farnborough Common towards the Royal Aircraft Factory taken during 1914. Author's collection

CHAPTER TWO

The B.E.2

Once development of the pusher F.E.1 and the canard S.E.1 was safely under way, the Factory's attention was finally drawn towards a tractor design, thereby completing the trio which formed Mervyn O'Gorman's basic classification of aeroplane types. Drawing upon both past experience and theoretical reasoning, O'Gorman, as Factory Superintendent, drew up a specification which listed those features he felt it would be desirable to include in the new machine. These included warping wings for lateral control, a swivelling tail skid to afford manoeuvrability on the ground, and a lifting tail to allow the main planes to be placed as far forward as possible to improve the pilot's view of the ground. The new machine was to be a tandem two-seater, with the passenger placed in the forward cockpit so that his weight was as near as possible to the centre of gravity, thereby avoiding any trim changes when the machine was flown solo.

At this time, however, the Factory still lacked any authority either to design or build new aeroplanes, and so a ruse similar to that which had been successfully used to create the S.E.1 was employed. In May 1911 a Voisin pusher, of outmoded design, had been donated to the War Office for use by the Air battalion. Damaged in a crash on 11 July, it was naturally sent to the Factory for repair. Thus, on 1 August the following letter was sent to the Director of Fortifications and Works at the War Office:

> With reference to the Voisin aeroplane recently presented by the Duke of Westminster and delivered to this Factory by the Wolsley [sic] Tool & Motor Co., I have to report that the method of controlling and steering this machine is obsolete and different from any present make; that the wood frame of the wings and struts and canvas covering have deteriorated to such a degree that they should be replaced if the machine is to be flown in safety.
>
> I therefore desire to recommend that I may be instructed to fit this machine with certain spare wings and struts which I have in stock and alter the control so that it is similar to the Farman type, and thus enable the machine to be flown by anyone qualified to fly a Farman type machine.
>
> I am in a position to effect these alterations quickly and economically and it would then be equal to a good Farman type machine.
>
> Signed T. Ridge.
> for Superintendent Army Aircraft Factory.

Of course, the Factory had no stock of wings and struts which would fit the machine, and they would have had to be built from scratch, but the 'little white lie' served its intended purpose for, on 12 August the War Office replied:

> With reference to your Memorandum dated 1st instant, No. 21/F, your proposal to carry out certain alterations and additions to the Voisin Aeroplane, which has recently been presented to the War Department by the Duke of Westminster, is approved.

The actual design work for the new machine was carried out largely by Geoffrey de Havilland, under the supervision of F.M. Green. Power was to be provided by the 60hp. V8 water-cooled Wolseley engine taken from the Voisin. Little else was reused, except perhaps a few metal fittings, for, as was to be expected, the new design bore no resemblance at all to its predecessor. Instead, it was a two-bay tractor biplane, the upper wing being of slightly greater span than the lower, and was rigged with neither stagger nor dihedral. Lateral control was by warping, the control column being as tall as practicable in order to keep stick forces as low as possible.

The long, slender fuselage was of cross-braced timber, formed in two sections, joined with fishplates just behind the rear cockpit, and with no top decking between the seats. A large radiator was mounted vertically in front of the forward centre section struts, where it must have severely restricted the crew's forward view, since they were obliged to look through it. However, in this position it would have gained the greatest benefit from the air movement created by the propeller, reducing the weight of water required to the minimum

Design Brief

1) Lateral control is to be obtained by warping a very large portion of both top and bottom planes, instead of warping a small portion. This is both powerful and more efficient.
2) A new form of landing chassis is to be designed, with adequate provision for absorbing vertical shocks by means of oil buffers and pneumatic absorbers.
3) Provision is to be made for steering the machine on the ground at slow speeds by means of a swivelling back skid placed under the tail (this facilitates landing in a restricted area).
4) The motor and propeller to be placed in front of the planes to give the pilot a better chance in case of a bad smash. The pilot is raised sufficiently above the bottom plane so that he gets a good view of the ground over the front edge of the bottom plane. This is inferior to the view in the S.E.1, but is at least as good as any other aeroplane with the engine in front.
5) The main surfaces are to be placed well in front of the machine and the stabilizing surfaces at the rear set at a considerably smaller angle. This ensures fore-and-aft stability, but I incline to retain some curvature in the upper surface of the tail as giving a better riding moment.
6) The rudder, and covered body will, I think, ensure sufficient directional stability. It is a matter of trial whether an extra vertical fin is to be fitted, and in any case this is very easy to do.
7) It is proposed to use a small amount of dihedral angle between the planes, probably 178°, i.e. 1°rise on each half plane.
8) The section of the planes in the new machine will not be dissimilar to those of the S.E.1.
9) The general construction of the machine will be improved considerably in detail, particularly with regard to the planes. Streamlined section struts are being used, also the main stay wires will be swaged to a streamline section. Every effort is being made to reduce head resistance as much as possible.

possible. A fully swivelling tail-skid was fitted, and the main undercarriage incorporated long skids to protect the propeller tips when the tail was raised during take off or landing.

A spade-shaped horizontal tail of true aerofoil section was mounted on top of the upper longerons, the rear fuselage's top decking ending at its leading edge. The elevators were made of steel tubing, fabric covered, as was the ear-shaped rudder, the latter being hung from an unbraced rudder post. There was no vertical fin.

Its exhaust pipes were long, terminating behind and below the rear cockpit, and incorporated car-type attenuators, leading to the machine being christened the Army's 'silent aeroplane' by a reporter from the *The Times*, who claimed that it could not be heard from 50yd away.

All in all, it was a considerable advance in aircraft design, particularly as it was only Geoffrey de Havilland's fourth design, and was much applauded by the aviation press. *Flight* magazine described it thus:

> The machine – from what we are allowed to see of it at the polite distance of a spectator among the casual public that frequents the plain on the 'off chance' – is a large biplane with an absolutely silent engine. It has been said that it is a remodelled version of the Duke of Westminster's old Voisin, but it seemed to us that there was more remodelling than anything else, and everything that one could see about the machine was of singular interest. In the control, the entire wing surfaces seem to be warped, which appears to give exceedingly powerful balancing action for the maintenance of lateral equilibrium. The detail construction also gives evidence of extreme care, and the application of the principle of streamline form together with the complete absence of visible rigging wires in the tail are both points worthy of comment.

The B.E.1 was taken out on to Farnborough Common, close to the Factory site, on Monday, 4 December 1911 and at 3.30p.m. made its first flight, with its designer at the controls. de Havilland's

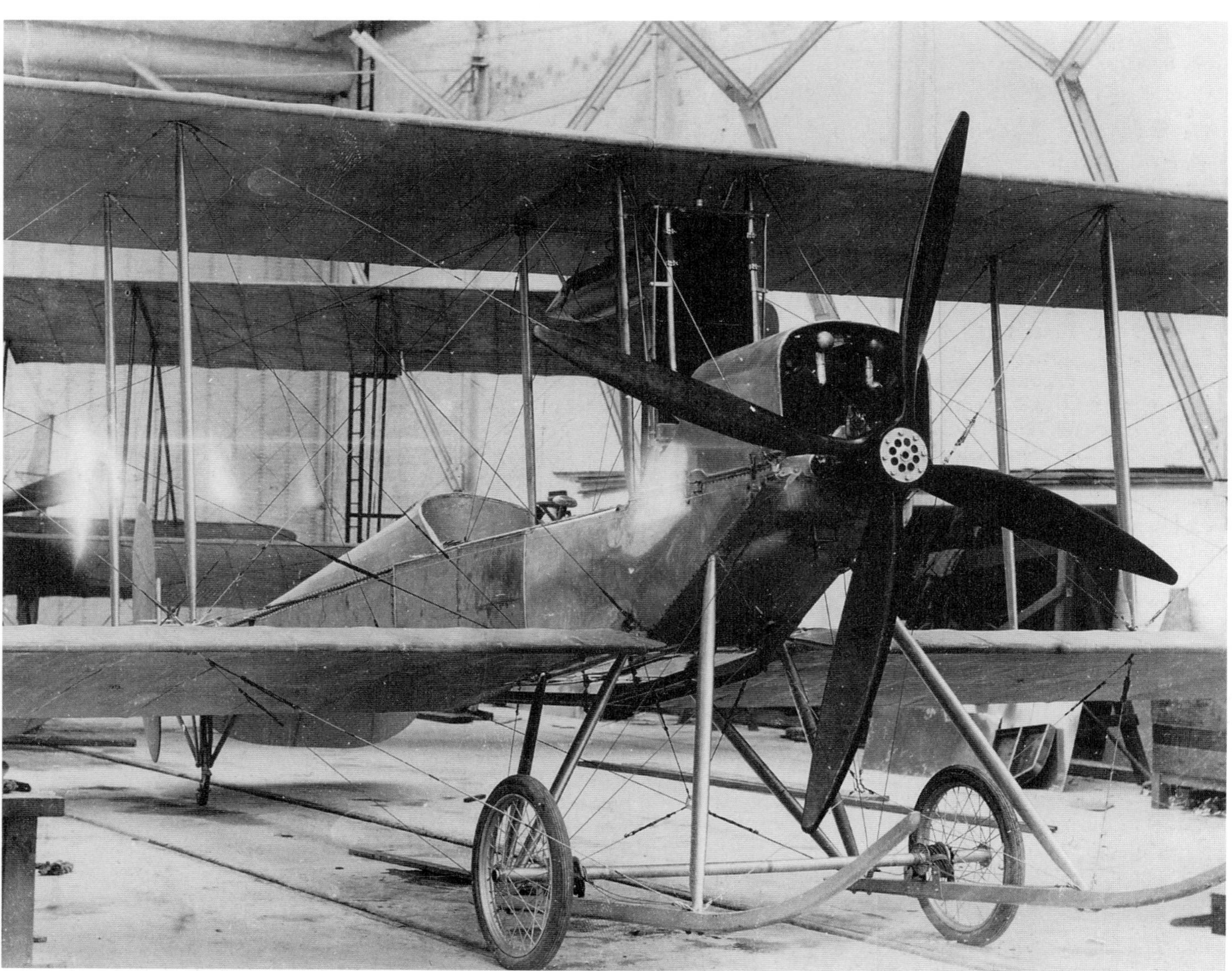

The B.E.1, apparently complete in the Factory's main workshop, with the F.E.2 in the background. The original photograph is clearly dated 1-10-11, but the B.E.1 did not fly for another two months. Crown copyright

logbook notes that the test flight covered three miles, and that he received 2s 6d (12½ pence) in flying pay for it. He also notes that the Wolseley carburettor did not allow throttling, and that it was therefore to be replaced with a Claudel. This may have proved more complicated than de Havilland had supposed, or maybe either he or the workshops were busy with other things, but for whatever reason the B.E.1 was not taken out again until after Christmas. On 27 December a total of ten flights were made, some of them with passengers, with de Havilland happily flying until it was too dark to continue, covering a total of about 50 miles (80km).

The machine's speed was tested and found to average 55mph (88km/h) and its pilot noted:

> Stability seems good. Engine is pulling 1,000 in air (should be 1,200).
>
> Carburettor (Claudel) is very good.
>
> Wheels should be put further back to take weight off tail. Elevator control requires gearing down.

By 1 January 1912 the wheels had been moved back 12in (30cm), shortening the take-off run, whilst the 7th saw it out again, now with the top wing rigged back 3in (7.6cm), and a baffle fixed in front of the carburettor, effecting a further small improvement in engine revolutions.

The next step was to introduce the dihedral which O'Gorman had wished for from the start, the wings being re-rigged to give an angle of about 1 degree on each plane. de Havilland thought that this was probably an improvement, but that further testing would be required before he could be certain.

On 12 January the machine was tested with a Zenith carburettor, but this was found to be less flexible than the Claudel, which was refitted in time for further flying the following day. A week later the propeller tips were cut down in a final desperate attempt to bring the engine speed up to its rated figure of 1,200 rev/min, the actual figure achieved being just twenty-five short of this target.

This completed the formal testing and development of the B.E.1. Geoffrey de Havilland used it for the remainder of the month to give passenger flights to factory staff and members of the Air Battalion. It was then flown on numerous occasions by E.W. Copland Perry, who had joined the Factory as a test pilot in February 1911, before being handed over to Capt Burke of the Air Battalion on 11 March.

It returned to the Factory again in June so that the ever troublesome Wolseley engine could be replaced by an air-cooled Renault, thus enabling the radiator to be removed, with consequent improvements both to the machine's performance and the crew's forward view.

Specification – B.E.1

Powerplant:	60hp Wolseley
Weights:	not known
Dimensions:	Upper span 36ft 7½in (11.78m); lower span 34ft 11½in (10.66m); chord 5ft 6in (1.68m); gap 6ft (1.83m); wing area 374sq ft (34.78sq m); dihedral nil; stagger nil
	Length 29ft 6½in (9.01m); height 10ft 2in (3.10m); tailplane area 52sq ft (4.84sq m); elevator area 25sq ft (2.33sq m); rudder area 12sq ft (1.12sq m); fin area nil
Performance:	Speed at sea level 59mph (94km/h); rate of climb 155ft/min (47.28m/min)

B.E.1 Certificate

This is to certify that the aeroplane B.E.1 has been thoroughly tested by me, and the mean speed of a ¾ mile course with a live load of 25 stone and sufficient petrol for one hour's flight is 58–59 m.p.h.

The rate of rising loaded as above has been tested up to 600 feet and found to be at the rate of 155 feet per minute.

The machine has been inverted and suspended from the centre and the wings loaded to three times the normal loading. On examination after this test the machine showed no sign of defect.

(signed) S. Heckstall-Smith.
for Superintendent, Army Aircraft Factory.

14th March 1912.
South Farnborough.

This document has, for many years, been regarded as the first-ever Certificate of Airworthiness, but in fact is not, for almost a full year earlier, on 16 March 1911, Mervyn O'Gorman had issued a similar certificate with regard to a Farman Biplane which had been repaired by the Balloon Factory on behalf of the Army.

A Sister Ship

On 1 February 1912, Geoffrey de Havilland turned his attention to the testing of a new machine. This was the B.E.2, which was so designated not to identify it as a separate design, but simply because it was the second machine in the B.E. series, and individual serial numbers were still in the future. In fact, it was virtually identical to its predecessor, except that its wings were of equal span, and it was powered, from the start, by a V8 Renault engine taken from the Breguet biplane from which it had ostensibly been 'reconstructed'. The down legs of the exhaust pipes passed through the fuselage, immediately behind the engine, thereby affording a small reduction in head resistance.

The B.E.2's first flight was made at 11.00a.m., its designer noting that it took off and climbed more quickly than did the B.E.1. He also noted that its engine speed was 1,720 rev/min. (The propeller speed would have been half of this, since, in the Renault engine, the propeller was not mounted directly on the crankshaft but onto an extension of the camshaft, thereby giving a 2:1 speed reduction.)

The new machine already incorporated the modifications made to its predecessor as a result of its initial flight trials, and so appears to have been satisfactory right from the start. de Havilland's log records four flights on 1 February, followed by further outings on the 2nd and 3rd, without any adjustments being required. Its rate of climb was noted to be 240ft (73m) per minute when flown solo, reducing to around 200ft (60m) with a passenger and sufficient petrol for 4½ hours' flying.

On 5 February de Havilland showed off the B.E.2 to members of the Advisory Committee for Aeronautics who were visiting the Factory, but the next day a cracked engine flywheel left it grounded. However, by the 21st the engine had been fully overhauled, and fitted with a Claudel carburettor similar to that which had proved so successful on the Wolseley engine of the B.E.1.

A superb study of the original B.E.2 inside the Royal Aircraft Factory workshops. Note that the exhausts pass through the fuselage and that the tailpipes are missing. The bulbous object alongside the starboard rear centre-section strut is a direct-driven engine rev counter. Crown Copyright – DERA

It seems to have brought about similar improvements to the Renault, increasing its speed to 1,900 rev/min., with consequent benefits to the aeroplane's performance. Confident that the engine was now in good shape de Havilland began to fly greater distances, covering 40 miles (64km) on 6 March and 200 miles (320km) a few days later. Petrol consumption worked out to be 11 miles per gallon (17km per 4.5 litres), or about six gallons (27 litres) per hour, a figure that would still have been considered respectable twenty or more years later.

Installation of a wireless set, designed and built by Factory staff specifically for use in aeroplanes (previous sets had been used only by airships), began on 16 March. Tests commenced on the 26th, continuing through the first weeks of April, and including the first ever wireless-controlled artillery shoot. The results of these trials were described as 'good', although with no indication of the ranges obtained. Also during April 1912 the B.E.2 was used in trials with several new test instruments developed at the Factory, including a Thrust Meter and an Accelerometer.

The B.E.2 underwent a further engine change at the end of April, receiving another V8 Renault, but this one rated at 70hp, the additional power presumably being required to cope with the next experiment on the Factory's agenda, that of adding floats to the undercarriage.

In the initial tests, conducted on 1 May, the new undercarriage proved unsatisfactory for 'rolling' (taxiing), and so was further modified before the 11th, when the machine was taken to Fleet Pond for flotation tests. These proved equally disappointing, the tail float being incorrectly set, which put too much weight onto the main floats, causing them to draw too much water for the fairly shallow pond. Adjustments were quickly made, enabling a take off to be made the same evening, although the floats were damaged on landing. Perhaps this was enough to disillusion completely the Factory's designers, for the amphibian undercarriage experiments were then discontinued, the machine having no floats fitted when de Havilland demonstrated it to the King and Queen during their visit to Farnborough on the 17th.

Further tests included flying with a meter fitted to test the tension in the wires, and trials of a new instrument, developed at the Factory, which measured the glide angle in flight. de Havilland even found time, on 19 June, to take his wife for a joyride.

The B.E. Range Extends

Allegedly reconstructed from the wreckage of a crashed Paulhan, the B.E.3, the third aeroplane in the B.E. series, was designed by John Kenworthy, assisted by H.P. Folland. It utilized the same wing structure as the B.E.1 and B.E.2, but with a pronounced forward stagger. The fuselage was faired to a circular cross-section, echoing the shape of its 50hp Gnome rotary engine; its rudder, although retaining the ear-like shape of the earlier machines, was built to be pivoted from the centre of its longer axis, giving a balanced surface of low aspect ratio. Its horizontal tail surfaces were also similar to those of its predecessors, although its elevator was a single, undivided surface.

It was first flown, by Geoffrey de Havilland, at 10.30a.m. on 3 May 1912, and made a number of passenger flights later the same day before flying was halted by a broken skid. It was out again three days later, after modifications to give more rudder movement, and to increase the washout to the wing-tips, but again broke its skids on landing, this time with damage to the propeller, presumably as a result of the

Geoffrey de Havilland in the cockpit of the rotary engined B.E.3. Whilst the family resemblance to the B.E.2 is obvious there are numerous differences, including the fuselage at mid gap and the low aspect ratio rudder. Author's collection

The B.E.8 or 'Bloater' which, like the B.E.3 from which it was developed, was powered by a rotary engine. Author's collection

The B.E.2. as it appeared during the Military Aeroplane Competition at Larkhill in August 1912. The pilot is its designer, Geoffrey de Havilland. The exhaust pipes have been modified and are now wholly external.
Author's collection

tips striking the ground. The undercarriage was therefore redesigned, and no further trouble recorded with it.

A second machine, the B.E.4, was built to the same design. This was powered initially by a similar 50hp Gnome engine provided by its 'parent' aircraft, a Bristol Boxkite, but was later fitted with a new Gnome of 70hp.

The B.E.3/4 layout was later embodied by John Kenworthy into the design of the rotary-engined B.E.8 series, which entered limited production, and served, in small numbers with the Royal Flying Corps (RFC).

The B.E.5, an alleged reconstruction of a Howard Wright, reverted to the original layout but was powered by the 60 hp ENV engine thus provided. This being water-cooled, a radiator was fixed to the forward centre section struts, exactly as the original installation in the B.E.1. It was eventually re-engined with a 70hp Renault, and thus became virtually identical to the B.E. 1 and 2.

B.E.2 at the Military Trials

Following several months of discussions, it was announced in December 1911 that the War Office was to hold a competition to select aeroplanes for military use. The conditions which entrants would need to fulfil included the following:

- To be able to carry a crew of two (jointly weighing up to 350lb) who should be able to communicate with each other, together with fuel and oil for 4½ hours' flying.
- To have a top speed of at least 55mph (88km/h), a glide angle of 1 in 6 or better, and to climb at least 200ft (60m) per minute, reaching an altitude of at least 4,500ft (1,370m).
- To take off in 100yd (91m), and to land without damage on any cultivated ground, pulling up within 75yd (68m).
- To have the best possible view of the country below, as well as to the sides.

In the end, a total of 32 entries was received, although eight of these failed to turn up at Larkhill, Salisbury Plain, where the trials were to be conducted by the closing date of 31 July 1912. The judges, appointed by the War Office, were:

Brig Gen David Henderson (Director of Military Training)
Capt Godfrey Paine R.N. (Commandant of the Central Flying School)
Maj F.H. Sykes (Officer Commanding Royal Flying Corps)
Mr Mervyn O'Gorman (Superintendent of the Royal Aircraft Factory)

Since O'Gorman was one of the judges and, like many of the test instruments employed to assess performance during the competition, the B.E.2 was a product of the Royal Aircraft Factory, it was clearly ineligible to win any of the cash prizes from the competition. Nonetheless it was flown down to Larkhill for use as a general

Military Aeroplane Competition Comparison Results

Test	*CODY*	*B.E.2*
Climb to 1,000ft	3 min 30 sec	2 min 55 sec
Maximum speed	72.4mph	73mph
Minimum speed	48.5mph	49mph
Speed range	23.9mph	24mph
Glide angle	6.2	6.5

runabout, and whilst there undertook some of the tests anyway, obtaining results as good as, or better than, those of the eventual winner, S.F. Cody. Cody's gigantic biplane was not dissimilar to that in which he had made the first flight in England some four years previously.

de Havilland arose early on 12 August and, accompanied by Maj Sykes, took off in the B.E.2 at around 5.00a.m. Climbing steadily in the cool, still air, they eventually reached an altitude of 10,560ft (3,218m), in only 45 minutes, and so not only gained the British Altitude record for flights with a passenger, but also bettered that for solo flights.

Into Production

In the early days of the RFC's existence the War Office employed the same policy of piecemeal acquisition of aeroplanes as it had with the Air Battalion, scarcely owning two which were alike. It was, of necessity, a time of trial and error, since nobody really knew what qualities would be required in military aeroplanes until their role was better defined. Conventions in aircraft design had yet to be set, and no machine was too unconventional to be tried.

However, by the early summer of 1912 a few types had clearly demonstrated a greater potential than had others, and so, in the interests of some degree of standardization, small batches of similar machines were ordered. The first orders were for three Avro biplanes, four Flanders monoplanes and a similar number of B.E.2s. This latter order was placed not with the Royal Aircraft Factory, which was still only intended to be a research establishment, but with Messrs Vickers, who were already well established as contractors to the War Office.

When the Military Aeroplane Competition, which was supposed to have revealed the perfect machine for the Army, was over, and the winner announced, even the War Office could see that Cody's design was not the Flying Corps' ideal mount. So, with more aeroplanes needed, further orders were placed for B.E.2s

These production machines were almost identical to the original B.E.2, but incorporated a number of detail changes and it seems probable that the designation B.E.2a was introduced to cover all production examples, this designation appearing on drawings dated as early as February 1912. The type is described in the Advisory Committee for Aeronautics, 'Report and Memorandum No. 66' dated 12 June 1912. That they are frequently referred to in contemporary documents simply as B.E.2s would have caused no confusion at the time, since all production aircraft were, in fact, of the same type, that is the B.E.2a.

Their engines were all 70hp V8 Renaults, the exhaust pipes running outside the fuselage and terminating below and to the rear of the pilot's cockpit, as in the B.E.1. The earliest production machines had wings of NPL3a aerofoil section, with overhanging tips to the upper wings, but these were later changed to equal-span wings of a deeper section. These became necessary when static load testing revealed that the rear spar had a lower factor of safety than the remainder of the wing structure and a deeper rear spar was introduced. The newer wings were set at an incidence angle of 3½ degrees, 1° shallower than previously, giving a small reduction in drag for a similar lift.

A new tailplane was also introduced for later production B.E.2as. This was of the same span, allowing the retention of the original elevators, but of a reduced chord, now being nearly semicircular in plan. No revision was made to the fuselage's rear decking, leaving a flat area ahead of the smaller tailplane.

The B.E.2a also incorporated a revised fuel system, the streamlined gravity tank which had been suspended below the upper centre section of the B.E.1 and 2 being replaced by an internal tank within the decking which was now fitted at the rear of the engine, ahead of the forward cockpit. The main pressure tank remained under the front seat, a hand pump being provided, usually on the port side of the fuselage near the ignition switch, by means of which the air pressure could be maintained. A decking was also fitted between the two cockpits and windscreens provided.

By February 1913 production aircraft from both the Vickers and British and Colonial companies were in RFC service. Since the War Office felt it would encourage the growth of the industry if its business was spread over as many firms as possible, further orders were placed with Sir W.G. Armstrong, Whitworth & Co.; Coventry Ordnance Works; and Handley-Page Ltd. Hewlett and Blondeau Ltd also built a number of B.E.2as which were then transferred to the Navy.

Specification – B.E.2a

Powerplant:	70hp Renault
Weights:	Empty 1,100lb (499kg); loaded 1,600lb (723kg)
Dimensions:	Upper span 36ft 11in (11.23m); chord 5ft 6in (1.68m); gap 6ft (1.83m); wing area 376sq ft (34.97sq m); dihedral 2 degrees; stagger –1½in (–0.04m)
	Length 28ft 4in (8.64m); height 10ft 8in (3.25m); tailplane area 34sq ft (3.162sq m); elevator area 25sq ft (2.33sq m); rudder area 12sq ft (1.12sq m); fin area nil
Performance:	Speed at sea level 74mph (118km/h); rate of climb 330ft/min (101m/min); endurance 3hr

B.E.2a in Service

The first production aircraft, the Bristol-built 217, was accepted by the RFC on 12 January 1913, and joined the B.E.1 (which had by now been given the serial number 201) on the strength of No.2 Squadron RFC at Farnborough on 7 February. Nos 4 and 6 Squadrons also received B.E.2as, adding the type to the assortment of designs with which all RFC squadrons were then equipped. The type was also operated by the Royal Naval Air Service (RNAS), as the RFC's naval

An early B.E.2a outside the RFC flight sheds at Farnborough. It has unequal span wings and lacks any decking between the cockpits. The radius rods which controlled axle movement can clearly be seen above the undercarriage skids. Crown copyright – DERA

B.E.2a 218 with its front cockpit faired over, covering the additional petrol tank which enabled Capt Longcroft to undertake several record-breaking cross-country flights. P.H.T. Green Collection

wing preferred to be called, at its Eastchurch station, and by the Australian Air Corps who purchased two from British and Colonial.

In February 1913 2 Squadron was transferred to a new base at Montrose in Scotland, and the commanding officer, Maj Burke, selected five of its pilots to make the journey by air. These included Capt J.H. Becke in B.E.2a No.217, and Capt Charles A.H. Longcroft in 218, the other aircraft being Maurice Farman's. The five machines left Farnborough on 17 February, reaching their destination on the 26th after many adventures, which included one aircraft undergoing an engine change in the field and the pilots spending one night in a lunatic asylum. Longcroft's 218 performed faultlessly throughout the journey, which then seems to have sparked off an interest in cross-country flying within the Squadron, Longcroft being particularly keen. On 21 May 1913, having been sent to Farnborough to collect a new machine, the Bristol-built B.E.2a no.273, he flew it straight back to Montrose, covering a distance of around 450 miles (720km) in one day. Leaving Farnborough at 5.25a.m. and stopping twice to refuel, he experienced no problems until nearing St Andrews when he ran into a bad storm. He pressed on regardless, landing at Montrose at 4.20p.m., his face bleeding where he had been struck by hailstones.

19 August saw Longcroft repeat the journey in B.E.2a 225, yet another Bristol-built machine, this time with the passenger seat occupied by Col F.H. Sykes. This aircraft had been fitted with an additional fuel tank, allowing the journey to be completed in 7 hours and 40 minutes with a single refuelling stop at Alnmouth in Northumberland. Longcroft's 'own' aircraft, the 218, was flown by him across to, and around, Ireland during September. It was then fitted with a special fuel tank, holding 53 gallons (240 litres), which had been built by Air Mechanic H.C. Bullock. This fitted into the forward cockpit, which was then faired over with fabric to improve streamlining, and on 22 November Longcroft flew non-stop from Montrose to Portsmouth, then back to Farnborough, covering over 550 miles (885km) in 7 hours and 20 minutes. For this magnificent effort Captain Longcroft justly won the Britannia Trophy for the best flight of the year.

However, 2 squadron's period at Montrose was marred by a tragic accident on 27 May 1913, when the starboard wing of the 205 (the erstwhile B.E.5, which had now been fitted with a Renault engine, effectively converting it into a B.E.2) collapsed in the air and the pilot, Lt Desmond Arthur, was thrown out and killed. An investigation concluded that the crash had been caused by a faulty repair to the rear spar of the upper wing. There was, however, no record of this repair having been carried out either at the Factory or by the RFC, which lead to a recommendation that all future repairs should be inspected and properly recorded.

The Montrose Ghost

On 27 May 1913 Lt. Desmond Arthur of 2 Squadron RFC, based at Montrose, was flying B.E. No.205 and was descending in a gliding turn at around 2,500ft (762m) when the starboard upper wing suddenly collapsed. He was thrown from the aircraft as it fell to the ground, his seat belt later being found to have broken.

Although it had only recently joined the Squadron, 205 was by no means a new machine. It had been built by the Royal Aircraft Factory, as B.E.5, back in June 1912, being powered originally by the 60hp water-cooled ENV engine taken from the earlier machine from which it had allegedly been 'reconstructed'. In February 1913 it had been fitted with an air-cooled Renault, thereby converting it into a standard B.E.2. and returned to the RFC, serving with 3 Squadron at Farnborough before being transferred to No.2.

Lt Arthur's crash was looked into by the Accident Investigation Committee of the Royal Aero Club, who found that the crash had been caused by a defective repair which had evidently come apart whilst the machine was in flight, resulting in the collapse of the whole wing. The rear spar had previously been broken near to the tip and repaired with a tapered splice 7½in (19cm) long which was so badly made that there were glue-filled gaps of up to ⅛in (0.3cm) between its two faces. No record of this repair having been carried out could be found.

It has been reported that, during 1916 Maj Cyril Fogin, commanding officer at Montrose, saw a figure in flying clothes walk across the airfield and then disappear near to the old mess. Other officers claimed to have seen the apparition too, but after August it appeared no more.

Montrose aerodrome was used again during World War II. One night, a single Hurricane was sent up to intercept an enemy aircraft reported to be in the area, but after half an hour the pilot had seen nothing and was instructed to return to base. The ground crews watched as the pilot made what seemed a perfect approach, but instead of landing he opened the throttle and climbed away for another circuit. The Hurricane landed at the third attempt, the pilot leaping from his cockpit demanding to know 'who was the fool who cut me out – some madman in a biplane baulked me just as I was touching down – a thing like a Tiger Moth'

Was this too the ghost of Desmond Arthur?

B.E.2 205 at Montrose. This was the machine in which Lt Desmond Arthur met his death due to a faulty repair to a wing spar. Author's collection

Further Development

The original B.E.2 did not enter RFC service, but was retained by the Royal Aircraft Factory for experimental work, and thus seems never to have been given a service serial number. A small number of production machines, including 601 and 602, were similarly employed. Modification of these aircraft was constant, not because of any perceived deficiency in their design, but as part of the Factory's continuing role

Lt Dawes with B.E.2a 225 in which he had just flown over from Ireland, Friday, 26 September 1913. The instrument panel was manufactured by Elliot Brothers Ltd and contained only an airspeed indicator, altimeter, rev. counter and watch. Author's collection

in research and development. The undercarriage, which, typically for the period, had no springing save that provided by the resilience of the bungee rubber cord used to secure the axle to the horizontal skid, was the first component to undergo development, probably because in his original design brief O'Gorman had expressed a

E.T. Busk

Edward Teshmaker Busk joined the Staff of the Royal Aircraft Factory on 10 June 1912 as Assistant Engineer in charge of Physics. Born 8 March 1886, he was educated at Harrow, and then at King's College, Cambridge, where he graduated with First Class Honours in the Mechanical Sciences Tripos. He then took up employment as an engineer with Halls & Co of Dartford, leaving during 1911 to conduct research into both the strain in wires and the nature and causes of wind gusts. Early in 1912 he learned to fly with the Aeronautical Syndicate at Hendon as a step towards moving into aeroplane design.

Once at Farnborough, he became involved in the study of aeroplane stability, and carried out a great deal of experimental work. By the autumn of 1913 he was able to design an aeroplane, the R.E.1, so that it would be inherently stable, automatically correcting for the effects of any bump or gust without action on the part of the pilot. He flew the machine 'hands off' in winds of up to 38mph, frequently carrying high-ranking officers as passengers and, on one occasion, demonstrating it before the King and Queen.

He then modified the B.E.2 to be similarly stable, rendering it a perfect platform for military reconnaissance, but met his death on 5 November 1914 when the machine he was flying caught fire in the air. He was posthumously awarded the Royal Aeronautical Society's Gold Medal and was replaced on the Factory staff by William Farren who was appointed Director of the R.A.E (as the Factory became) during World War Two.

A B.E.2 fitted with an early form of oleo undercarriage in May 1913. The purpose of the object strapped to the front starboard centre-section strut is not known. Crown copyright – DERA

wish to improve upon that system. Several forms of oleo undercarriage were tried, the final design having a single front wheel (to prevent nose-over) fixed to the apex of a triangulated structure, with two sturdy hydraulic oleo legs to absorb the landing shocks of the main wheels. This design was adopted for a number of later Factory designs including the F.E.2b and R.E.7 but proved too heavy for the B.E., adversely affecting both its speed and climb.

In the early days of aviation many people thought that aircraft, such as those of the Wright Brothers, which required constant correction by the pilot in order to maintain a steady course, would prove unsuitable for military purposes since the pilot's attention would be diverted from essential matters such as observation. As early as January 1909 the great scientist F.W. Lanchester had stated that:

> The future of flight as a useful and practical means of navigation will depend upon the abolition of hand-maintained equilibrium, and the substitution of automatic stability.

Some engineers sought to achieve this stability by means of pendulums and gyroscopes, in effect anticipating the modern automatic pilot but, as Mervyn O'Gorman reported in 1913 when asked to comment upon a proposal made by Sebastian De Ferranti, founder of the Ferranti firm of electrical engineers:

> The principle is good, but the amount of 'working out' to be done at present would appear to make it impracticable, unless very considerable sums of money are to be sunk into experiments upon this line alone.

Such considerable sums of money were not available, and in any event O'Gorman and the Royal Aircraft Factory sought to achieve the desired stability by aerodynamic means, just as J.W. Dunne had tried to do, a young Cambridge graduate, Edward Busk, being engaged for that express purpose.

Busk's investigation into aeroplane stability led to the fitting of interplane struts whose upper ends had a considerably increased chord, thereby providing a fin area which was intended to reduce the rolling moment caused by yaw. In another experiment, B.E.2a No.601 was fitted with two curved fins, each with an area of 6sq ft (0.5m), above the top wing, one over each pair of centre section struts. They had vertical leading edges about which they could be pivoted, although it is now unclear how this was achieved. The same aircraft was fitted with a rectangular tailplane of high aspect ratio mounted on top of the fuselage in place of the original surface, and braced from a kingpost fitted on the fuselage centreline. This tailplane, designated T3, had the same overall area as the semi-circular tailplane (T2), which it replaced. The original spade-shaped tailplane was retrospectively designated T1.

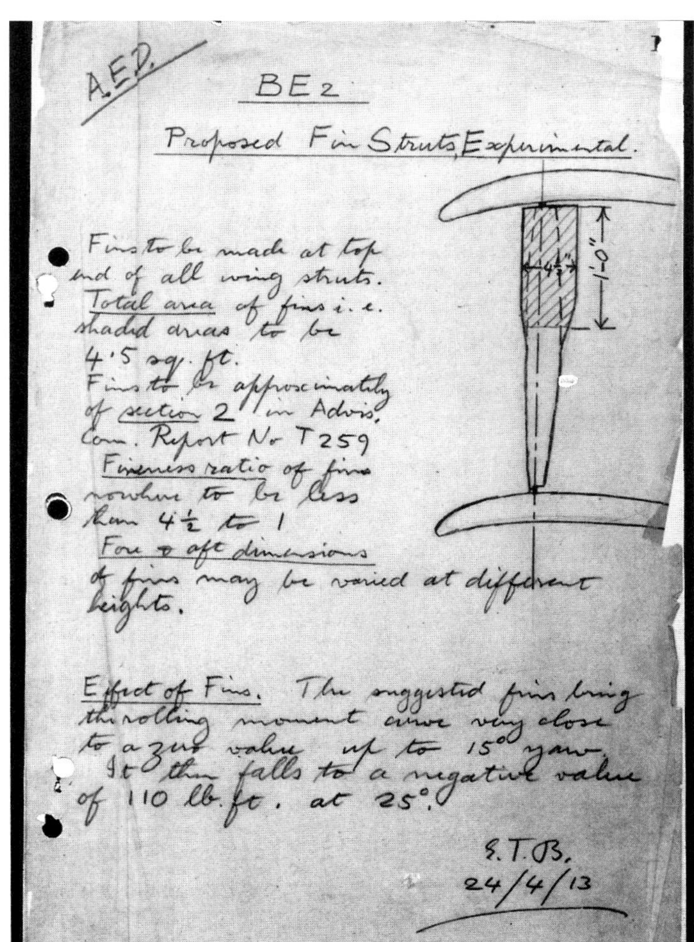

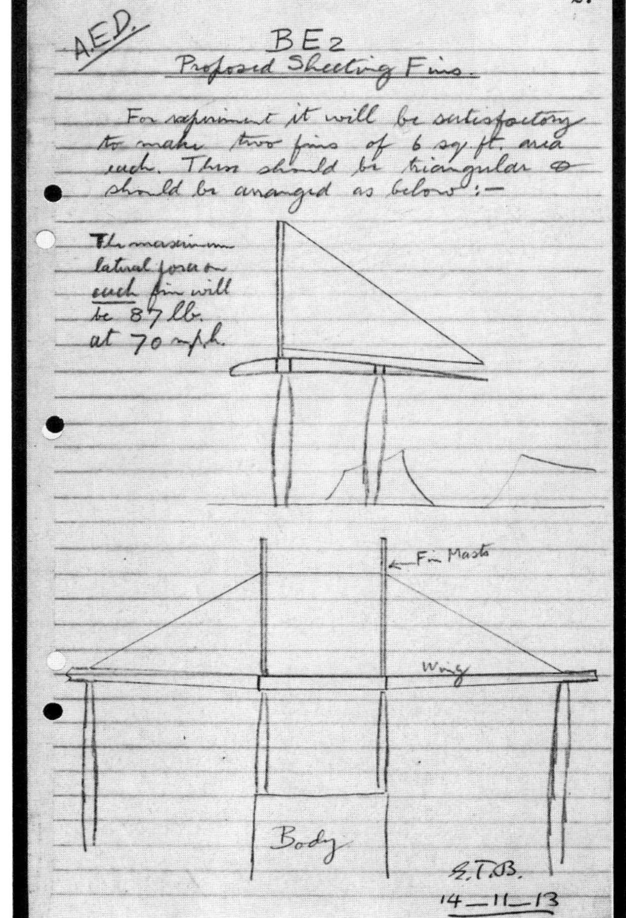

Pages from E.T. Busk's notebook demonstrates his continual concern with aeroplane

In addition to the oleo undercarriage this B.E.2 has been fitted with experimental interplane struts, designed by E.T. Busk to improve directional stability. Author's collection

A later B.E.2, probably 601, with a decking between the engine and the passenger cockpit. The fin areas above the upper centre section were part of the Factory's investigations into aeroplane stability, as was the modified tailplane. Imperial War Museum

Whilst these and other modifications were being tested in flight, the B.E. airframe was being subjected to static testing in the Farnborough workshops. The original B.E.2, after over 100 hours of flying, in all weathers, was inverted and loaded to six times its normal load, the only damage being that a small pin in the warp mechanism sheared. This was replaced and the test repeated without failure.

A wing was static loaded to twice the normal load and then warped up and down to an angle several degrees greater than the maximum possible in flight, for 350,000 times without damage. An attempt to repeat the experiment at 3½ times normal load had to be abandoned when the test machine broke! Initially, these loading tests were conducted by simply shovelling the required weight of loose sand onto the wing that was being tested, but this rather crude method was soon superseded by the use of sealed bags of lead shot.

In May 1914 the Advisory Committee published 'Report and Memorandum No.127' which was entitled 'Precautions taken as to the Strength of Details on the B.E. Class Aeroplane' and which described these tests and many others, stating that B.E. wings had been loaded to 8.4 times normal before failure, and that the machine had an overall factor of safety of seven.

The next development of the B.E.2 appears to have been intended to improve the crew's comfort rather than the aeroplane's performance. It comprised the introduction of a new fuselage top decking, with much smaller cockpit cut-outs, affording better protection against the elements. Modifications were also made to the control runs, the cables now being external to the fuselage to facilitate inspection and maintenance.

Early in 1914 orders for this new variant, the B.E.2b, were placed with Armstrong-Whitworth, Jonques Aviation Works and the Whitehead Aircraft Co., thus continuing the policy of spreading the War Office's business across the entire industry. This type was just coming into service at the outbreak of the World War I in August, although it had already been superseded by yet another variant.

At this time the primary, almost the only, role for military aeroplanes was reconnaissance, for which a steady platform was considered essential. Tentative experiments involving dropping bombs or fitting machine-guns had certainly taken place, but remained secondary to the need to develop the perfect reconnaissance machine. Edward Busk's research into stability had resulted, late in 1913, in the creation of what was undoubtedly the world's first inherently stable aeroplane, the R.E.1., of which two prototypes were built in the Farnborough workshops. However, this machine, for some reason which is now unclear, was never adopted for production, and instead Busk incorporated many of its principal design features into a new revision of the B.E. airframe, the B.E.2c.

Although the War Office had by now realized that the Factory was building new aeroplanes to its own designs, and indeed on 14 November 1913 had officially granted it authority to do so, the spirit of 'reconstruction' clearly lived on at Farnborough. The prototype B.E.2c was created by modifying B.E.2a No.602, although a little

(Top) **The wing structure of a B.E.2 is tested to destruction by loading it with sand in March 1913. In later years, bags of lead shot were substituted for the loose sand.** Author's collection

(Bottom) **The point of collapse; the failure appears to have occurred at the rear spar. As a result of such tests, a modified aerofoil section, which allowed for a deeper spar, was introduced.** Crown copyright – DERA

B.E.2b 2884 showing the smaller cockpit cut-outs which gave improved weather protection to the occupants and distinguished the type from earlier variants. Author's collection

Specification – B.E.2c

Powerplant:	90hp RAF1a
Weights:	Empty 1,370lb (621kg); loaded 2,142lb (972kg)
Dimensions:	Span 37ft (11.29m); chord 5ft 6in (1.68m); gap 6ft (1.83m); wing area 354sq ft (32.92sq m); dihedral 3½ degrees; stagger 24in (0.61m)
	Length 27ft 3in (8.31m); height 11ft 1½in (3.39m); tailplane area 36sq ft (3.35sq m); elevator area 27q ft (2.51sq m); rudder area 12sq ft (1.12sq m); fin area 4sq ft (0.37sq m)
Performance:	Speed at sea level 86mph (138km/h); rate of climb 500ft/min (153m/min); endurance 3hr

more of the parent aircraft was used than on previous occasions. The new machine was given staggered mainplanes with pronounced dihedral, ailerons now being employed for lateral control. This allowed the introduction of a new, deeper aerofoil section, RAF6, since the wings no longer needed to be sufficiently flexible to allow 'warping'. Incidence bracing was now similarly possible.

A rectangular tailplane, similar to the experimental unit T3, was fitted but mounted midway between the longerons, rather than on top of the fuselage as previously. Four bracing wires ran from it to the rudder post, ahead of which was now a triangular fin.

The fuselage had the top decking with smaller cockpit cut-outs similar to those introduced with the 2b, its lower front longerons being redesigned to accommodate the repositioned spar attachment points necessitated by the staggered wings, the lower wing having moved 24in (60cm) to the rear. The engine and undercarriage remained unaltered. The B.E.2c made its first flights on 30 May 1914, Busk occupying the pilot's seat for three of its four outings.

In early June 1914, the RFC's entire contingent of aeroplanes gathered together at Netheravon for what was termed a 'concentration camp'. Pilots from 2 squadron naturally flew their aircraft down from Montrose in order to attend. On 9 June Maj W. Sefton-Branker, then the Whitehall Officer in charge of RFC supplies, and an indifferent pilot, flew the B.E.2c down to Netheravon from Farnborough. So effective was the machine's inherent stability that, after having taken off, climbed to 2,000ft (609m), and set course, he was able to busy himself writing an account of the countryside over which he flew, not touching the control column again until he required to land. Thus the Royal Aircraft Factory had effectively created the stable observation platform which the pre-war Army was convinced it needed.

On 19 June, 602 returned to Netheravon remaining there until the 26th, during which time it was flown by a number of service pilots. In July, it was assigned to

They Called Them RAF 2cs

Oh! they found a bit of iron what
Some bloke had thrown away,
And the R.A.F. said, 'This is just the thing
We've sought for many a day.'
They built a weird machine,
The strangest engine ever seen,
And they'd quite forgotten that the thing was rotten,
And they shoved it in a flying machine.
Then they ordered simply thousands more,
And sent them out to fight.
When the blokes who had to fly them swore,
The R.A.F. said, 'They're all right
The 'bus is stable as can be,
We invented every bit ourselves, you see!'.
They were so darn' slow, they wouldn't go,
And they called them R.A.F.2cs!

RAF 1a Engine

The Royal Aircraft Factory's first indigenous aircraft engine was an air-cooled V8 providing 90hp from a swept volume of around 9 litres at a crankshaft speed of 1,800rpm. This relatively high speed was made possible by mounting the propeller on an extension of the camshaft, which was positioned within the 'vee' between the two banks of cylinders where it operated the side inlet valves directly, and the overhead exhaust valves via pushrods. This simple but effective reduction gear was one of several features copied from the Renault which had inspired the engine's overall design. The two sets of cylinders were staggered, the right-hand bank being slightly forward of the left so that each connecting rod could have its own big-end journal. The cylinder heads were integral with the cylinders, which were of iron, their cooling fins cast on, a departure from Renault practice intended to eliminate the ever troublesome cylinder head gasket. The design included for a cowl or scoop to be fitted above the cylinder heads, and for baffles to direct the airflow around each cylinder to ensure each was cooled equally.

Lubrication was by splash, assisted by a light flywheel which dipped into the sump and transferred oil into channels which led to the crankshaft bearings. Breather pipes reminiscent of ships' ventilators were fitted at the forward end of each cylinder bank to blow an oil mist onto the exposed valve gear.

In a bench test on 23 April 1914 during which it ran faultlessly for 6 hours it produced a steady 78 brake horsepower, consuming 50½ gallons (227 litres) of petrol.

No.4 Squadron. In service the B.E.2c soon acquired the nickname 'Stability Jane', the type later becoming known, more simply, as the 'Quirk'.

A second prototype B.E.2c was created by rebuilding the aeroplane that had played a significant role in its initial development, B.E.2a No.601. This differed from the first prototype, 602, in that it was powered, not by a standard 70hp Renault, but by the Royal Aircraft Factory's own design, the RAF1. This was dimensionally similar to the Renault, being loosely based upon it, but gave an additional 20hp. Flight testing began towards the end of May 1914, and soon established the merits of the Factory's engine, which went into production by the Daimler Company, and others, as the RAF1a, becoming the standard powerplant for the B.E.2c as soon as it was available in sufficient numbers.

With testing of the RAF engine completed, 601 remained at Farnborough, joining the small fleet of test vehicles. However, on 5 November 1914 a leaking petrol tank led to its catching fire in the air. It crashed on Laffan's Plain, killing its pilot and originator, Edward Busk.

War

At the outbreak of war on 4 August 1914, the Royal Flying Corps was mobilized and Nos 2, 3, 4 and 5 Squadrons were sent to France as soon as they could be made ready. They crossed the Channel on the 13th, and took with them every available aeroplane, 64 in all, leaving only the worst few behind for training replacement pilots, and an ill-matched assortment they were: Henri Farman and Maurice Farman pushers, Avros, Bleriots, and, of course, B.E.2s. Indeed, the first British aeroplane to land in France was B.E.2a No.327 of 2 Squadron, piloted by Capt F.F. Waldron.

Just a few days later, Lt G.W. Mapplebeck of 4 Squadron, piloting a B.E.2a, shared with Lt Joubert de la Ferte's 3 Sqn Bleriot the distinction of carrying out the RFC's first ever wartime reconnaissance mission. On 26 April 1915, during the Battle of Neuve Chapelle, 2nd Lt William B. Rhodes Moorhouse of 2 Squadron was sent to bomb the railway junction at Courtrai, and so prevent enemy reinforcements from reaching the battle zone. Flying B.E.2b No.687, and armed only with a single 112lb (50kg) bomb he descended to around 300ft (90m) to be sure of hitting his target. Although successful, he was wounded in the stomach, thigh and hand by the fusillade of fire from troops on the ground, but managed to return to his base at Estaires near Merville to give his report and so prevent another pilot being sent to repeat the raid. He died in hospital the next day, and was later awarded a posthumous Victoria Cross for his courage and self-sacrifice.

Mass Production

The expansion of the Flying Services to meet the demands of war naturally led to the placing of production orders for large numbers of aeroplanes, of all available types. In this, the B.E.2 had an advantage over its commercial rivals, in that it had been designed in a drawing office, not in chalk on the factory floor, as was still common practice in the trade. Fully detailed drawings of every single component, no matter how simple, had already been prepared, thereby allowing its manufacture by anyone with the necessary skills in wood-

This early B.E.2c is 1099, the first built by Wm Beardmore. This photograph presumably shows its handover to the RNAS, with which it served at Whitley Bay. Author's collection

Early production B.E.2c, with Renault engine and skid undercarriage. Built by Bristol, it was presented by the Overseas Club; later presentation aircraft had the donor's name more discreetly marked. The union flag on the rudder was the only national marking carried in the early days of the war. Seen here at Farnborough in May 1915, 1695 served with 12 Squadron until it was wrecked in a crash 2 February 1916. Author's collection

Production – B.E.2/2a/2b

B.E.2/2a:
46; 47; 202; 267; 272 – Royal Aircraft Factory.
383; 385 – Armstrong Whitworth.
217; 218; 220; 222; 225–42; 245 248–250; 273; 449 – British & Colonial.
318; 347-349; 384; 474 – Coventry Ordnance Works.
299; 321 – Grahame-White.
460; 461 – Handley-Page.
49; 50 – Hewlett & Blondeau.
314; 316; 317; 320; 336; 372 – Vickers.
441; 442; 447; 452–4. 327–9; 331–2; 368; 457; 465–6;471; 475; 477-8; 602–2; 612; 622; 635; 667–8; 709 – Unknown.

B.E.2b:
A376 – Royal Aircraft Factory.
396 – British & Colonial.
2175; 2180; 2770–2819 – Jonques.
2884-9 – Whitehead Aviation.
484; 487–8; 492–3; 646; 650; 666; 676; 687; 705; 722; 733; 746. – Unknown.

A B.E.2b fuselage in service as an airship car with an additional fuel tank fixed to the underside of the fuselage. The large diameter pipe behind the propeller kept the airship's ballonet inflated, thus enabling the non-rigid envelope to retain its shape. J.M. Bruce/G.S. Leslie Collection

and metalworking, regardless of their lack of previous experience with aeroplanes. Orders for the B.E.2c were placed first with aircraft firms experienced in volume production, a sensible precaution intended to ensure that initial deliveries were received as quickly as possible, and then with companies from outside the established aircraft industry. Firms whose previous products had been furniture, carriages, motor cars or agricultural machinery had both the right equipment and the skilled tradesmen required for building aeroplanes, and so accepted orders to manufacture the B.E.2c. The first companies thus entering aircraft manufacture were Messrs G. & J. Weir and the Daimler Motor Car Company, the latter laid out an aerodrome beside their works so that completed machines could be test flown, and dispatched by air.

The first production example was accepted by the RFC on 19 December 1914, and the type began to replace earlier variants and other machines in front-line squadrons, the older machines being returned to England for use in training establishments. By the end of 1915, of the sixteen RFC squadrons on the Western Front, twelve were operating B.E.2cs, although not all of these were fully equipped with the type.

The first ever night bombing raid by a British Unit was made on 19/20 February 1916 by two B.E.2cs of 4 Squadron. The target was an enemy aerodrome at Cambrai and the machines, piloted by Capt E.D.Horsfall and Capt J.E.Tennant, were flown solo to increase their bomb load.

A number of B.E.2 fuselages, minus wings and tail surfaces, were employed as cars for S-S type non-rigid airships. Their wheels were frequently removed, landings being made on the skids alone, as no forward motion was necessary. Large additional fuel tanks were fitted below the cockpit area, giving a substantial increase in endurance.

Although the death of Edward Busk was a tragic blow to British aeronautical research, it did not stop development of the B.E.2, any more than the loss of Geoffrey de Havilland to private industry had done, for by this time the Royal Aircraft Factory had dozens of talented designers on its staff.

The Factory's oleo undercarriage looks too heavy for this B.E.2c. It found better use on the F.E.2b. J.M. Bruce/G.S. Leslie Collection

Within a comparatively short time the twin-skid undercarriage had been replaced, not with one of the cumbersome oleo types, but with a simple 'vee' type, the axle being lashed within its apexes with 38ft (11m) of ⅜in (0.95cm) bungee rubber shock cord on each side. This new undercarriage was first tested fitted to 1749 on 7 January 1915, and was adopted at the same time that the RAF1a replaced the Renault as the standard powerplant. A cowling, covering the underside of the engine sump and improving streamlining, was introduced with it. The exhausts were also modified, with two exhaust pipes, one from each bank of cylinders, turning up in front of the centre-section struts to terminate just above the upper wing.

The instruments, which had originally comprised little more than an altimeter and an air speed indicator, now included a compass and a watch. A dial type air speed indicator replaced the original fluid column type. The brass domed ceramic ignition switch (actually a domestic light switch) remained outside the pilot's cockpit, where the mechanic swinging the propeller could see for himself whether it was up or down.

The landing and flying wires, which were originally of plain cable, were replaced with a new form of swaged streamlined wires which had been invented by the Royal Aircraft Factory, and which were named, with obvious logic, 'Rafwires'. These wires soon superseded cable bracing on many other aircraft types, eventually becoming the standard form of bracing wire for all biplanes.

These modifications were thought to make the new B.E.2c sufficiently different to earlier versions that a small leaflet entitled 'A Note for Flyers of B.E.2c Aeroplanes fitted with RAF 1A Engines, V-type

A Note for Flyers of B.E.2c Aeroplanes Fitted with RAF1A Engines, V-Type Undercarriages and Rafwires

1. *Adjustment* – The aeroplane should be so adjusted that it is trim when flying at 'cruising' speed – from 65 to 70 miles per hour. At this speed the machine will then fly without the controls.

2. *Revolutions on the ground* – On the ground, the engine revolutions should be between 1,480 and 1,520 per min.; but under no circumstances should this, or any other engine, be allowed to run on full throttle until after it has warmed up, and the oil is circulating freely throughout the engine. This will require at least 10 mins. slow running.

3. *Climbing speeds* – With full tanks and passenger, the best climbing speed is about 55 miles per hour, and the engine revolutions at this speed should be 1,600 per min.

During a test made by the Aeronautical Inspection Department, a climb to 6,000 ft. in 13 mins. 35 secs was obtained; and on service at least 6,000 ft. in 16 mins. may be expected.

4. *Maximum speed* – At the maximum speed of the aeroplane, when flying at a low altitude, the engine revolutions will approximate to 1,850 per min.; but at this speed, the fuel consumption will reach 9 gallons of petrol per hour, and if the maximum time in the air is desired, the normal engine revolutions of 1,600 per min. should be maintained.

5. *Landing speed* – The landing speed is much the same as with a Renault engined B.E.2c – about 40 to 41 miles per hour; but there is a strong tendency for flyers to alight at too high a speed until they become accustomed to flying this machine, owing to its higher normal speed – 89.6 miles per hour on an Aeronautical Inspection Department test, or 87 miles per hour under service conditions. It should be noted that the gliding angle of this machine is finer than that of the old B.E.'s.

6. *Fuel consumption* – The petrol consumption at the normal engine speed of 1,600 revs. per min. is 7¼ gallons per hour; but this will vary with the elevation at which the flight is made, being reduced somewhat as the height is increased.

2650, a later B.E.2c, with 'vee' undercarriage and RAF1a engine complete with sump cowling. The gun mounting would allow the observer to fire obliquely forwards, avoiding his own propeller. Author's collection

Undercarriages and Rafwires' was prepared. Copies, dated 4 May 1915 were printed by HMSO and distributed to all squadrons operating the type.

In early 1916 the B.E.2c underwent its final major modification with the substitution of wings of the newly developed RAF14 section for those of RAF6. These new wings could be set at a slightly greater angle of incidence, thereby offering some small improvement in the machine's rate of climb without any increase in drag.

Streamlining seems to have paid little part in this wireless installation. The exhaust pipes have been shortened in such a way as to ensure that anyone in the front cockpit would get the full benefit of their fumes. A. Thomas

Armament

The B.E.2 was conceived as a general purpose/reconnaissance aeroplane to fill the needs of the pre-war army, and was never intended to be armed. However, like much equipment in that war of ever-changing technology it was soon pressed into a role for which it had never been designed, not because it was particularly appropriate to that role, but simply because it was available. Thus it was occasionally employed as a bomber, carrying either four 20lb (9kg) bombs in underwing racks, or a single 112lb (50kg) bomb beneath the fuselage; heavier loads of up to a dozen 20lb (9kg) bombs could be carried if the observer was left behind.

This camera installation was typical, the pilot needing to lean out to change plates, whilst the observer kept a watchful eye for enemy fighters, fortunately rarer in the desert, where this photograph was taken, than over the Western Front. J.M. Bruce/G.S. Leslie Collection

In the early days of the war virtually all aircraft, on both sides, were similarly unarmed, but their crews soon began to carry revolvers, or rifles, with which to fire at any enemy machines they happened to encounter. Although a few attempts were made to fit machine-guns on crude mountings fabricated in squadron workshops, none was very successful. Placing the observer in the forward cockpit, whilst done for sound aerodynamic reasons, left him surrounded by struts and wires, making the operation of any defensive armament a tricky operation. In addition, the lack of any synchronization gear, which would have allowed a gun to fire forward through the propeller disc without hitting the blades, made the installation of any offensive armament almost impossible.

The first officially adopted Lewis gun mounting appears to have been the No.1 Mk.1 fixed bracket, often known officially as the 'candlestick' type which fixed to the fuselage side and into which a spike, or pin, fixed to the gun was inserted, allowing it to be swivelled around as required. Thus the gun could be used both for offence, and defence as the occasion demanded, but it relied entirely on the skill of its user to avoid shooting into his own machine. This was later superseded by the No.1 Mk.2 which fixed to the centre-section strut.

This was followed by the No.2 Mk.1 mounting in which the gun's pivot pin was placed into a socket on a bar, which was fixed between the front centre-section struts and could be moved up and down to facilitate aiming. It had been invented by Lt Medlicott of 2 Squadron, and so was often referred to as the 'Medlicott Mount'. A wire guard, which restricted muzzle movement, was often employed to prevent the observer hitting his own propeller.

A mounting which fixed a Lewis gun to the fuselage side, its muzzle held in place by cross-wires, was intended primarily for use by single-seaters, but found its way on to a number of B.E.2cs too, thereby providing the more aggressively minded pilots with some means of joining the fray.

The initial solution offered to the problem of firing rearwards, as required for defence, was the No.10 Mk.1 or 'Goalpost' mounting, which fixed between the two cockpits. Although moderately effective it must have been unnerving in use as it brought the observer's gun barrel within a few inches of the pilot's head. However, as it was unusual for more than one gun to be carried the observer was obliged to transfer his weapon from one mounting to another as occasion demanded.

A carefully posed photograph showing how an observer might, with a lot of luck, attack an enemy aircraft. The Lewis gun has a Norman vane foresight not usually seen on active service. J.M. Bruce/G.S. Leslie Collection

(Below) **Defence against an attack from the rear was possible, with a Lewis gun on a Strange mounting, provided that the enemy remained high. There was no defence against attack from below the tail.** J.M. Bruce/G.S. Leslie Collection

The 'Strange' mounting, named after its inventor, Capt L.A. Strange of 12 Squadron, was a swivelling pillar mounting, its Lewis gun being fixed to a toothed quadrant so that it could be elevated. It was positioned midway between the two cockpits so that it could be used either defensively by the observer or offensively by the pilot, eliminating the need for the gun to switch mountings. It was improved later by the provision of a quick release fitting designed by Sgt Hutton of 39 Squadron, making manoeuvre easier.

However, these various gun mountings were by no means universally adopted, some machines having one mounting, some another and a few remaining unarmed.

This B.E.2c, on service in the Middle East, has gun mountings on each rear centre-section strut, as well as bomb racks, and rails for Le Prieur rockets on the interplane struts. J.M. Bruce/G.S.Leslie Collection

The Pulpit

In mid-1915 an attempt was made to provide a fighting machine based upon the B.E.2c but armed with a forward-firing machine-gun. Wind tunnel research confirmed that it would be possible to overcome the lack of any effective synchronization gear by placing the observer in a separate nacelle, ahead of the propeller, and so gaining the arc of fire which could normally only be offered by a pusher, without losing the aerodynamic advantages of the tractor layout.

The prototype was created from the Bristol-built B.E.2c No.1700 by moving the engine back into the space previously occupied by the forward cockpit, and fitting a plywood nacelle onto a bearing on a forward extension of the propeller shaft, the propeller itself now being about 15in (38cm) ahead of the upper wing. This nacelle was provided with steel tube struts

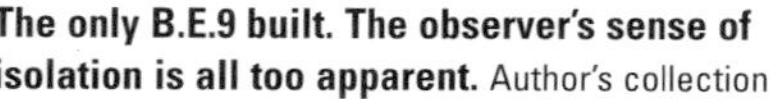

The only B.E.9 built. The observer's sense of isolation is all too apparent. Author's collection

(Below) **A head-on view of the B.E.9 taken 17 August 1915.** Crown copyright – DERA

to support it from the undercarriage, and was prevented from revolving with the propeller by bracing wires from the wings. A steel hoop was provided at the rear of the nacelle to offer its occupant some protection from the propeller, or to at least remind him of its presence! An enlarged fin was fitted to offset the increase in keel ahead of the machine's centre of pressure. A wider centre section was provided, not to increase the lift, but to allow the struts to be splayed outwards clear of the engine. Standard B.E.2c outer wing panels and horizontal tail surfaces were used. Although officially designated the B.E.9, it quickly acquired the nickname 'The Pulpit'.

It was test-flown by Frank Goodden on 14 August 1915 and four days later was shown to the King and Queen during their official visit to Farnborough. By 1 September it had been flown to the Central Flying School, whose report (CFS No.132) was generally favourable, commenting that the observer's view and field of fire were excellent and that its stability was also very good. Communication between the pilot and observer was noted to be poor, and it was suggested that it should be fitted both with dual controls, and with some form of telephone between the two cockpits. Remarkably, the top speed was 82mph (130km/h), little less than that of the B.E.2c.

B.E.9 in flight over Farnborough, 18 September 1915. Crown copyright – DERA

On 11 September, with the dual controls fitted, it was flown across to France for evaluation by front-line pilots. It was collected from the depot at St Omer by Capt L.G. Hawker and taken to 6 Squadron, from where, on the 21st, it moved to 16 Squadron, whose C.O., Maj H.C.T. Dowding, considered it to be dangerous for the passenger.

Whilst with 8 Squadron, Lt D.A. Glen flew it over the lines, and engaged in an inconclusive combat with a Fokker monoplane. It was also flown over the lines by Marshal of the Royal Air Force Lord Douglas of Kirtleside (then Lt W.S. Douglas), whose logbook records that it was very stable, but sluggish. On 22 December Lt Douglas was detailed to return 1700 to the depot at St Omer. As a result of these trials it was concluded that the type could not be recommended for production, and it was therefore returned to England on 9 January 1916, its eventual fate being unrecorded. A planned improvement, the B.E.9a, in which the engine was to have been replaced with the more powerful RAF4a, was therefore not proceeded with.

Another development of the basic B.E. layout was the B.E.10, which had a steel tube fuselage, with a deep top decking, a high aspect ratio fin, a rudder and the oleo undercarriage, with a small buffer nose wheel, which eventually found favour for the F.E.2b. Its ailerons were full span, and could be used together as flaps. In order to simplify production its wing ribs were pressed from sheet alloy. No prototype was built at Farnborough, but an order for four machines was placed with the British and Colonial Aeroplane Co. at Bristol, where its unusual construction led to its being dubbed the 'gas-pipe aeroplane'. However, this order was soon cancelled when it was realized that its manufacture would require extensive changes to production methods, and that it would therefore be more expedient to continue to manufacture the B.E.2c.

Production B.E.2c/d/e

B.E.2c:
1780–1800; 2000–2029 – Armstrong Whitworth.
964–975; 1123–46; 3999; 8606–29; 9951–10000 – Blackburn.
1099-1122; 8714-9475 – Wm. Beardmore.
1652-1747; 4070-4219 – British & Colonial.
2030-2129; 2570-2669 – Daimler.
1183-88 – Eastbourne Aviation.
1147-70; 8293–8500 – Grahame-White.
976–87; 1189–94 – Hewlett & Blondeau.
988–999 – Martin & Handyside.
2670–2769 – Ruston, Proctor & Co.
1424–35 – South Coast Aviation.
952–63; 1075–98; 1748–79;4710–25; 5413–41; 7321–45 – Vickers.
4300–4599 – G & J Weir.
2470–2569; 5384–5403 – Wolseley Motors.
B728; B792; B8794; B8819; B9444B9459; B9993; F9627 –Rebuilds.
4016; 4019; 5616 – Unknown.

B.E.2d:
5730–5879; 7058–7257 – Ruston, Proctor & Co.
6728–6827; A1792–1891 – Vulcan Motor.
B705; B707–8; B719; B3954; B8825C9988–9; C9995; F4218; F9567; F9571; H8256. – Rebuilds.

B.E.2e:
A1261–1310; C7001-7100 – Barclay Curle.
A2733–2982; A8626–8725; B4401–4600; C1701–1753 (cancelled) – British & Colonial.
B6151–6200– British Caudron.
A1361–1410; C6901–7000 – William Denny.
A1311–1360; C7101–7200 –Napier & Miller.
N5770–5794. (cancelled) – Robey.
A1792–1891; B3651–3750 – Vulcan Motor.
A3049–3168 – Wolseley Motors.
B702; B706; B709–710; B712; B719; B722–5; B728; B748; B770; B772; B790; B797; B4004; B4006; B4022–3; B4026; B8820; B8828; B8831; B8835; B8849; B8854; B8863; B9453–4; B9457; B9469; B9474; B9938; B9940–1; B9957; B9998 –Rebuilds.

Note: Some aircraft ordered as B.E.2c or B.E.2d were completed as B.E.2e, thus becoming B.E.2f or g.

'Fokker Fodder'

Poorly armed as the B.E.2c was, few other aircraft, whether friend or foe, were better armed and, although losses were inevitable, its crews scored an occasional victory too.

However, the advent at the front in late 1915 of the Fokker Monoplane which was armed with a fixed machine-gun synchronized to fire forward through the propeller disc, added a new dimension to aerial warfare. The Fokker was a true fighter plane, the first to enter service with Germany's air arm, and it was able to overcome the B.E.'s poor defence with comparative ease, for in combat the British machine's stability was no longer to its advantage, and losses began to mount. The RFC in France quickly requested that the B.E.2 should be replaced with a machine capable of defending itself against the Fokkers, but none was available. Fortunately for B.E. crews the Fokkers were introduced in ones and twos as they became available, and were never really numerous, with around one hundred being in service by the spring of 1916. Nonetheless, the increased casualties provided ammunition for the enemies of the Royal Aircraft Factory, which many aircraft manufacturers still saw as an unwelcome rival, deriving from the fact that the existence of 'official' designs, such as those for the B.E.2, had made it possible for the government to put aircraft manufacture out to competitive tender, thereby limiting profits. The manufacturers' principal champion was Charles G. Grey, editor of *The Aeroplane*, undoubtedly influenced by the fact that the trade placed advertisements in his journal, whereas the Factory did not.

As the losses continued, the Press, in reporting the casualties, made frequent references to the 'Fokker Scourge', with both RFC pilots, and their mounts being dismissed as helpless 'Fokker Fodder'.

The situation was dramatically brought to the attention of Parliament on 22 March 1916 when the newly elected Member for East Hertfordshire, Mr Noel Pemberton-Billing, whilst attacking the management of Britain's air services, declared:

> ... I do not intend to deal with the colossal blunders of the Royal Flying Corps, but may I refer briefly to the hundreds, nay thousands of machines which have been ordered and which have been referred to by our pilots at the front as 'Fokker Fodder'. Every one of our pilots knows that when he steps into them if he gets back it will be more by luck and by his skill than by any mechanical assistance he will get from the people who provide him with the machines. I do not want to touch a dramatic note this afternoon but if I did I would suggest that a number of our gallant officers in the Royal Flying Corps have been rather murdered than killed ...

These remarks were widely reported in the Press, as was the reply by the Under-secretary of State for War, Mr Tennant, who asserted that the Government had no need of such strong language to bring their attention to a situation of which they were already aware, and suggested that the word 'murder' ought not to have been used. Pemberton-Billing responded by repeating the accusation and declaring that, if challenged, he could produce such evidence as would shock the house, to which Tennant replied that he should either withdraw the charge or produce his evidence.

Thus when, one week later, on 29 March, the Air Services were again the subject of debate, Pemberton-Billing presented his evidence, quoting emotionally from letters from parents whose sons had been shot down and stating:

> ... if the officials who are responsible for deciding the type of the machines in which our officers take to the air fail, either by ignorance, intrigue or incompetence, to provide them with the best machines that this country can produce they are guilty of a crime for which only a fastidious mind can fail to find a name ...
>
> Our machines are dispatched to France in most cases as aeroplanes only. On their arrival the local squadron smiths do their best to convert them into weapons of war. A gun is stuck on here and a bomb hung on there. The performance of the machine loses 10 to 20 per cent of its efficiency. For example, the official speed of the B.E.2c is something less than 80 miles an hour. That in all conscience is bad enough when the machine is called upon to fight a Fokker or other German aeroplane with a speed of 110 miles an hour [The Fokker EIII was actually capable of 88mph], whereas by the time it has been turned into this travesty of a weapon of war its speed is reduced to about 68 miles an hour.

The debate continued, eventually moving on to Britain's defence against aerial attack,

The Pilot's Psalm

The B.E.2c is my 'bus, therefore I shall want.
He maketh me to come down in green pastures.
He leadeth me where I will not go.
He maketh me to be sick; he leadeth me astray on all cross-county flights.
Yea, though I fly over no-man's land where mine enemies would compass me about, I fear much evil, for thou art with me, thy joystick and thy prop discomfort me.
Thou preparest a crash before me in the presence of mine enemies, thy R.A.F. anointeth my hair with oil, thy tank leaketh badly.
Surely to goodness thou shalt not follow me all the days of my life, else I shall dwell in the House of Colney Hatch forever.

Noel Pemberton-Billing

To describe Noel Pemberton-Billing as a colourful character is a gross understatement, as he led a life so full and so varied that it all but defies description.

Born in Hampstead on 31 January 1881, the son of a Birmingham iron-founder, he ran away to sea at the age of 14, ending up in South Africa, where he joined the Natal Mounted Police. Wounded twice in the Boer War, he returned to England and opened one of the first ever petrol stations at Kingston-upon-Thames. Ahead of its time, it failed, and Pemberton-Billing returned to South Africa, where he founded a motoring magazine.

By 1904 he was back in England once more and becoming interested in aviation. He designed and built a number of aeroplanes, although none was successful. In 1909 he opened an aerodrome and aviators' colony at Fambridge in Essex but, once again, he was ahead of the times and this venture failed too.

In 1913 he learned to fly in a single day, in order to win a bet that it could not be done, then returned to aeroplane design, founding what was to become the 'Supermarine' company although, typically, he sold it before it achieved any real success.

When the war broke out his company designed and built a single-seater scout in just a week, but orders for this, PB9, inevitably known as the 'seven day bus', were not forthcoming. As a Temporary Acting Flight Lieutenant in the RNAS he was largely responsible for planning the bombing raid on the Zeppelin factory at Freidrichshafen on Lake Constance.

In January 1916 he resigned his commission to stand for Parliament and on 10 March became M.P. for East Hertfordshire, styling himself the 'First Air Member'. Just twelve days later he shocked the House, and the nation, by claiming that British pilots were being 'rather murdered than killed' by being sent to war in aircraft which were outdated and outclassed, and so brought about an enquiry into the management of RFC and the role of the Royal Aircraft Factory.

Post-war he ran a radio station in Australia, then moved to America. He returned to England in 1928 and attempted to market a form of motor caravan which he called a 'Land Yacht'. He tried, unsuccessfully, to re-enter Parliament in 1929 and throughout his life proposed numerous ideas for improvements in aeroplane design, but none were adopted. He died on 11 November 1948.

and concluded with Mr Tennant promising that he would request that the Prime Minister set up a small independent body to investigate the allegations put before the House by Mr Pemberton-Billing.

At the conclusion of the debate, Lt-Gen Sir David Henderson, who had been present in the public gallery, sought a meeting with Mr Tennant, agreeing that an inquiry should be called. As Director General of Military Aeronautics, and therefore one of those against whom Pemberton-Billing's accusations were levelled, he felt compelled to tender his resignation, but this was not accepted, at least until the conclusions of the inquiry were known.

The following day, the Army Council announced that a Committee of Inquiry was to be appointed under the chairmanship of Richard Burbidge, the General Manager, and later Managing Director, of Harrods, the famous London department store. The other committee members were Charles A. Parsons and H.F. Donaldson, with Mr R.H. Griffith acting as secretary. Its terms of reference were:

> To enquire and report whether, within the resources placed by the War Office at the disposal of the Royal Aircraft Factory and the limits imposed by War Office orders, the organization and management of the factory are efficient, and to give the Army Council the benefit of their suggestions on any points of the interior administration of the factory which seem to them capable of improvement.

Mr Pemberton-Billing seems to have been unimpressed by these arrangements, and continued his campaign against what he perceived as the mismanagement of Britain's Air Services. On 2 May 1916 he asked the House of Commons whether, as a result of his allegations regarding the inefficiency of the type, a decision had yet been taken to send no more B.E.2cs to France. He received the reply that no such decision had been taken, for no better machine was yet available, although several were being developed, both by the Royal Aircraft Factory and by commercial companies.

The constant attacks upon War Office policy led to the appointment, just five days later, of another Committee of Inquiry, chaired by a High Court judge, Mr Justice Bailhache, to inquire into the administration and command of the Royal Flying Corps.

Meanwhile, the Burbidge Committee performed its task with commendable efficiency, taking evidence from Mervyn O'Gorman, Maj Heckstall-Smith, the Factory's Assistant Superintendent, and Lt Gen Sir David Henderson. Its report to the War Office is dated 12 May 1916, and states:

> The functions of the Royal Aircraft Factory we understand to include original designs of aeroplanes and engines, improvement of existing designs, manufacture of experimental aeroplanes, engines and their parts, and aeronautical devices; study of and experimental work in all material used in an aeroplane; preparation of drawings and specifications for contractors, and, in certain cases, supervision of manufacture; repair of aeroplanes and engines, and provision of aeroplane and engine spare parts for maintenance; production of aeroplanes in limited quantity; and emergency work of all kinds to assist contractors or make good the failure of contractors.
>
> From which it is apparent that the War Office has laid it down that the Royal Aircraft Factory should be devoted to experimental rather than manufacturing purposes.
>
> The Royal Aircraft Factory cannot therefore be regarded as an establishment working on strictly commercial lines; it is rather a very large experimental laboratory, probably the largest in the United Kingdom, where experiments are carried out to full scale, therefore expenses must necessarily be high …
>
> The Royal Aircraft Factory has produced 77 new machines in all since the commencement of the war, while trade supplies have exceeded 2,120 machines.

The report went on to describe the structure and organization of the Factory, and to define the process by which a new design was made, stating that it usually took from six to nine months from the first preliminary sketch to preparation of finalized drawings ready for volume production. Its conclusions included:

> We are of the opinion that such an experimental establishment as the Royal Aircraft Factory should be in existence. That on its present wages cost the Factory efficiency could be enhanced as an experimental place and a substantially increased volume of finished work produced provided a sharp line of demarcation be drawn between experimentation and commercial productivity, and the factory be reorganized and managed as nearly as possible upon a commercial and engineering basis.
>
> From information afforded both at Farnborough and London we conclude that the standard of efficiency required by the War Office for Royal Aircraft Factory finished products is regarded as met, both as to construction and design.
>
> The existing undesirable trade feeling referred to we consider should be met and, if possible, overcome, as its existence can hardly fail to have a detrimental effect on all concerned. We do not consider that the competition of the Royal Aircraft Factory with the Trade should, if reasonably administered, be the cause of any detrimental friction or trade feeling.

The report, together with comments by the recently formed Air Board, was published on 19 July as Parliamentary Paper Cd 8191, although certain figures were prudently omitted 'in the public interest'. Since it made no criticism, other than a suggestion that the stores could be better managed, and instead suggested that the Factory could actually build more production machines, it was far from the report that Pemberton-Billing would have hoped for.

The Report of the Bailhache Inquiry into the management of the Flying Corps took longer to produce. The committee,

Pilots' Opinions

Pilots who flew the B.E.2c had the following memories of it:

'It was very much better in manoeuvre than the DH6 [the machine in which he had learned to fly], and more comfortable. It was more exact to fly, and lighter on the controls, more like a D.H. Moth.'
Lt Philip B. Townsend, RFC/RAF

'It took an enormous effort to get it into a spin at all, and then it immediately came out, almost by itself.'
Lt H. Thompson, RNAS

'The machine wanted to stay on a level keel. You could steep turn it but it took an effort.'
Capt C. Chabot, RFC

'By the late summer of 1915 the RFC had not yet progressed much beyond the two seat general purpose aeroplane, the most effective of which was still the B.E.2c.'
Lt W. Sholto-Douglas, RFC

'The beauty of the B.E.2c was that you could adjust a spring to hold the elevator in position for level flying, then ignore the bumps and fly 'hands-off'. The machine would right itself from whatever position it got into provided you had enough height.
Flt Cdr W.G. Moore, RNAS

Note: Ranks given are those held at the time of flying the B.E.2c and not those to which the pilots later rose.

which included Mr J.H. Balfour-Browne KC, Mr J.G. Butcher KC, MP. Mr Edward Short KC, MP, the Hon. Sir Charles Parsons FRS, and Mr Charles Bright FRS, held its first meeting, in public, on Tuesday, 16 May. Its terms of reference were stated to be:

> To inquire into and report upon the administration and command of the Royal Flying Corps, with particular reference to the charges made both in Parliament and elsewhere against the officers responsible for that administration and command, and to make any recommendations in relation thereto.

Initially, Mr Pemberton-Billing declined to give evidence, stating that, since he had made allegations against both flying Services, an inquiry solely into the command of the RFC was not an adequate response to his demands, particularly as the committee comprised a judge, three lawyers, a retired civil engineer and an expert on steam turbines. However, eventually both he and Mr Joynston-Hicks MP gave their evidence, as did Gen Henderson, Gen Smith-Dorrien, Lord Montagu of Beaulieu, a number of junior officers from both Air Services, and several people engaged in aircraft manufacture, in all a total of 54 witnesses being consulted. One witness, Algernon Berriman, the Daimler Company's chief engineer, stated that:

> The RAF engine and the B.E.2c have their defects, but they form a combination that has been instrumental in enabling the Royal Flying Corps to perform invaluable service in France.

The committee's final report was published in December and dealt at length with the difficulties naturally experienced in setting up a new branch of the armed forces, and in foreseeing with any accuracy exactly what equipment it would need, and in what quantities. The report stated that the Royal Aircraft Factory should be judged by its greatest achievement, the B.E.2c, which was aerodynamically sound, and capable of being mass-produced by companies which had never previously built aeroplanes. In conclusion, it answered thus the charges that had initiated its formation:

> No one could complain if Mr Pemberton-Billing had asked that these cases be enquired into to ascertain whether the deaths of these men could have been prevented. But based upon these incidents a charge of criminal negligence, or murder is an abuse of language and entirely unjustified.

Brought down intact, this B.E.2c was test-flown by its captors and German national markings were therefore applied. Author's collection

In fact, the B.E.2c was far from being the most vulnerable machine in front-line service, for in mid-1916 its rate of loss, as a percentage of the total number employed in France, was actually lower than for the many other types of machine. So the B.E.2c was left to soldier on, pending its eventual replacement by newer aircraft specifically designed for the aerial war over the Western Front.

Home Defence

There was, however, one combat role for which the B.E.2 was far from ill-suited, that of home defence. The first Zeppelin raid, on the night of 19 January 1915, although causing little damage, claimed the lives of two elderly people, and so brought about a sense of outrage that the enemy should visit the war upon defenceless civilians. As the raids continued, sporadic but wholly unopposed, the feeling grew that the Government should do more to protect the population. The defence of the British Isles was traditionally placed in the hands of the Admiralty, and so the first Zeppelin to be defeated, LZ37, was brought down over Belgium by Flt Sub-Lieut Rex Warneford, an RNAS pilot stationed near Dunkirk, who managed to coax his Morane monoplane high enough to drop a bomb on to it. Warneford, killed in a crash only a few weeks later, received the Victoria Cross for this action.

Later, with public anxiety still growing, it became clear that the RNAS was unable to cope unaided, and so the RFC was given responsibility of the defence of the east coast. A chain of strategically placed landing grounds was established, aeroplanes being stationed at each ready to intercept the raiders. In this role the B.E.2c's stability remained to its advantage, facilitating flying during night-time and landing by the poor light of a few flares. In the home defence role the B.E.2c was usually flown solo, the forward cockpit being faired over, and it was armed with small bombs, Ranken darts and a single Lewis gun.

However, it took a B.E.2c almost an hour to reach 10,000ft (3,048m), the lowest altitude at which Zeppelins were usually encountered, and its normal endurance at this height was around two hours. The RNAS at Chatham therefore conducted experiments in which a B.E.2c was carried, suspended below an SS type airship which could then patrol at altitude, releasing the aeroplane only when a target was sighted. Initial trials were conducted in August 1915 but the control gear proved defective and no release was achieved. In a further trial on 21 February 1916, the aeroplane released accidentally whilst at 4,000ft (1,220m), overturning in the process. One crew member, Lt Cdr Ireland, was thrown

The Destruction of the SL11

To: The Officer Commanding No.39 H.D. Squadron.

Sir:
I have the honour to make the following report on night patrol made by me on the night of the 2/3 instant. I went up at about 11.08p.m. on the night of the second with instructions to patrol between Sutton's Farm and Joyce Green.

I climbed to 10,000 feet in fifty-three minutes. I counted what I thought were ten sets of flares – there were a few clouds below me, but on the whole it was a beautifully clear night. I saw nothing until 1.10a.m. when two searchlights picked up a Zeppelin S.E. of Woolwich. The clouds had collected in this quarter and the searchlights had some difficulty in keeping on the airship. By this time I had managed to climb to 12,000 feet and I made in the direction of the Zeppelin – which was being fired on by a few anti-aircraft guns – hoping to cut it off on its way eastward. I very slowly gained on it for about ten minutes. I judged it to be about 800 feet below me and I sacrificed some speed in order to keep the height. It went behind some clouds, avoiding the searchlight, and I lost sight of it. After fifteen minutes of fruitless search I returned to my patrol.

I managed to pick up and distinguish my flares again. At about 1.50a.m. I noticed a red glow in the N.E. of London. Taking it to be an outbreak of fire, I went in that direction. At 2.05a.m. a Zeppelin was picked up by searchlights over N.N.E. London (as far as I could judge).

Remembering my last failure, I sacrificed height (I was at about 12,900 feet) for speed and nosed down in the direction of the Zeppelin. I saw shells bursting and night tracers flying around it. When I drew closer I noticed that the anti-aircraft aim was too high or too low, also a good many shells burst about 800 feet behind – a few tracers went right over. I could hear the bursts when about 3,000 feet from the Zeppelin. I flew about 800 feet below it from bow to stern and distributed one drum along it (alternate New Brock and Pomeroy). It seemed to have no effect; I therefore moved to one side and gave them another drum along the side – also without effect. I then got behind it and by this time I was very close – 500 feet or less below, and concentrated one drum on one part (underneath rear). I was then at a height of 11,500 feet when attacking the Zeppelin.

I had hardly finished the drum before I saw the part fired at, glow. In a few seconds the whole rear part was blazing. When the third drum was fired there were no searchlights on the Zeppelin, and no anti-aircraft was firing. I quickly got out of the way of the falling, blazing Zeppelin and, being very excited, fired off a few Very lights and dropped a parachute flare.

Having little oil or petrol left, I returned to Sutton's Farm, landing at 2.45a.m. On landing, I found the Zeppelin gunners had shot away the machine-gun wire guard, the rear part of my centre-section, and had pierced the main spar several times.

I have the honour to be, sir,
Your obedient servant,
(signed) W. Leefe-Robinson, Lieutenant. R.F.C.

The forward fuselage of 2092, in which Lt W Leefe-Robinson shot down the airship SL11. The windscreen has hinged sides and could be folded flat. The internal switches control navigation lights, the external switch the ignition. The instrument panel remains as on early examples, although with the addition of an Admiralty pattern compass.
J.M. Bruce/G.S. Leslie Collection

out, the other, Cdr N.F. Usborne, being killed when the machine crashed in the goods yard at Strood railway station. The experiments were therefore discontinued, leaving the RNAS B.E.2cs to climb to patrol height under their own power.

On the night of 31 March 1916, 2nd Lt Alfred de B. Brandon, flying a B.E.2c from Hainault Farm, encountered Zeppelin LZ15, which had already suffered a hit from anti-aircraft fire, causing it to lose gas. Brandon attacked it with explosive darts, no doubt contributing to its eventual descent into the sea whilst on its journey home.

The first German airship to be brought down over British soil was the wooden-framed Schutte-Lanz SL11 which was shot down on the night of 2/3 September 1916 by Lt William Leefe-Robinson of 39 Squadron RFC flying B.E.2c No. 2092 based at Sutton's Farm near Hornchurch in Essex. Leefe-Robinson, who was awarded the Victoria Cross for the action, fired several drums of incendiary ammunition at the airship which then caught fire, crashing near Cuffley in Hertfordshire, its flaming descent visible over a wide area which included much of North London.

Just three weeks later 39 Squadron scored again when 2nd Lt Frederick Sowery, flying B.E.2c No.4112, shot down Zeppelin L32 over Potters Bar. On 1 October, 2nd Lt W.J. Tempest, also of 39 Squadron, brought down L31 whilst flying 4577 and on 27 November 2nd Lt I.V. Pyott of 36 Squadron destroyed the L34, his mount being B.E.2c No.2738. Finally, the following night, L21 was the subject of three separate attacks by B.E.2cs from RNAS Yarmouth, with Flt Lt Egbert Cadbury in 8625, Flt Sub Lt G.W.R. Fane flying 8420, and Flt Sub Lt E.L. Pulling in 8626, the last-named officer being officially credited with the victory. Before the year was out, 2nd Lt Brandon had contributed to the destruction of yet another Zeppelin, L33, and the public's fears were laid to rest.

Development and Experiment

In mid-1916 an attempt was made to protect the B.E.2c against small arms fire from the ground by the introduction of what was

A B.E.2c with what was officially called 'heavy armour' applied. Although possibly proof against small arms fire from the ground, the effect of over 400lb (181kg) of steel plate on the machine's performance is easily imagined. Author's collection

known as 'Heavy Armour'. This comprised sheets of ¼in (6mm) steel plate fastened to the sides, front and underside of the forward fuselage, extending as far back as the rear of the pilot's cockpit. Although effective, this armour added some 445lb (200kg) to the aeroplane's overall weight, with a consequent reduction in performance. Nonetheless, at least fifteen aircraft fitted with the armour, served in France throughout the winter of 1916/17, but by the following spring all had been either returned to England or stripped of their armour.

On 22 November 1916, B.E.2c No.4721 was assigned to the ill-founded School of Aerial Gunnery at Loch Doon in Scotland. It was converted into a seaplane by fitting a central pontoon float to the skids of its early pattern undercarriage, a small float replacing its tail-skid. These floats were made by the well-known boat building company S.E. Saunders Ltd. Later, two further small floats were fitted, one under each wing-tip in place of the normal under-wing-skid, in order to improve stability on the water. Unfortunately, the aircraft sank in the Loch, and the experiment was discontinued.

Both the stability and viceless performance of the B.E.2c made it an ideal vehicle upon which to test many experimental devices, and so it was used to test several forms of air brakes including one in which interplane struts of greatly increased chord could be turned at right angles to the airflow by means of a control in the pilot's cockpit.

The B.E.2c also provided a platform for the testing of the 'Guardian Angel' parachute which had been invented by the retired engineer Ernest Calthrop. This static-line parachute became common issue to balloon observers but proved too bulky to be adopted for use in aeroplanes.

The hydraulically operated C.C. interrupter gear, which was devised by George Constantinesco, was fitted to a B.E.2c for testing in August 1916, together with a belt-fed Vickers gun, and proved highly successful. Since the gear ran at twice engine speed, the gun's rate of fire was not greatly affected when the engine was throttled down, and it could be adapted to any engine. It was adopted as the standard interrupter gear for future designs, but no attempt was made to fit it to front-line B.E.2cs.

The design staff at the Royal Aircraft Factory carried out numerous experiments intended to offset the falling off in engine performance which occurs at altitude and, to this end, introduced both engine superchargers and variable pitch propellers, these devices naturally being tested upon Farnborough's favourite workhorse, the B.E.2c. Although successful, neither was adopted, principally because the small improvement in performance could not justify the increase in weight and complication.

Like her allies, Britain was quick to see that the 150hp Hispano-Suiza 8Aa V8 engine, which first appeared in mid-1915, represented a breakthrough in engine design. An order for fifty was placed in August and negotiations undertaken so that it could be built under licence in British factories. When the first example was received in February 1916 it was installed, rather crudely, in B.E.2c No.4133, the work being undertaken at No.1 Aircraft Depot at St Omer, with flight testing beginning on 13

An experimental supercharger fitted to the RAF1a of a B.E.2c in December 1915. Crown copyright – DERA

March. Another installation was made at Farnborough, the aircraft chosen being 2599. In both cases, cooling was provided by German-made Hazet radiators positioned beside the observer's cockpit. Although it was first planned that the initial batch of Hispano-Suiza engines should all be installed into B.E.2cs, thus bringing about a welcome boost in performance, it was later decided that they would be better employed in an aeroplane specifically designed to take advantage of their unique features.

B.E.2d, e, f and g

In mid-1915 plans were produced for another variation of the B.E. formula, the B.E.2d. Dimensionally similar to the '2c, this new version was fitted with dual controls, but retained the same crew positions, although the sides of the forward cockpit were cut a little lower. Since the rudder cables, and the torque tube linking the two control columns now passed under the observer's seat, the petrol tank which had

B.E.2c 2599 fitted with a 150hp Hispano-Suiza engine, 13 December 1916. The engine is cooled by radiators mounted above the cylinder heads. Crown Copyright – DERA

previously occupied that space was eliminated and replaced by a tank in the upper decking separating the cockpits. In addition, the capacity of the main fuel tank was increased by 5 gallons (22 litres), and a large gravity tank provided under the port upper wing, close to its root, thus bringing the total fuel capacity to 41 gallons (186 litre) (compared to 32 gallons (145 litres) in the '2c), giving a generous increase in endurance, albeit at the expense of performance. The rigging notes for the type called for an extra 6ft (1.8m) of rubber shock cord to each wheel, presumably to cope with the weight of the additional petrol.

Orders were placed with the British and Colonial Aeroplane Co., Ruston Proctor Ltd, and the Vulcan Motor and Engineering Co. However, before any production examples were ready for service, yet another variant, the B.E.2e, of which great things were expected, had already been designed and so few B.E.2ds ever saw active service. Instead, they ended up at training establishments where their dual controls and five-hour endurance gave them a considerable advantage over other types.

One unit, serving in East Africa, and therefore occasionally needing to cover greater distances than the B.E.2c's normal range, even devised a method of in-flight refuelling which worked in the following manner: after take-off fuel was used from the gravity tank behind the engine until this was almost empty, and air pressure was then pumped into the main tank by means of the hand pump, forcing petrol back into the gravity tank. The pressure in the main tank, which was under the observer's seat, was then released, the filler cap unscrewed and the tank topped up from 2 gallon (9 litres) cans stowed in the observer's cockpit.

By 1915 aerodynamic research was beginning to make aircraft design into a science, rather than an art. It was known that, although structurally superior, particularly with the thin aerofoil sections in use at the time, the biplane was aerodynamically less efficient than a monoplane of equivalent wing area. This loss of efficiency, which was caused by interference between the airstreams flowing over the two planes, could reduce the overall lift by up to 17 per cent, although this could be reduced both by staggering the wings, and by increasing the gap between them. Therefore, in order to improve the B.E.2's

The large gravity tank which distinguished the B.E.2d, seen here under the upper port wing, was frequently removed in service, the reduction in endurance being accepted in order to gain an improvement in performance. Author's collection

performance at altitude, a new wing cell was designed in which the span of the upper wing was increased and that of the lower wing reduced, thereby creating a large overhang which would have the efficiency of a monoplane wing. This arrangement also allowed the elimination of the outer pair of interplane struts, the overhang being braced from inverted-vee kingposts positioned above the remaining pair of struts. A single, slender strut connected the ailerons. These new wings were designed with outwardly raked tips, since wind tunnel research had demonstrated that this shape was more efficient than any other, delaying wing-tip stall sufficiently that the wings could be rigged at constant incidence without 'wash-out'. This wing-tip shape was echoed in a new tailplane of reduced area. A new, larger fin with a curved leading edge, which first appeared on production B.E.2cs in January 1916, was adopted for this new variant, the B.E.2e, as were the dual controls and external gravity tank of the '2d.

The prototype was created in the usual Factory manner, by the conversion of an existing machine, in this case the Bristol-built B.E.2c No.4111 which arrived at Farnborough on 3 November 1915. Completed ready for inspection on 14 February 1916, the B.E.2e made its first flight four days later and proved a considerable improvement on earlier variants. Lateral control was considered 'very much better', with landing easier, and its climb was almost 10 per cent faster than that of the '2c.

On 1 March 1916 Mervyn O'Gorman informed the War Office that the speed of the B.E.2e was 97mph (156km/h) at ground level, which would give about 90mph (144km/h) at 6,000ft (1,828m), although this was with the uprated RAF1b engine, which was planned to supersede the earlier model. Although, in the end, this engine was not adopted for mass production, and the 90hp RAF1a remained the standard powerplant, the B.E.2e's speed at 6,000ft (1,828m) was 82mph (132km/h), some 10 per cent faster than the '2c. These improvements in performance were sufficient to prompt the War Office not only to adopt the type for future production, but also to inform contractors that all B.E.2c and d aircraft currently on order should be completed as '2es. However, when these machines reached Squadron service it was found that, although externally similar, they were actually of three separate and distinct types, the B.E.2c fuselage fitted with the new wings and tail surfaces, the B.E.2d fuselage similarly equipped, and the B.E.2e as designed. Some had dual controls, whilst others did not, and each had a different arrangement of fuel tanks, those converted from the B.E.2c having an 18 gallon (81 litres) tank under the observer's seat and a 14 gallon (63 litres) gravity tank in the decking immediately behind the engine, whilst those with the dual control fuselage of the B.E.2d had a 19 gallon (86 litres) tank behind the engine, a 10 gallon (45 litres) tank in the decking between the cockpits, and a 12 gallon (54 litres) gravity tank under the upper wing. This situation created a great deal of confusion, especially in maintenance and in the provision of spares, and so, on 2 October 1916 the RFC headquarters in France instructed that in future B.E.2c fuselages with '2e wings would be designated B.E.2f and that B.E.2d fuselages similarly equipped would henceforth become the B.E.2g. Wherever possible, B.E.2fs would be kept together in the same squadrons. The use of these designations was largely confined to France, although eventually

16 Squadron B.E.2e A3168 clearly shows its long upper wing extensions and single bay bracing. On 17 April this aircraft was shot down by Manfred von Richtofen, his 47th victory. B. Robertson

Specification – B.E.2e

Powerplant:	90hp RAF1a
Weights:	Empty 1,431lb (649kg); loaded 2,100lb (953kg)
Dimensions:	Upper span 40ft 6in (12.35m); lower span 30ft 6in (9.30m); chord 5ft 6in (1.68m); gap 6ft (1.83m); wing area 360sq ft (33.48sq m); dihedral 3½ degrees; stagger 24in (0.61m)
	Length 27ft 3in (8.31m); height 11ft 9in (3.58m); tailplane area 24sq ft (2.23sq m); elevator area 22sq ft (2.05sq m); rudder area 12sq ft (1.12sq m); fin area 8sq ft (0.74sq m)
Performance:	Speed at sea level 88mph (141km/h); endurance 3hr

Unidentified B.E.2e with a neat installation of a Hispano-Suiza engine. Few such conversions were made, the engine being in great demand for other aircraft.
J.M. Bruce/G.S. Leslie Collection

aircraft which had been sent out as B.E.2es were returned to England as '2fs and '2gs.

However, whatever their designation, the B.E.2es remained as poorly armed as their predecessors and, despite their improvement in performance, losses continued to mount, and so replacement with a wholly new design grew ever more pressing.

In addition, a rumour grew up amongst Service personnel to the effect that the long extensions to the upper wing were structurally unsound, some pilots even claiming to have seen them flap in flight, and it was suggested that they would collapse if the machine were to be manoeuvred violently, as was frequently essential if under attack. Although these allegations were investigated by the Royal Aircraft Factory, and proved to be wholly unfounded, the rumours persisted, prompting some crews to treat their mounts with undue caution, further increasing their vulnerability.

Markings

Early B.E.2s, like all aeroplanes of that period, were given no specific finish, other than the 'dope' used to waterproof the fabric and to render it taut, and were thus a pale straw colour, easily stained with oil and with age. Serial numbers were painted in large black numerals on their rudders, exactly as the type designations of the earliest variants had been previously.

The first months of the war saw no change in this finish, but early in 1915 national markings, in the form of Union flags, were painted onto the rudders, above the serial number, and onto the undersides of the lower wings. These markings were superseded by roundels and rudder stripes when it was realized that the flag could be mistaken for the German cross patee, thereby attracting the fusillade of small arms fire from the men in the trenches that the markings were intended to prevent.

Later examples had their fuselage and upper surfaces finished in P.C.10, an olive/brown pigmented cellulose coating developed by Dr J.E. Ramsbottom, head of Chemistry at the Royal Aircraft Factory. Its function was not only to provide camouflage, but also to protect the fabric from deterioration due to the effects of ultra-violet light. Undersurfaces remained clear doped, the P.C.10 usually overlapped onto them by approximately 1½in (3.8cm), thereby giving a well-defined outline. Plywood deckings were also finished in P.C.10, with metal panels being either in a similar coloured finish, or painted battleship grey.

Individual markings were officially restricted to Squadron codes and identification letters or numerals, plus, in the case of presentation machines, the identity of the donor. Occasionally, a pet name or similar talisman was added by the crew. However, aircraft serving with training establishments were, very occasionally, given more elaborate finishes.

The B.E.12

In mid-1915, when, before the advent of the 'Fokker scourge', the B.E.2c was still rightly regarded as an effective front-line aircraft, an attempt had been made to create an uprated version for those operations, for which it was usually flown solo, such as long-range reconnaissance or bombing. The initial plan was to replace the standard V8 engine with a 150hp Hispano-Suiza, but this engine was in very short supply and so the V12 RAF4a, which was rated at 140hp, was used instead. The forward cockpit was eliminated to accommodate its greater length, with the fuel tank occupying the space thus created in order to maintain the centre of gravity in its original

The prototype B.E.12. Its engine mountings are level with the upper longerons and tandem air scoops are fitted over the engine. Later examples had the engine lowered to improve the view over the enlarged air scoop. Author's collection

The prototype B.E.12 on Farnborough Common, 20 July 1915 showing its inverted 'Y' exhaust. The RFC flight sheds, familiar to generations of SBAC air show goers as the 'Black Sheds' are visible in the background. Crown copyright – DERA

position. Two small air scoops were fitted in tandem, and the exhaust pipes manifolded together into a central inverted 'Y'.

The prototype was created by the conversion of Bristol built-B.E.2c No.1697, a 'Vee' undercarriage being substituted for the twin-skid type with which it had originally been fitted, and its Renault engine being returned to store for reuse elsewhere. The prototype was completed, ready for inspection, by 28 July 1915, although it was still regarded by the Air Inspection Department (AID) as a B.E.2c. Test flights began the same day and appear to have been satisfactory, with few, if any, modifications being suggested beyond the provision of a larger fuel tank.

Although this aeroplane was much faster than the B.E.2c, Mervyn O' Gorman was quick to point out to the War Office that it was still, in effect, a B.E.2, and could easily be flown by anyone familiar with the earlier machine, particularly if they did not fully open the throttle until they were used to the additional power.

Designated the B.E.12, it was ordered into production in the autumn, the first order, Contract No.87A123 for fifty machines, being placed with the Standard Motor Co. Subsequent orders were placed with Coventry Ordnance Works, and the Daimler Co. Production examples differed from the prototype in that a single large scoop was fitted to supply cooling air to the engine, the engine bearers being lowered in order to restore the pilot's view over it. An underwing gravity tank, similar to that designed for the B.E.2d, was added, and the larger fin was substituted for the triangular pattern with which the prototype had initially been fitted. Since the aircraft's intended role was reconnaissance, camera mountings were provided as standard on the starboard side of the fuselage.

Specification – B.E.12

Powerplant:	140hp RAF4a
Weights:	Empty 1,635lb (741kg); loaded 2,553lb (1,158kg)
Dimensions:	Span 37ft (11.29m); chord 5ft 6in (1.68m); gap 6ft (1.83m); wing area 354sq ft (32.92sq m); dihedral 3½ degrees; stagger 24in (0.61m)
	Length 27ft 3in (8.31m); height 11ft 1½in (3.39m); tailplane area 24sq ft (2.23sq m); elevator area 22sq ft (2.05sq m); rudder area 12sq ft (1.12sq m); fin area 8sq ft (0.74sq m)
Performance:	Speed at sea level 102mph (163km/h); endurance 3hr

There was, initially, no plan for the B.E.12 to be armed, and it was not until after it had been placed in production that any attempt was made to fit a gun to the prototype. The initial installation, completed by 16 March 1916, was of a Lewis gun fixed to fire forwards. This included steel wedges fixed to the rear of the propeller blades to deflect any bullets which might otherwise have damaged them, there being no synchronization gear available. Later, when such a gear had been developed, it was, of course, adopted, but was judged only moderately successful as it proved ineffective with the engine throttled back, a situation which frequently occurred as the stick forces in a dive under full power proved too great for easy recovery. This was eventually overcome by adopting the B.E.2e type tailplane.

The final gun installation, which included a belt-fed Vickers gun and the Vickers-Challenger gear, proved effective, although the presence of the air scoop prevented the gun's installation in the favoured location immediately in front of the pilot, and its eventual position external to the cockpit on the port side of the fuselage made clearing jams difficult. The gun's sights were similarly positioned, with a bead sight on the forward centre-section strut and the sighting ring on the rear strut, the pilot having to lean out to port in order to make use of them.

Production B.E.12

B.E.12:
6478–6677 – Daimler.
6138–6185 – Standard Motor.
B701; B720–1; B749; B1500; B8826; B9462; B9950 – Rebuilds.

B.E.12a:
A4006–4055; A6301–6350 – Daimler.
A562–611 – Coventry Ordnance Works.

B.E.12b:
C3081–3280. (many completed as B.E.12) –Daimler.
B718; C9992 – Rebuilds.

B.E.12 with the Standard Vickers gun, plus a Strange mounting for a Lewis Gun. J.M. Bruce/G.S. Leslie Collection

(Above) **A beautifully finished production B.E.12a, built by Daimler but apparently unarmed when this photograph was taken.** Author's collection

(Right) **This B.E.12b lacks an armament but appears to have a mounting for a Lewis gun on the rear centre-section struts.** J.M. Bruce/G.S. Leslie Collection

An experimental installation was made of the six-pounder Davis gun fitted to the starboard side of the fuselage and arranged to fire upwards at an angle of 45 degrees in order to attack Zeppelins. Ten rounds were carried, the gun being returned to the horizontal for loading, and, when not in use, a bracket supported its muzzle when in the lowered position. Whatever the results of these trials, it was not adopted for Service use.

Production machines were slow in reaching the front, largely due to teething troubles with the RAF4a engine, which was, incidentally, being manufactured by two of the contractors building the B.E.12, the Daimler and Standard motor companies. The first production machine was at Farnborough by the end of March 1916, with the first few examples coming into service in May, although the type did not reach Squadron strength until the end of July. In view of the changed nature of aerial warfare it was immediately pressed into service as a single-seat fighter, a role for which its lack of manoeuvrability made it wholly unsuited. Fortunately, and rarely in that war, common sense prevailed and by September the B.E.12 had been returned to a role for which it had originally been designed, that of a light bomber. It also served as a night fighter, with similar distinction to the plane it replaced, the B.E.2c, and on 17 June 1917 the Zeppelin L48 fell to the gun of 6610, flown by Lt L.P. Watkins of 37 Squadron.

Following the introduction of the single bay wing structure which distinguished the

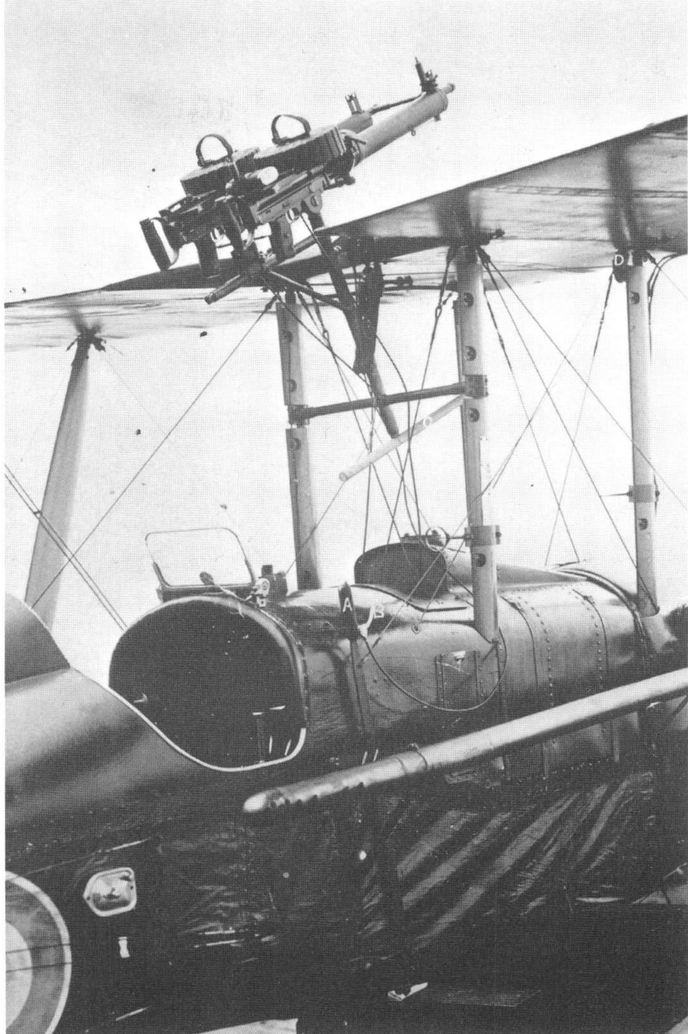

(Above) **A twin Lewis gun installation on a B.E.12b complete with a complex mechanism to lower it for loading. The sights are on the starboard centre-section struts. The slope of the reversed fuel tank can clearly be seen.** J.M. Bruce/G.S. Leslie Collection

B.E.12 with experimental transparent covering to the rear fuselage designed to make the aircraft less visible in flight. J.M. Bruce/G.S. Leslie Collection

B.E.2e, a similar modification was also planned for the B.E.12 in order to bring about a similar increase in climb rate. The first installation, on 6511, included horn-balanced ailerons on the upper wing, but these made the handling 'unpleasant' and plain ailerons, like those of the B.E.2e, were adopted instead. It has been suggested that this version was initially designated the B.E.12Ae, although documentary evidence is lacking; in any event, it is probable that the new wing was being tested with a view to its introduction, not only on the B.E.12 but also on the other types using the same wing structure, the B.E.2e and R.E.8. The new variant was officially designated B.E.12a, with orders, each for fifty aircraft, being placed with Daimler and the Coventry Ordnance Works. However, pilots seem to have preferred the earlier version and so, when it was decided to bring out a variant, the B.E.12b, powered by the 200hp Hispano-Suiza engine, it was the earlier airframe, with equal span, two bay wings, which formed the basis of the new machine. A two-blade propeller was used, as was a car-type frontal radiator, and the standard fuel tank was retained. However, as this had a sloping top surface, fairing the RAF engine's air scoop into the fuselage shape, this was reversed so that the backward slope thus obtained would offer less drag. Intended purely for home defence, the increase in power enabling it to climb to the heights at which Zeppelins now operated, it was armed with a Lewis gun above the upper wing, its muzzle flashes thus shielded from the pilot's view. Navigation lights were provided, and holt flare brackets were fitted under the lower wing-tips. An order for 100 machines was placed with the Daimler Co. but, with Zeppelin raids growing less frequent, and the Hispano engine being in short supply, at least some of these machines were eventually completed as standard B.E.12s, with the RAF4a engine.

B.E.2cs operated by the RNAS often had alternative engines, this example being powered by the most common of those alternatives, the Curtiss OX5. J.M. Bruce/G.S. Leslie Collection

Ubiquitous Service

The 1914–18 war was indeed a *world* war, involving many nations and covering numerous battle zones, with the B.E.2, in one form or another, serving almost everywhere. In addition to its extensive use in a wide variety of roles, along the length of the Western Front, in Home Defence and in training units, the B.E.2 served wherever the Royal Flying Corps went. Thus 26 Squadron operated the B.E.2c in East Africa, whilst 31 Squadron flew it on India's North-west Frontier. Both 14 and 17 Squadrons flew the type in Egypt before moving even further afield, 14 Squadron to Palestine and 17 to Mesopotamia. Also serving in Mesopotamia was 30 Squadron whose B.E.2cs flew numerous relief missions to the town of Kut, where Gen Townshend and 1,300 troops were besieged. Each machine carried 50lb (22kg) of badly needed food, medical supplies and other essentials on each lower wing root, and 50lb more, in two 25lb (11kg) bags attached to the undercarriage.

Although it has frequently been claimed, with some justification, that the

Training Units were allowed more colourful markings than active service squadrons, as this B.E.2c, based at Turnberry, clearly shows. Note that it has been fitted with the larger fin introduced for the B.E.2e. Author's collection

Admiralty preferred the products of private industry to those of the Royal Aircraft Factory (which had, after all, been established expressly to supply the needs of the Army), the RNAS did operate a considerable number of B.E.2s. Several B.E.2as, forming part of the Eastchurch Squadron, served with distinction at Dunkirk during the early months of the war. Later, the RNAS, like the RFC, operated the B.E.2c as a night fighter for home defence, as well as for anti-submarine patrols for training. Many of these, particularly in the latter roles, were fitted with alternative engines, notably the 90hp V8 Curtiss OX5 or 75hp straight six Rolls-Royce Hawk. Since both of these engines were water-cooled, their installation necessitated the provision of car-type frontal radiators, and they were frequently fitted with two-bladed propellers in lieu of the four-blade type always preferred by the Royal Aircraft Factory's designers.

Amongst the first foreign nations to employ the type was Australia, with a number of B.E.2as serving at the Central Flying School at Point Cook in 1914/15. The Australian Flying Corps also acquired at least fifteen B.E.2cs, four of which are known to have seen service in the Middle East with No.1 (Australian) Squadron. One pilot who flew the type there was Capt Ross Smith, who found fame in 1919 when, together with his brother Keith, he flew Vickers Vimy G-EAOU from England to Australia within thirty days, thereby winning a substantial prize. In addition, some 23 B.E.2es joined the Australian air service and were flown by pilots of Nos. 1, 3, 4 and 7 Squadrons. Nos. 1 and 4 Squadrons also operated the single-seater B.E.12, a total of 27 such aircraft eventually being acquired by Australia.

The B.E.2c also served with the 6ème Escadrille of the Aviation Militaire Belge, where its performance was greatly improved by the substitution of the 150hp Hispano-Suiza engine for the standard RAF1a. The Belgian installation of this engine was far more practical than any of the British attempts, with a two-blade propeller, a neat cowling and a circular frontal radiator. In an equally practical modification, the crew positions were reversed and the observer, now in the rear cockpit, was given a Lewis gun on a ring mounting. Initially, these were French Eteve mountings, but later examples had the cockpit sides built up to accommodate the British Scarff ring. A forward-firing Vickers gun was also provided, creating a wholly different machine to its British counterpart. Similar modifications were not carried out to British machines for several reasons: the Hispano-Suiza engine was never available in sufficient numbers even for those types expressly designed around it; and new designs in which the observer occupied the rear cockpit, and in which adequate armament was provided, were by 1916 already under manufacture.

Following their replacement on the Western Front by less obviously vulnerable designs, B.E.2es were returned to England so that they could be reassigned to less demanding roles. Many were allocated to training units, joining the B.E.2cs previously relegated to that role by the advent of the '2e, where their outdated performance was no handicap to giving experience to tyro pilots. Although the majority were retained by the Royal Flying Corps, a few were sold on. Thus a total of twenty-nine machines, including Nos 6790 to 6801 and 7109 to 7123, joined the Imperial Russian Air Service just prior to the Revolution. In August 1918 a dozen examples joined the United States Air Service at their training bases in England. Others went to Greece, Estonia and South Africa.

Of the seventeen B.E.2es sold to Norway in 1917, where they frequently operated on specially designed ski undercarriages, one remained in service until 1928 and, remarkably, two survived to be preserved in museums.

B.E.2e G-EAVS has racing numbers applied, although in which race it planned to compete is not known. Author's collection

Decorated for the 1923 RAF pageant this was the B.E.2xyz, otherwise known as 'Ooh er'. It has been re-rigged with back stagger, fitted with a (false) second undercarriage for inverted landings, and generally dressed up for the part. It did not fly in this condition. Author's collection

Post-War

Following the Armistice in November 1918 the Royal Air Force was, naturally, drastically reduced in size, leaving no place in its peacetime line-up for the obsolete and frequently ill-regarded B.E.2, which by then was half as old as powered flight itself.

The redundant aeroplanes were quickly disposed of, the majority being sold for a pittance to be broken up for scrap. Their wheels ended up on farm carts, their wing panels became fences, or formed roofs for garden sheds. However, at least ten B.E.2es managed to escape such wanton destruction, and found their way onto the Register of Civil Aircraft when it was introduced in 1919, their legendary inherent stability making them ideally suited to private flying. In addition, at least one example, its identity now unknown, must have been retained by the RAF, for it appeared at an early Hendon Pageant as a comic turn, the B.E.2xyz. Colourfully painted and decorated, it was re-rigged with reduced, possibly negative, stagger, and fitted with a weather-cock, and a second, dummy, undercarriage above the upper centre section, for inverted landings. This machine too was eventually broken up.

Two examples joined the civil register in Australia, C7198 becoming VH-UBB, and C6986 becoming G-AUBF and later VH-UBF. In 1921 the latter machine, together with an Avro 504, formed the entire fleet of the newly formed 'Queensland And Northern Territory Aerial Services Ltd' (QANTAS) and earned its keep giving joyrides and demonstration flights. When its working life was over it was preserved for a time but was eventually destroyed in a hangar fire. Its engine survives to this day, as do two original B.E.2es and three '2cs, as well as several accurate reproductions, and a number of less accurate representations of the type.

Preserved Examples

Original Aircraft

B.E.2c – 2699 –	Imperial War Museum, Lambeth, London.
B.E.2c – 5878 –	National Aviation Collection, Ottowa, Canada.
B.E.2c – 9969 –	Musée de l'Air et l'Espace, Le Bourget, Paris.
B.E.2e – A1235 –	Peter Jackson, New Zealand, following restoration by AJD Engineering.
B.E.2e – A1380 (131) –	Kongelige Norsk Luftforssvarte Collection, Gardermoen, Norway.

Reproductions

B.E.2a (cockpit only) –	RAF Museum, Hendon, London.
B.E.2b – '687' –	RAF Museum, Hendon, London.
B.E.2c (airworthy) –	US Army Museum, Fort Rucker, Alabama.
B.E.2c. (static) –	Yorkshire Air Museum, Elvington, York.

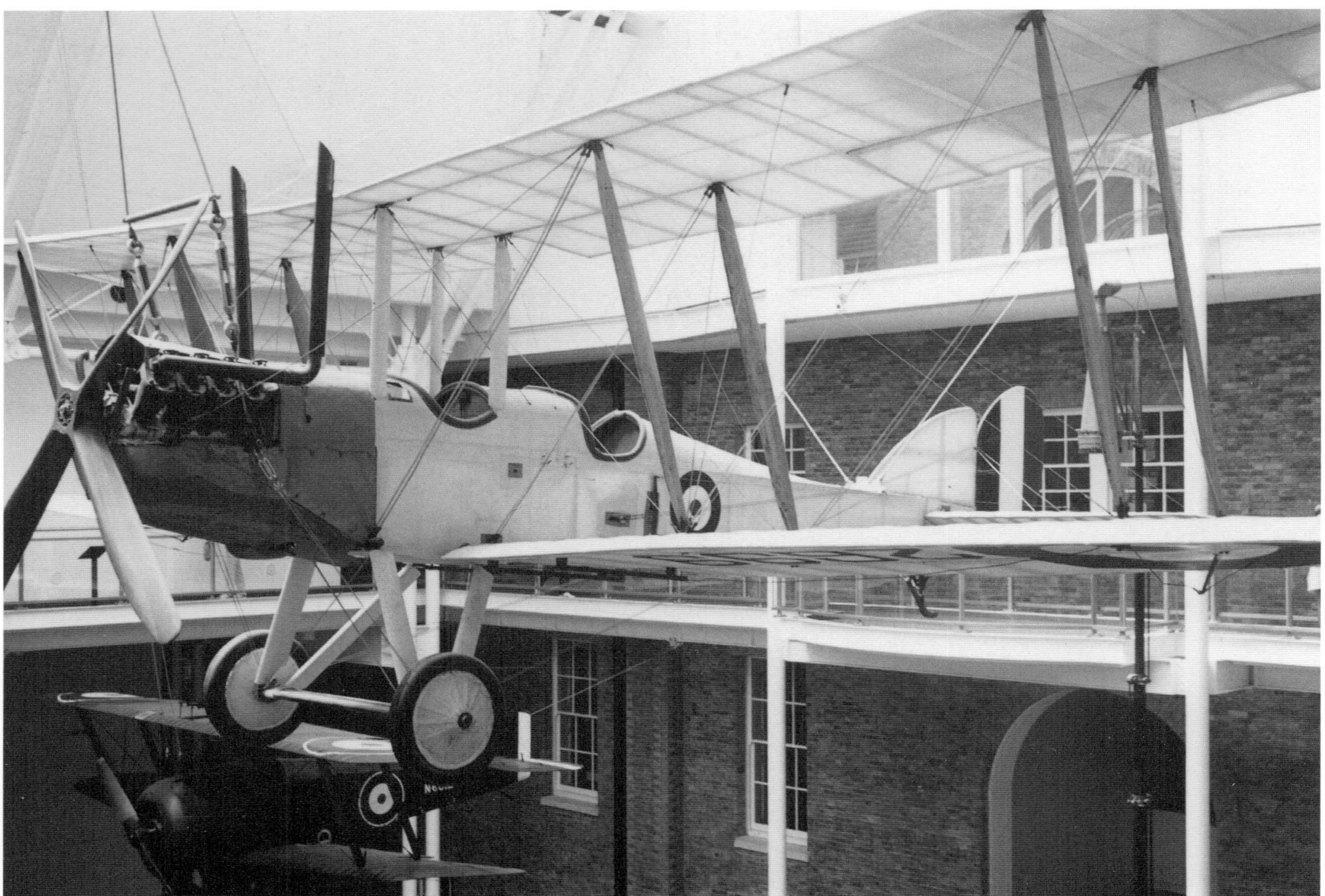

The beautifully preserved B.E.2c now displayed by the Imperial War Museum in London. Author's collection

CHAPTER THREE

The R.E.8

By the autumn of 1915, long before any political controversy had erupted, the Royal Flying Corps in France had already realized that the B.E.2 series was obsolescent. Therefore a request was issued for a replacement aircraft which would take over its reconnaissance and artillery observation duties, but which would be capable of defending itself against attack by enemy aircraft, especially those which were now equipped with forward-firing machine-guns. The Royal Aircraft Factory's response to this request, produced by a design team led by Stanley W. Hiscocks, was the R.E.8. The choice of designation is interesting, since the new machine had nothing in common with the earlier R.E. series, which had grown from the neat, almost dainty R.E.1 (which had itself played a part in the development of the B.E.2c), into the cumbersome R.E.7 which was, at that time, being employed as a bomber.

The R.E.1, which had arisen directly out of investigations into aeroplane stability conducted by a Royal Aircraft Factory team headed by E.T. Busk, was a single bay biplane with staggered wings. As originally built, lateral control was by warp, but ailerons were soon substituted, and the dihedral was progressively increased from 1 degree to 3. The first example, 607, was completed during March 1913 and was retained at Farnborough for continued development. A second machine, 608, had a slightly longer fuselage and a balanced rudder, both modifications being intended to improve directional stability. It served with 6 Squadron until the outbreak of war, then transferred to No.2, but was wrecked in a forced landing on 1 September 1914 and was not rebuilt.

The R.E.2 was an altogether larger aeroplane, with two bay wings, tail surfaces similar to those of the B.E.3, and like the R.E.1 was, initially, powered by a 70hp Renault engine. Following successful test flights, it was mounted on floats and in this form became known as the H.R.E.2, or Hydro Reconnaissance Experimental. In order to offset the keel area of the floats a new, enlarged rudder was fitted, together with a fin, the rudder being mounted above the fuselage to keep it clear of the water and to avoid any need to modify the existing one-piece elevator. Tested on Fleet pond, it failed to take off satisfactorily even after the engine had been changed for a 100hp Renault. It was therefore converted back to a wheeled undercarriage, the new fin and

Arising from E.T. Busk's work on aeroplane stability, the R.E.1 was intended to perform the reconnaissance role eventually assigned to the B.E.2c. Author's collection

The R.E.2 in floatplane form. Its rudder has been lifted high to keep it clear of the water, retaining the one-piece elevator originally fitted. Author's collection

Specification – R.E.1	
Powerplant:	70hp Renault
Weights:	Empty 1,000lb (454kg); loaded 1,580lb (717kg)
Dimensions:	Span 34ft (10.37m); chord 5ft 6in (1.68m)
Performance:	Speed at sea level 78mph (125km/h); initial climb 600ft/min (183m/min)

Specification – R.E.2	
Powerplant:	70hp Renault
Weights:	not known
Dimensions:	Span 45ft 3½in (13.81m); chord 6ft (1.83m); length 32ft 3in (9.84m); height 12ft 2in (3.71m)
Performance:	Speed at sea level 60mph (96km/h)

rudder being retained, and it served briefly with the RNAS.

A further machine, built to the same modified design but powered by a 120hp Austro-Daimler, was given the designation R.E.3. Another example, the R.E.4, which was to have been modified so as to allow it to operate from small fields, was not proceeded with.

The R.E.5 followed a similar layout, and was again powered by the 120hp Austro-Daimler engine. Its forward fuselage was of steel tube, with its rudder of both a modified shape and more conventional location. A batch of twenty-four was ordered 'off the drawing board', a safe enough action considering that the type was very similar to previous designs which were already in service. The order was financed, at least in part,

The R.E.3 retained the high rudder position of the modified R.E.2, and was generally similar except for its 120hp Austro-Daimler engine. J.M. Bruce/G.S. Leslie Collection

Specification – R.E.3	
Powerplant:	120hp Austro-Daimler
Weights:	not known
Dimensions:	Span 45ft 3½in (13.81m); chord 6ft (1.83m); length 32ft 3in (9.84m); height 12ft 2in (3.71m)
Performance:	not known

The sturdy R.E.5. Like most aeroplanes in service at the outbreak of war it was unarmed. Author's collection

Specification – R.E.5	
Powerplant:	120hp Austro-Daimler
Weights:	not known
Dimensions:	Upper span 57ft 2½in (17.45m); lower span 45ft 3½in (13.81m); chord 6ft (1.83m)
Performance:	Speed at sea level 78mph (125km/h); initial climb 400ft/min (122m/min)

with £25,000 paid to the War Office by the Admiralty in exchange for the Army's airships, which were all transferred to the Navy on 1 January 1914. This transfer, incidentally, left the Farnborough airship sheds largely redundant, although some years later they became the home of the Southern Aeroplane Repair Depot which produced rebuilt aeroplanes for the RFC.

The first R.E.5 was completed on 26 January 1914, the remainder following fairly quickly. Some examples, including the fifth and sixth machines to be built, had extensions to the upper wing, supported by inclined struts, increasing its span by some 15ft (4.5m). This provided a considerable increase in lift, enabling Factory test pilot Norman Spratt to coax No.380 to an altitude of 18,900ft (5,760m) on 14 May 1914, a feat which many RFC pilots tried, unsuccessfully to emulate, although 17,000ft (5,180m) was fairly readily attainable.

A float plane variant, the R.E.6, was proposed but not built and the next version, the R.E.7, again followed the same basic

Fitted with wing extensions, the R.E.7 was clearly well suited to its role as a bomber. Author's collection

A Rolls-Royce-powered R.E.7 complete with a third, gunner's cockpit behind the wings. It lent nothing to its supposed successor, the R.E.8. Author's collection

overall design, including the extended upper wing, although with several modifications. The centre section was eliminated, the upper wings joining above the fuselage centre line and supported on inverted vee struts. A new higher aspect ratio tailplane replaced the previous design, and the engine was changed to the Factory's own 140hp RAF4a. Although orders were placed for several hundred, the R.E.7, as designed, was considered underpowered for its intended role as a bomber and several other engine types, including the Sunbeam Maori and Rolls-Royce Falcon, were fitted as available. In common with most aeroplanes of its day, the observer was carried in the front cockpit, and a number of the higher powered versions were modified to include a third cockpit behind the wings, housing the gunner. It was withdrawn from active service from mid-1917, and relegated to less arduous duties, a number ending their days as target tugs.

The R.E.8 owed nothing to these previous designs, and in general appearance had much more in common with the B.E.2 it was intended to replace. However, it was designed, from the start, for Corps Reconnaissance duties, and included many features intended to enhance its performance in that role. Its designation was therefore intended not only to define its role, but also to divorce it, in people's opinions, from the already ill-regarded B.E. series that it was to supersede. Whilst the B.E.2 had been designed to be the best flying machine that the technology of the time could conceive, the R.E.8 was designed specifically for its role in war, with the parallel aim of correcting all the perceived deficiencies of the earlier design.

The pilot was placed in the front cockpit where he had a good view of the ground

Specification – R.E.7

Powerplant:	150hp RAF4a
Weights:	Empty 2,140lb (970kg); loaded 3,349lb (1,159kg)
Dimensions:	Upper span 57ft 2in (17.44m); lower span 42ft (12.81m); chord 5ft 6in (1.68m); length 31ft 10½in (3.32m); height 12ft 7in (3.84m)
Performance:	not known

R.E.7 Production

2185–2234 – Coventry Ordnance Works.
2235–2236 – Unknown.
2237–2266; 6016–6115 (cancelled) – Austin Motors.
2287–2336; 7455–7594 (cancelled) – Napier.
2348–2447 – Siddeley-Deasey.
6828–6927 (cancelled) – G. & J. Weir.

ahead of the leading edge of the lower wing, and the observer was in the rear, where recent experience had shown he needed to be in order to defend against enemy fighters. Since this placed him well behind the centre of gravity the aircraft would be dangerously nose heavy if flown solo and production machines had the words 'Do not fly with less than 150lb. in the Gunner's compartment' stencilled on the fuselage side, leading many a pilot's log-book to record his non-existent passenger's name as 'Lt. Sandbags'.

Guns were to be provided for both crew members. The earliest surviving drawing, No.A9429, a preliminary fuselage layout, shows the observer's Lewis gun on a pillar mount which extended high enough to enable him to fire forwards, at an angle, over the top wing, as well as to the sides and to the rear. Ten spare 47-round ammunition drums were to be provided, and the shape of the rear fuselage was carefully contoured, with its cross-sectional area kept as small as possible so as to offer the least possible impediment to the field of fire. As originally designed, the pilot's gun was also a Lewis, positioned inside the cockpit so that the drum could be changed, albeit with some difficulty, as the gun was on a level with the pilot's right calf. Four spare drums were provided, two stowed on each side of the cockpit. A bowden cable brought the trigger control onto the upper right longeron, so that the pilot would be forced to fly left-handed when he wished to fire the gun. Sights were to be fitted to both sides of the cockpit, adjacent to the windscreen, thereby avoiding the obstruction created by the engine's air scoop and allowing the pilot to use whichever eye he preferred. Since the British had still to perfect a synchronization gear, steel bullet deflectors were to be fitted to the propeller blades, that shown on drawing No.A9429 being of the wrong hand for the 140hp V12 RAF4a engine which was to be the R.E.8's normal powerplant. The engine exhaust pipes terminated just above the leading edge of the upper wing in a manner similar to that employed on the B.E.2c. The cooling air which was forced down onto the engine by the scoop was directed around the cylinders by sheet metal baffles.

The fuselage was wider than that of the B.E.2 series, as indeed it had to be in order to accommodate all the equipment the cockpits were intended to contain, the longerons ending at the point where the forward undercarriage legs and centre-section struts were attached. Its construction was entirely conventional, with wooden longerons, metal fittings and wire crossbracing. The upper longerons were straight and made in one piece, but the lower ones were built up from three separate sections, joined by fishplates in order to achieve the necessary angles. The engine mountings were slightly narrower than the fuselage frame, leaving a neatly faired step in the fuselage side, through which the internally mounted front gun was to fire.

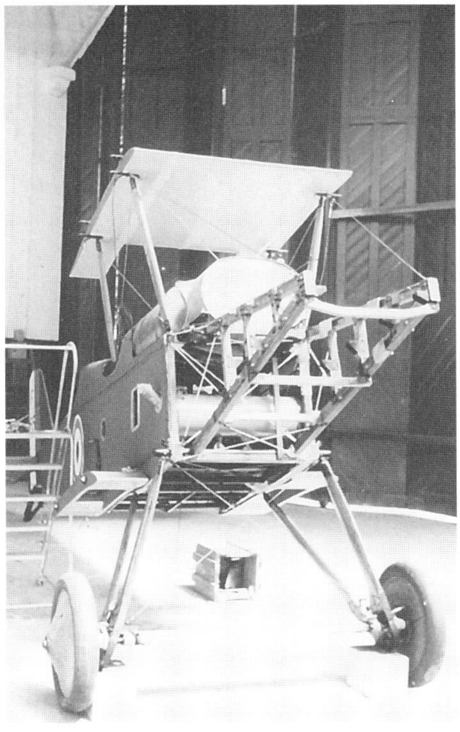

This view of F3556 under restoration at Duxford in 1980 clearly shows the width of the fuselage compared with the narrower engine mounts. Author's collection

Dual controls were included from the start, those in the rear cockpit being merely for emergency use, for although there was a conventional control column this only operated the elevators and was positioned at the right-hand side of the cockpit, clipped out of the way when not actually in use. The rudder was to be moved by means of a handgrip on the cable passing through the cockpit on the port side, a conventional throttle lever being positioned just above it. Whilst the pilot was provided with the wicker seat normal for the period, the observer's need for mobility was recognized and a small swivel seat was provided in the rear cockpit. The pilot's cockpit was provided with a semi-conical windscreen with a cut-out below it

R.E.8 pilot's cockpit, the trim wheel (bottom right) has the misleading message 'Faster – Slower'. Ahead of it is the Very pistol holster, switches for the cockpit lights, and the RAF MkII compass. The instruments are oil pressure, rev counter, air speed indicator, altimeter, watch holder and clinometer. Author's collection

to allow light onto the instrument panel. Although a similar windscreen was designed for the rear cockpit, this was either deleted, or, if fitted, was removed in service since it interfered with communication between the crew.

The preliminary drawing shows provision for a camera to be installed under the pilot's seat and for a larger camera, if required, to be fitted into the rear cockpit, alongside the observer. Wireless was to be a standard fitting too, the aerial drum being positioned by the observer's left shoulder, with morse keys fitted to the port upper longeron in both cockpits. An R.L. Tube, which was an electrically primed chute for the dropping of flares, smoke markers and incendiary bombs, was also fitted in the front cockpit, on the port side.

Two petrol tanks were to be provided – a main pressure tank holding 38 gallons (173 litres) positioned over the pilot's legs, with a 10 gallon (45 litres) gravity tank immediately behind the engine. There was also an allowance for 3½ gallons (16 litres) of oil in a tank immediately behind the engine.

The wings were virtually identical to those of the B.E.2e, with the broader fuselage and wider centre section of the new machine increasing their overall span by approximately 2ft (60cm). They retained the generous dihedral which had always been a feature of Farnborough designs so as to ensure lateral stability and thus allow the pilot to concentrate on his reconnaissance duties. The upper ailerons were made in two parts, but were joined by small metal plates and acted together. Each pair of upper and lower ailerons was linked by a single slender strut which, like the interplane struts, was of solid ash. Picket rings were provided below each set of interplane struts so as to allow the machine to be tied down when not in use.

In order to keep the landing run short, the wings were designed to have a large angle of incidence when on the ground and so provide a braking effect. As a result, the machine flew with its tail held high, which, viewed in conjunction with the slope of the engine's air scoop, exaggerated by the engines being set at a slight upward angle, gave the machine a curious 'broken back' profile in flight.

The tailplane and elevators were also copied from the earlier design, but were mounted so that their incidence could be varied in flight by means of a control wheel on the right-hand side of the pilot's cockpit, and the aircraft was thereby trimmed to fly level 'hands-off'. A small metal plate with the words 'FASTER' and 'SLOWER' indicated which way the wheel should be turned. The distinctive fin and rudder of the B.E.2 was not adopted for the R.E.8, wholly new surfaces being designed instead. Preliminary drawing No.A9429 shows a constant chord, high-aspect ratio rudder, with the tail-skid attached directly to it, together with an angular fin not dissimilar to that later fitted to the S.E.5. However, for some unexplained reason, although the fin area of other designs, most notably the B.E.2, was being increased in size, this design was modified pre-manufacture to include a broader rudder but a fin of much reduced area.

The instrumentation was typical of the period, comprising a rev/counter, oil pressure gauge, air speed indicator (ASI); altimeter, bubble clinometer and watch. It was fitted on the left of the instrument panel, leaving a space at the right for the starting magneto, and the rather bulky compass. A canvas Very pistol holster was provided on the starboard side of the cockpit forward of the trim wheel and almost level with the pilot's right knee. The pitot head for the ASI was fitted to the forward port interplane strut, its tubes running along the leading edge of the top wing and down the centre-section strut.

Prototypes

Two prototypes, 7996 and 7997, were built, the former being given its pre-flight inspection on 16 June 1916. Unusually for a Royal Aircraft Factory machine, it appears to have been fitted with a two-blade propeller. This was without the bullet deflector plates shown on the preliminary drawing, even though a Lewis gun was fitted in the forward cockpit. Frank Goodden took it up for a ten-minute test flight at 8.30pm on the following day.

Pilots' Opinions

Although historians have frequently criticized the R.E.8, particularly in recent years, those who flew it remember it differently:

'It was cosy and comfortable, lovely to fly. It would do anything asked of it up to its limited ability. It was very good on sideslips. I never had any difficulty in 157 hours, 90 of it over the lines. The engine never let me down, and I shall always think of it as a very fine aircraft.

I once deliberately spun an R.E.8, and recovered, which gave me confidence in it.'

Lt P.B. Townsend, RFC/RAF.

'They were adequately manoeuvrable for their purpose. I did not find any difficulty with the R.E.8 although I converted on to it (with small fin) without any dual or 'familiarization'.

The handling qualities differed considerably from those of the B.E.; it was lighter on the rudder and heavier on the stick both in pitch and roll (partly due to the rather short stick).

The R.E.8 had an excellent view for both pilot and gunner, and the gunner had a good field of fire; it was pleasant to fly and could be flown hands off for long periods; it could use small landing fields.'

Wg Cdr H.M. Yeatman, RFC/RAF.

The prototype R.E.8, photographed on Farnborough Common. Author's collection

Although critical of many details, he made no adverse comments regarding the machine's handling either on the ground or in the air, and found its performance to be all that had been expected of it. It was then flown down to the CFS testing flight at Upavon for their evaluation, receiving a similarly favourable report.

The second prototype was fitted with a four-blade propeller and was inspected on 28 June, but appears not to have been test-flown until 5 July, when Goodden took it up. On the 16th he flew it over to France for assessment by the RFC in the field, with F.M. Green, the Factory's chief engineer, in the rear seat, presumably so that he would be on the spot to deal with criticisms or suggestions for modification. Two days later Goodden demonstrated it to Maj Gen H.R.M. Brooke-Popham, commander of the 3rd Wing, who reported enthusiastically on its performance, informing Gen Trenchard that its top speed was 103mph (165km/h), and that it was 'very handy, and easily manoeuvred'. He also reported that it landed very slowly and then pulled up quickly, confirming that its designers had achieved their object. Although he too was critical of details, it was clear that the R.E.8 would meet the RFC's needs.

Maurice Baring, who as Gen Trenchard's aide was present at No.2 Aircraft Depot at Candas, noted in his account of the war (*Flying Corps Headquarters 1914-18, London, 1968*) that on 18 July 1916:

> R.E.8 is at the A.D. [Aircraft Depot] Its camera needs a larger case. The machine is to be kept a fortnight so that the gun mounting and camera can be altered to what we want.

Unfortunately, Baring does not specify exactly what modifications were required, but in any case they were not started straight away as the following day the R.E.8 was flown by a number of Service pilots, including Col C.A.H. Longcroft who had made so many pre-war record-breaking long-distance flights in a B.E.2. Experienced observers were also invited to examine and fly in the new machine. Again, opinion was generally favourable, although Longcroft thought it heavy on turns. Further flight trials were made on the 21st, Baring again being present, and on the 26th Brooke-Popham submitted a list of the modifications required by the RFC. Some would be carried out at the depot before 7997 was returned to Farnborough, where the more involved modifications could be undertaken. These included moving the pilot's gun to outside the cockpit on the port side, thus echoing the installation on the B.E.12, and allowing the R.L. tube to be transferred to starboard so that the pilot could use his right hand to load it. He also requested that the observer's seat be lowered, and his upward view improved by covering the centre section with transparent cellon.

On 12 August, 7997 was flown back to Farnborough by Capt R.H. Mayo, Goodden and Green having returned long before, and the modifications put in hand. By the 31st the tailplane adjustment had been modified and the gunner's seat lowered, although there is no evidence that the centre section was modified or its covering changed. The tail-skid was mounted so that it could swivel independently of the rudder, which had its lower edge cut back to allow room for it to do so. Since the Vickers-Challenger gun synchronization gear was now available, a belt fed Vickers gun now replaced the pilot's Lewis, although this was installed within the cockpit rather than outside as Brooke-Popham had requested. Its trigger was moved from the starboard longeron to a more conventional (and convenient) position on the pilot's control

This R.E.8 has its centre section covered in transparent cellon to improve the crew's upward view.
Author's collection

column. An Aldis optical gunsight was fitted to starboard, a single ring-and-bead sight being retained to port.

The capacity of the petrol tanks was redefined, that of the main tank now being 37½ gallons (170 litres) and the gravity tank 10½ (45 litres), their total capacity thus remaining unaltered. However, the capacity of the oil tank was now 6 gallons (27 litres), suggesting that the consumption of the RAF4a had been underestimated when the original design was prepared. The camera, designed specifically for the R.E.8 by Thornton-Pickard, was moved from under the pilot's seat to the rear cockpit, where the plates could be changed more easily.

Into Production

Given the deteriorating situation both on the Western front, where the Fokker was in ascendance, and in Parliament, where Noel Pemberton-Billing had begun his campaign against the management of the RFC, it is, perhaps, not surprising that the first production order was placed before either of the two prototypes had flown. However, this order was for just fifty machines, and was placed with the Royal Aircraft Factory itself. As the serial number block allocated, A66 to A115, suggests that the order was placed was early as April 1916, it is possible that it was done so that War Office staff could honestly inform their critics that a replacement was already in production.

A66, the first production R.E.8 preparing to take off. Its Vickers gun is mounted internally. J.M. Bruce/G.S. Leslie Collection

An early R.E.8 with its observer's Lewis gun on a Bowker Mounting. J.M. Bruce/G.S. Leslie Collection

These production machines naturally needed to incorporate all the post-trials modifications, thus delaying completion, and yet the first example, A66, was ready for final inspection by the AID on 13 September 1916, just two weeks after the much-modified prototype 7997 had been similarly inspected. The first dozen or so examples were completed with the pilot's Vickers gun mounted internally, firing through the break in the fuselage sides were the narrow engine mounting met the wider fuselage. Later examples had the gun mounted externally, as the RFC had requested, and were fitted with the Vickers-Challenger mechanical synchronization gear, its long operating rod clearly visible below and forward of the gun. The gun mountings comprised a frame fabricated from steel tube, two additional vertical wooden fuselage members being introduced to provide attachment points for the frame. The ammunition belt was stored in a wooden box, mounted across the fuselage, a sliding door being provided in the starboard fuselage side for reloading.

All early production aircraft had the small triangular dorsal and ventral fins as fitted to the prototype and steel tube undercarriage legs with streamlined wooden fairings. The observer's Lewis gun was mounted on a fairly basic swivelling pillar, the Bowker mounting quickly replacing this, and the much more satisfactory Scarff ring being substituted.

There is no record that the last few machines, A110–A115, in the Royal Aircraft Factory's initial batch of fifty were ever completed. This was possibly as a direct result of the conclusions of the Burbidge Enquiry into the Factory's affairs, or simply because they had more pressing demands upon workshop space. This lack of a handful of machines could hardly be considered critical, as by the time A66 first flew orders had already been placed with at least three other manufacturers. On 25 August, the Austin Motor Co. was awarded contract No.87/A/488 for 100 aircraft; Siddeley-Deasey was awarded contract 87/A/486 on the 30th and a further contract, 87/A/785, for an additional 150 machines on 6 September. By the end of September further orders, to Daimler, Napier & Miller, Standard and the Coventry Ordnance Works had brought the total to 1,200, a significant commitment to an aeroplane which had yet to see active service. However, this commitment was entirely justified given the situation in France and the R.E.8's superiority to the aircraft then in service – it is only with the benefit of hindsight that it is possible to say that, had the War Office waited a few months, even better aeroplanes might have been available. The need was immediate, and in the opinion of the author, the War Office's action in ordering the R.E.8 at that moment in time was entirely correct.

R.E.8 production at Siddeley-Deasey's Parkside Works, Coventry. The fins and rudders have been distorted by the wide-angle lens employed. P.H.T. Green Collection

Into Service

The R.E.8 first saw active service with 52 Squadron, a newly formed unit which arrived in France on 21 November 1916 equipped with aircraft taken from the batch built at Farnborough. However, its debut was not the signal success for which both designers and operators had hoped, as initially its engine proved rather unreliable, due to poor lubrication. Although this was soon resolved, 52 Squadron unfortunately suffered numerous crashes, the aircraft often spinning into the ground from low altitude. Fires frequently resulted from these crashes, as there was no fire wall to separate the engine from the petrol tanks, and so if in a crash the hot engine was pushed back it would rupture the tanks and spill the remaining fuel. 52 Squadron's pilots were mostly newly qualified, their training brief unlikely to have included instruction in spin recovery. It was therefore decided that they should exchange aeroplanes with the more experienced crews of 34 Squadron, commanded by Maj Blount, who were then operating the B.E.2e. The swap took place early in 1917, both parties appearing happy with their new acquisitions. However, the introduction of the R.E.8 was greeted with apprehension by some crews who, for whatever reason, regarded the long upper wing extension which it had inherited from the B.E.2e as structurally unsound, and the tragic crashes experienced by 52 Squadron did nothing to enhance its reputation. Lord Cowdray, the then President of the Air Board, discerned that it would be appropriate to conduct trials to establish just how prone to spinning the new machine actually was, as it had been suggested that the vertical tail surfaces might be too small to counteract the torque reaction of the propeller, particularly when climbing.

Three variants were tested: a standard production machine; one with an enlarged fin; and one in which the engine's angle of upthrust had been reduced. The report of these tests, written by Lt Col F.C. Jenkins and dated 5 March 1917, states:

> In carrying out these tests, I came to the conclusion that this machine can only be spun by determined effort, or by inexperienced flying. In the latter case, it might be due to such an elementary error as taking off with insufficient speed and attempting to turn without sufficient bank.

Although this early production R.E.8 is fitted with a Scarff ring, no Lewis gun is mounted thereon as these were usually removed between sorties. The operating rod for the Vickers-Challenger gear can be seen on the fuselage side, ahead of the front cockpit. Author's collection

In addition, it was suggested that inexperienced pilots might find the trimming instructions 'Trim for climbing when getting off the ground by turning the wheel half way', which had been stencilled on the fuselage side by order of the Director of Aeronautical Equipment, to be misleading. It was also felt that the instruction greatly increased the risk of a stall occurring should the engine cut during the climb. These instructions were therefore deleted, with effect from 14 May 1917, on the instructions of Brooke-Popham.

A brief note for the guidance of pilots, explaining how the R.E.8 should be flown, was then written by Maj J.A. Chamier DSO, former C.O. of 34 Squadron, whose crews were now successfully operating the type. The 'Note', in addition to giving sound, practical advice for pilots, went on to offer similarly useful advice to observers, by suggesting that they ought not to stand up to look over their pilot's shoulder whilst landing, an action which resulted from them finding themselves sitting in the rear seat for the first time with their forward view impaired.

Then, it having been established that the crashes were almost certainly due to pilot error, brought about by woefully inadequate training, and that the R.E.8 was perfectly safe with its original fin, the Royal Aircraft Factory's designers set about changing it. In addition to the modifications made during the spinning trials a

Extracts from 'NOTES FOR THE GUIDANCE OF PILOTS' by Maj J.A. Chamier DSO

This is a splendid flying machine but it is not a perambulator and requires, at first, a little care.

In the R.E.8 the chief thing to remember is that the machine gives very little indication of losing its speed until it suddenly shows an uncontrollable tendency to dive which cannot be corrected in time if you are near the ground.

All the recent accidents in R.E.8s can be equally divided into two classes:

a) With the engine pulling.
b) With the engine off.

a) With the engine pulling the machine will not stall at 50 mph but it is not advisable to get the speed as low as this. The only accident which is likely to occur with the engine on is spinning, or more correctly swinging tail. This is caused by having too little bank for the amount of rudder used. It can be stopped immediately by increasing the bank and taking off the rudder.

You will find the rudder control in every case of spinning or swing tail will become very stiff, and you may not be able to get it very central but you should aim (without putting on sufficient pressure to break anything) to do this.

b) With the engine off the only thing to avoid is gliding too slowly. I have already told you that with the engine on the machine will not stall at 50 mph, but at 65 mph or below, when gliding, the machine suddenly loses speed. This is particularly the case when making a turn to enter the aerodrome as the extra resistance caused by the rudder is sufficient to bring down the pace …

One more point as regards losing speed. Observers must be cautioned that when an aeroplane is gliding down from work over the lines they must not stand up in order to look over the pilot's shoulder for the fun of the thing, as the extra head resistance caused may lead to the aeroplane falling below its critical gliding speed, and so bring about an accident.

A3186, built by Austin, has a larger dorsal fin but retains the original small triangular ventral fin. Author's collection

A3654 has both upper and lower fins enlarged. It is seen here with the fuselage fabric unlaced for inspection. Author's collection

B6557 of 142 Squadron, fitted with a steel tube undercarriage. As was usual when on the ground, the Lewis gun has been removed. Author's collection

(Below) **This unidentified R.E.8, seen here with its crew, has a Lewis gun on a Foster mounting in addition to its standard armament. A later production example, its Vickers gun is controlled by the hydraulic C.C. gear.** J.M. Bruce/G.S. Leslie Collection

number of other experiments were tried: A3468 and A4598 were each fitted with enlarged fins of different types, both being of around 12sq ft (1sq m) in area. A4572 was tested with a new fin and a balanced rudder, and the original prototype 7996 was fitted with modified ailerons. As a result of these various trials the fin area of production aircraft was increased. Initially only the main, dorsal fin was modified, its root chord being increased to bring the junction of its leading edge with the fuselage forward of the horizontal tailplane, thus increasing its overall area. Soon afterwards, the area of the ventral fin was also enlarged, its chord being similarly extended and its leading edge given a rounded profile. This form of fin then became the standard for all further production aircraft.

first, the pair being fired together. These double-yoked guns became affectionately known in the squadrons as 'Huntley and Palmer', although any connection with the famous biscuit makers is highly unlikely! Other variations in armament were not unknown, with at least one machine, E20 of 4 Squadron being fitted with an over-wing Lewis gun on a Foster mounting, the Vickers and observer's Lewis being retained.

An experimental installation of the Le Prieur gunsight, a development of the ring-and-bead sight, in which the bead could be adjusted to compensate for deflection, was made late in 1916. However, it was quickly condemned as being over complicated, clumsy to use and dangerous in a crash, and was not adopted.

or by whom, is not known, and there is no surviving record of its effectiveness.

Since the aircraft had a constant tendency, caused by a natural reaction to the torque of the propeller and its slipstream corkscrewing around the fuselage to turn to the right, a piece of ⅜in (0.95cm) diameter rubber shock cord was fixed to the left side of the rudder bar so as to provide a gentle pressure which would otherwise have had to be provided by the pilot's foot. The tension, and thus the turning moment created, could be adjusted by means of a bowden cable which terminated at a control lever mounted on the upper port longeron within the pilot's cockpit.

From July 1917, the Claudel-Hobson carburettors with which the RAF4a had originally been fitted were superseded by

Further Modifications

As with other designs, the original steel tube undercarriage legs appear to have proved less than satisfactory in service, and new undercarriage legs of solid ash were introduced for later production machines, starting in the autumn of 1917. These were joined at the apex of the their 'vee' with steel facing plates on each side, to which the axle and rubber shock cords were also attached. The steel tube axle and 700 × 100 wheels remained unchanged.

The hydraulic Constantinesco synchronization gear which, unlike previous mechanical gears, could be fitted to any aeroplane engine without the need for custom-made parts, and which proved far superior, was naturally adopted for the R.E.8 as soon as it became available. A cut-out was made in the cockpit floor panel to accommodate the fluid reservoir which was installed low down on the starboard side, the gun being fitted with the type-B trigger motor and Hyland type-C loading handle. The first machines to have the C.C. gear were A3630, built by Daimler, and A3730, built by Siddeley-Deasey.

The R.E.8's armament was also improved by replacing the webbing ammunition belt for the Vickers gun with Prideaux disintegrating links, which not only eliminated some of the jamming to which that gun was prone, but also increased the storage capacity from 300 to 500 rounds. The observer's firepower was also frequently increased on active service by the provision of a second Lewis gun, mounted on the Scarff ring alongside the

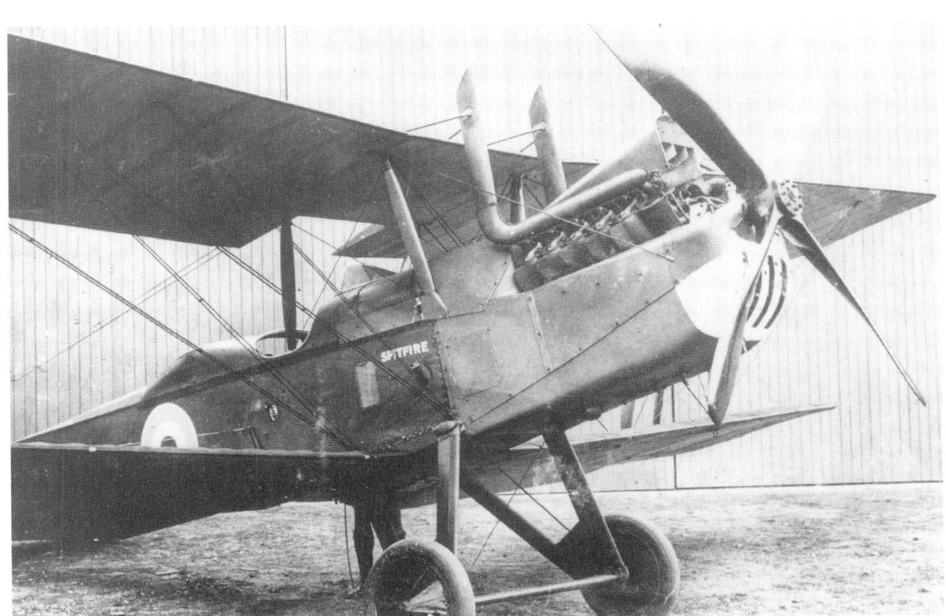

A 50 Squadron R.E.8, A4192, showing details of the engine's air scoop and the baffles which directed cooling air around the engine cylinders. P.H.T. Green Collection

At least one R.E.8, serving with 30 Squadron in Mesopotamia, was experimentally fitted with the 6-pounder Davis non-recoiling gun (which worked by discharging an equal mass in both directions) for ground-attack work. The weapon was installed alongside the fuselage, firing downwards at an angle, in a manner similar to that previously adopted for the B.E.12, from which it was most probably 'borrowed'. It was loaded by the occupant of the rear cockpit, but how it was sighted,

units manufactured by Messrs Brown and Barlow, thereby bringing about an ever-welcome improvement in engine performance. The original lower engine cowling fitted closely to the sump, with fairings over the carburettors, and the introduction of a deeper and more rounded sump cowling may have been connected with this change of carburettor.

Brig Gen Brooke-Popham continued to press for the R.E.8's centre section to be covered in a transparent material, and

Squadron Service

The R.E.8 is known to have been operated by the following units:

Western Front Nos. 4, 5, 6, 7, 9, 12, 13, 15, 16, 21, 34, 42, 52, 53 and 59 Squadrons. Nos 4 and 69 (Australian) Squadrons, and 6[eme] Escadrille, L'Aviation Militaire Belge.

The type also served with the Headquarters Communications Squadron, and the Communications flight attached to 56 Squadron.

Italy 34 and 42 Squadrons.

Palestine 14, 113, 142, and 67 (Australian) Squadrons.

Mesopotamia 30 and 63 Squadrons.

Home Defence 50, 76, and 77 Squadrons.

Training Nos. 7, 8, 9, 13, 15, 16, 17, 20, 23, 25, 26, 31, 35, 38, 39, 42, 46,51, 52, 53, 57, 59, 60, 64, 66 and 110. 2, 5, and 35 Training Depot Station.

Also the Wireless and Observer School, Brooklands, and the Aerial Observation School, Heliopolis.

Post-War RAF Contingent, Archangel, Russia.
6 Squadron, Basra, Mesopotamia.
141 Squadron, Ireland (one aircraft only).

twelve examples were built with an insert of Triplex glass in the area between the spars. The first machine to be so fitted was the A3701, built by Siddeley-Deasey, which arrived in France on 12 June 1917. On 15 October 1917, Brooke-Popham requested that a quarter of all production aircraft should have the insert, but a shortage of Triplex glass prevented even such limited use, and only a small number, all built by Siddeley-Deasey, were ever fitted with it.

On Active Service

Like the B.E.2, which it replaced, the R.E.8 seems to have served everywhere that the RFC, and later the RAF, went to war, with well over 4,000 being built before the Armistice brought production to an end. Its crews, with typical British affection, christened it 'Harry Tate' after the well-known Music Hall comedian with whose name its designation so nearly rhymed, and learned to forgive its shortcomings. In early February 1917, 21 squadron was equipped with the R.E.8 and was joined by the newly formed 59 Squadron on the 23rd of that month. Nos 6, 13, 42 and 53 Squadrons all received the new machine in April, followed by 4, 5, 7, 9, 12, 15 and 16 in May and June. It was in June, too, that 52 Squadron, its pilots now veterans of six months' service, was re-equipped with the type. Finally, in September 1917, 69 (Australian) Squadron brought its R.E.8s to France. Thus it equipped fifteen of the twenty-five corps/reconnaissance squadrons based on the Western Front, so that the presence of an R.E.8 on artillery observation duty, plodding its lonely figure of eight at around 4,000ft (1,220m) over the lines, became as familiar a sight in the sky as the

Harry Tate

Born in 1873, Ronald Macdonald Hutchinson became a Music Hall comedian and was at the height of his fame in the period just before and during World War I. He took the stage name 'Harry Tate' from that of his former employers, the sugar refiners, Henry Tate & Sons of Liverpool (now incorporated into 'Tate & Lyle'). His name became common Service slang for the R.E.8, with which it so nearly rhymed. He died in 1940.

This R.E.8, built by the Coventry Ordnance Works, has the deeper sump cowling fitted to many later machines. Unusually its Lewis gun has its jacket still fitted. Author's collection

Ammunition dropping by parachute as practised by an R.E.8 of 3 Squadron AFC in July 1918. The apparatus was built by L.J. Wackett and was mounted on a modified Cooper bomb rack. National Library of Australia via A.H. Rowe

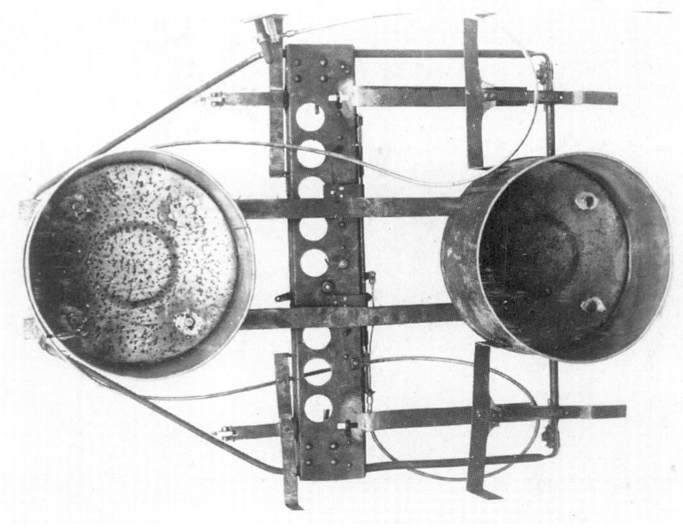

An underside view of Lawrence Wackett's ammunition carrier. The two cut-down oil drums held the parachutes. National Library of Australia via A.H. Rowe

(Left) **This machine is fitted with bomb rails below the lower wing. The absence of the operating rod of a Vickers-Challenger gear indicates that this is a later R.E.8, with the hydraulic C.C. gear.** J.M. Bruce/G.S. Leslie Collection

(Below) **An R.E.8 observer demonstrating the degree to which he was able to fire his Lewis gun forwards.** J.M. Bruce/G.S. Leslie Collection

sun or the stars. On 7 June 1917, during the Battle of Messines, the R.E.8s of 21 Squadron directed the fire of British artillery so accurately that seventy-two enemy batteries were put out of action, saving the lives of many a British 'Tommy'. The Battle of Ypres, two months later, saw 16 Squadron win similar distinction, not just for the accuracy of its artillery work, but also for photographic missions and contact patrols.

On 4 July 1918, the R.E.8s of 3 Squadron (AFC) and 9 Squadron (RFC) began to drop supplies of ammunition to the infantry using a system devised by Capt Lawrence J. Wackett, commander of 3 Squadron's 'B' Flight. The technique involved an aircraft carrying two wooden boxes, each containing 1,200 cartridges, on a rack attached to a modified Cooper bomb carrier fixed below the fuselage. Purpose-made parachutes then ensured that the boxes reached the ground undamaged. A remarkable degree of accuracy was soon being achieved, the boxes often landing within 10yd (9m) of the aiming point. The scheme was a great success, with up to 100,000 rounds being dropped in a single day.

September 1917 saw the R.E.8 add night bombing to its other roles, two 112lb (50kg), or larger numbers of lighter bombs being the usual load. Thus loaded, the top speed of the R.E.8 was reduced by around 5mph (8km/h), and 10 minutes was added to its climb to 10,000ft (3,048m), although such an altitude was never required.

Thus the R.E.8 performed its duties well, with credit both to its designers and its crews, but it remained what it had been designed to be, a reconnaissance two-seater. Although its top speed was only a few miles an hour less than that of its principal opponent, the German Albatros, it was nonetheless unable to run for home if attacked, and had no choice except to stand and fight. This it was frequently able to do to very good effect.

For example, on 16 August 1917, when the Battle of Langemark had brought about increased aerial activity, an R.E.8 from 7 Squadron was attacked by two Albatroses over Poelcapelle but managed to shoot one down, the other then breaking off the attack. Later the same day, another 7 Squadron R.E.8 was attacked by a patrol of eight Albatroses, but again they gave up the attack after one of their number was shot down. An R.E.8 crew from 21 Squadron faced even greater odds that day when they ran into no less than nine enemy fighters, but they too turned away when the observer's Lewis gun sent one of them down out of control. Then on the 21st, Lts N. Sharples and M.A. O'Callaghan were flying A4381 when they were attacked by Oberleutnant E. Von Dostler, the commander of *Jasta* 6, who, despite being a holder of the famed 'Blue Max' with twenty-six combat victories, fell to the guns of his would-be victim.

In December, Lt J.L. Sandy and Sgt H.F. Hughes of 69 (Australian) Squadron were attacked by a patrol of six Albatros fighters, and managed to shoot down one of them, the enemy machine landing in allied territory and so being captured virtually intact. The arrival of two more R.E.8s made the contest a little more even, and another Albatros was brought down before the fight broke up. Unfortunately, Lt Sandy had been shot dead and his observer mortally wounded, yet their R.E.8 flew on in wide circles until it finally ran out of fuel and glided down to a crash landing some 50 miles (80km) away.

The morning of 9 June 1918 saw Lts R.C. Armstrong and F.J. Mart of 3 Squadron Australian Flying Corps as No.69 (A) Squadron had now become attack an enemy Halberstadt two-seater whilst flying R.E.8 D4689, forcing it to land at their own aerodrome at Flesselles. The German crew were taken prisoner, and their machine returned to Australia as a war trophy. One R.E.8 crew who appear to have been particularly pugnacious were Lts Croye Rothes-Pithey and Hervey Rhodes of 12 Squadron. Pithey was a South African from the Orange Free State, Rhodes a Lancastrian who had served in the Infantry since 1914, transferring to the RFC early in 1918. Their first victory, on 7 May 1918, was over an enemy kite balloon. One month later they were on a photographic mission in B7715 when they were spotted by a patrol of nine Pfalz D IIIs. The enemy machines attacked successively in pairs, Rhodes managing to shoot down three of them before the enemy finally gave up the fight. For this action the pair were each awarded a well-deserved DFC, but their career together was still far from over. On 21 August they were attacked by four Fokker D VIIs, sending one of them out of control before their R.E.8.'s petrol tank was shot through, forcing them to make a hasty return to their base. Just one week later they brought down a DFW two-seater whilst flying R.E.8 F6097, and on 30 August they were attacked by a patrol of seven Fokkers, managing to bring one of them down before the arrival of other British aircraft broke up the action. In mid-September Rhodes was posted home for pilot training, and their highly successful partnership came to an end.

This R.E.8 crew appear ready for action. Their cockpits were placed closely together for ease of communication. Details of the pilot's instrument panel appear to have been deleted by the censor.
J.M. Bruce/G.S. Leslie Collection

Inevitably, of course, the R.E.8 crews did not always emerge victorious from combat. On 13 April, for example, two R.E.8s of 59 Squadron based at Bellevue were ordered to photograph the railway junction at Drocourt-Queant, four more machines from the same squadron accompanying them to afford some protection. This was 'Bloody April', when the German Air Service had considerable superiority over the Western Front, but the crews took comfort from the promised presence of patrols of six F.E.2ds, a flight of SPADs and 48 Squadron's Bristol Fighters all operating in the same area. However, the SPADs were late taking off, the F.E.s lost formation and nothing had been seen of the Bristols when the six R.E.8s were attacked en route by a similar number of Albatroses from von Richtofen's *Jasta* 11. All six British machines were shot down within a few minutes, A3190 by the 'Red Baron' himself, with ten out of the twelve crew members being killed.

However, on 21 April the following year the R.E.8 was instrumental in the death of von Richtofen, for two machines from 3 (AFC) Squadron were photographing an area west of Hamel when they were attacked by four Fokkers from Richtofen's *Jasta*. Two of the enemy aircraft were hit by bullets from the observers' guns and broke off the engagement. British anti-aircraft

R.E.8 Production

7996–7; A66–115; A3506–30 – Royal Aircraft Factory.
A3169–3268; A4261–4410; B5851–5900 – Austin.
A4664–4763; B6631–6730; B7681–7730; C5026–5125; D6701–6850 – Coventry Ordnance Works.
A3521–3680; A4161–4260; B3401–3450; B5001–5150; C2231–3080; F3548–3747 – Daimler.
A3832–3931; B2251–2300; C4551–4600; D3836–3910 (cancelled) D4811–4960; E1101–50 – Napier.
A3405–3504; A3681–3830; B6451–6624; E1–300; E1151–1260; F1553–1602; F3246–3345 – Siddeley-Deasey.
A4411–4560; A4564–4663; D1501–1600; D4661–4810; F1665–1764 – Standard Motor.

In addition to these production machines a considerable number of 'new' aircraft were assembled at Repair Depots from spare parts and salvage. These rebuilt aircraft included:

A7000; B730; B732; B737–8; B741–2; B750; B753; B755–760; B764–5; B780–3; B786–7; B791–3; B798; B810–811; B814; B820–25; B830; B832–3; B835–7; B840–6; B853; B876; B1498; B4021; B4028–30; B4032–6; B4038; B4040; B4045–6; B4048; B4050–1; B4054–7; B4059–60; B4062; B4065; B4067; B4069; B4075; B4086; B4089–90; B4093–4; B4097; B4101; B4103–6; B4109; B4118; B4134; B7734; B7738–40; B7754; B7761; B7802–5; B7827; B7834; B7853; B7887; B7893; B7917; B8097; B8798; B8872; B8874; B8876–8; B8880–91; B8893–8900; B8909; B9473; B9997; C3381; C3433; C4282; C4294; D4966–7; D4970; D4972; D4980–1; D4996; D4998; D9737–9; D9790–99; F662–3; F666; F669; F672; F675–7; F681–5; F687; F689–90; F694; F699–700; F5871–2; F5874–5; F5879–82; F5885; F5891; F5895; F5897; F5899; F5901–2; F5909; F5976; F6005; F6007; F6010; F6012–9; F6044–50; F6085; F6091; F6097; F6203–4; F6218; F6270; F6273; F6277; F6279; F6299; H6843; H6845; H6857; H6865; H6870; H6879; H6896; H6900; H7017–38; H7040–57; H7136–43; H7182–93; H7207; H7262–8; H8121.

Three R.E.8s in service in the Middle East. The nearest aeroplane has a steel tube undercarriage. Author's collection

guns opened fire on the German machines as the fight drifted westwards over the lines, attracting the attention of a flight of Sopwith Camels from 209 Squadron led by Capt Roy Brown. And so the 'Red Baron' was brought down.

The first R.E.8 to reach Mesopotamia joined 63 Squadron, then based at Basra, on 14 September 1917 and was joined by another two days later. Unfortunately, these two machines were both lost on their first flight over the Turkish lines, one due to engine failure and the other in combat with a Halberstadt. However, by the end of October these had been replaced and the Squadron was fully equipped with the type. Meanwhile, 30 Squadron received its first R.E.8 on 17 October 1917 and had acquired a full complement before the end of the year. The two squadrons performed sterling service throughout the Mesopotamia campaign, the aircraft of 63 Squadron at one time each averaging 10 hours flying per day.

The R.E.8 served in Palestine too, although it was not until late in 1918 that any squadron was wholly equipped with the type. Throughout the autumn of 1917, 67 (Australian) Squadron operated a mixed collection of aircraft which included five R.E.8s, as did 113 Squadron which was formed at Ismailia in Egypt and transferred to Palestine in September 1917. A year later, it had sixteen R.E.8s, as did 14 Squadron, whilst 142 squadron, based at Jerusalem, had five.

On 19 September 1918, aircraft from 113 Squadron aided the Infantry by laying smoke screens, each dropping a series of smoke candles in order to create a screen up to 400yd (365m) long. Four days later, the same aircraft dropped a total of 122 20lb (9kg) bombs on the retreating Turkish forces on the Es Salt/Amman Road, hastening their defeat. At the end of the month the R.E.8s of 14 and 113 squadrons were used to transport badly needed fuel to El Affule aerodrome, a total of 928 gallons (4,220 litres) of petrol, and 156 gallons (709 litres) of oil being flown in.

In November 1917, 34 and 42 Squadrons were transferred from France to Italy as part of a British detachment sent to help

Seen in the Egyptian desert, C5108 has been fitted with a much larger fin, probably made locally. Author's collection

For pilot training the Scarff ring was replaced with a new decking and windscreen, forming a second cockpit. Standard dual controls were fitted. J.M. Bruce/G.S. Leslie Collection

render assistance to the Italians. No.34 arrived at its new base near Milan on 14 November, and had its R.E.8s reassembled and operational by the 17th, whilst 42 Squadron was sent to Istrana, flying its first missions on 9 December.

During the Italian offensive on the River Piave in July 1918, a small number British R.E.8s were placed under the direct control of the Italian Army, flying artillery observation missions from an aerodrome at Malcontenta. They often carried Italian observers, but returned daily to their own base for maintenance by British ground crews. A few R.E.8s even made their way to Russia, sent to Archangel in August 1918 to reinforce the small RAF detachment that was operating there.

During 1917 a total of twenty-two R.E.8s was sold to Belgium for use by the 6[eme]. Escadrille of l'Aviation Militaire Belge, entering service during July. By the end of the year their engines, like those of the B.E.2cs which they superseded, had been replaced by the V8 water-cooled Hispano-Suiza, the R.E.8s thereby acquiring frontal radiators and extensively louvred engine cowlings resembling those of the similarly powered SPAD fighter. One of these aircraft survives to this day in the Musée Royal de l'Armée in Brussels.

Home Establishment

A considerable number of R.E.8s served with training squadrons, providing advanced training both for scout and two-seater pilots. In this role, the Scarff ring, guns and R.L. tube were all removed, and the fuselage's upper decking was modified so that the rear cockpit cut-out resembled that of the forward cockpit. A standard wicker pilot's seat was substituted for the observer's small swivel perch, and his rather rudimentary dual controls were replaced with a conventional stick and rudder bar. In order to make room for the rear rudder bar, it was necessary for the elevator cross shaft to be raised and for the foot step which was normally fitted on the port side of the fuselage to be removed. A tailplane trimmer adjustment wheel was provided too. The map table, holders for spare Lewis drums and the wireless were usually also removed. Although a throttle control lever was a standard fitting in the rear cockpit, in training aircraft this was frequently moved back to a more convenient position aft of the fourth vertical fuselage side-strut. However, there is no record that any instrumentation was installed in the rear cockpit.

A training unit R.E.8 with a greatly enlarged upper fin, possibly based on that of a B.E.2e. Author's collection

Many of these training aircraft were fitted with a greatly enlarged fin, usually fabricated in the squadron workshops and often based upon that first created at 42 Squadron, whereby a stock B.E.2e fin was fitted and its upper edge extended to meet the top of the rudder with a 1in (2.54cm) diameter 22swg tube, the whole being covered with fabric. Despite the Air Board having prepared a drawing of the 42 squadron fin, the finished shape of these enlarged fins varied considerably, some having a smooth outline, others a noticeable kink towards the top where the outline of the B.E. fin was modified to meet the R.E.8s rudder. Other shapes and designs were almost equally common, with triangular fins and angular shapes closely resembling that shown on the original preliminary layout drawing A9429 also appearing, not only on training aircraft, but also on active service machines in France and even in the Middle East.

The R.E.8 was also pressed into service for home defence, and in this role was frequently equipped with navigation lights, and with brackets for Holt flares to facilitate landing at night.

Markings

The standard finish for all R.E.8s intended for service on the Western front or for home establishment was P.C.10, with the redder-tinted P.C.12 being substituted on aircraft being sent to the Middle East. The pigmented finish was applied to the fabric covering of the fuselage and fin and to the upper surfaces of the wings, tailplane and elevators, being allowed to overlap onto the undersides of these surfaces by 1–1½in (2.54–3.8cm) and so giving them a noticeable outline or border. It was also applied to

The appearance of this R.E.8, possibly C2626, has been transformed by a B.E.2e-style fin and a racy colour scheme. Author's collection

the fairings of the steel tube undercarriage legs and to the metal engine cowlings, although these were more usually painted Battleship Grey. The interplane struts were frequently also painted Battleship Grey, as were outer portions of the propeller blades, their hubs being left in natural mahogany.

In accordance with the system then in use, the rudder was painted with three stripes in the national colours of red, white and blue, with red at the trailing edge, and the entire surface being covered. Roundels were painted, as large as possible, on the fuselage sides, usually just aft of the rear cockpit, and the extremities of the outer surfaces of the wings. Early examples had these roundels immediately inboard of the interplane struts in accordance with a ruling then in force that markings should not lap on to the ailerons. Following complaints that the darker blue introduced during 1917 was hard to distinguish from the surrounding P.C.10 finish, a narrow outer circle of white was added.

Squadron markings, comprising stripes or geometric symbols, were usually painted in white, as were letters or numbers to distinguish individual machines, these being applied to the fuselage sides and often repeated on the upper wing. Presentation aircraft also had the name of their sponsor stencilled on the fuselage side, usually aft of the roundel. Although the practice was officially frowned upon, some crews nonetheless managed to christen their machines with the name of a loved one or some other reminder of more gentle times, these names being similarly painted on the fuselage side. Occasionally, crews chose to name their mount after their home town, or some other place they held dear, thereby causing confusion between such machines and true presentation aircraft.

Aircraft stationed in training squadrons, where regulations appear to have been somewhat less stringently enforced, occasionally acquired more colourful markings, but, perhaps because the type was not regarded with a great deal of affection, there were few instances of R.E.8s being decorated in this way.

R.E.9, A3561, fitted with a Sunbeam 'Maori' engine. The fuselage is similar to that of the R.E.8, but the wings have two-bay bracing. Author's collection

Continued Development

As a result of the Burbidge Inquiry, the Royal Aircraft Factory was no longer permitted to undertake the design of new aeroplanes, but instead was expected to pursue research and improve and develop existing designs. Thus efforts to develop the R.E.8 continued throughout its service career, not only in an attempt improve its performance, but also in the interests of aeronautical experiment, the results of which were intended to benefit the whole aircraft industry.

On 31 August 1917, B738, one of the aircraft retained at Farnborough for experiment, was flown with what was described as a 'small balanced rudder' and by 16 September had been fitted with elevators of reduced chord. Aircraft designers, seeking enhanced manoeuvrability, had for some time been introducing ever bigger control surfaces, only to find them growing less effective as their area increased, causing the Royal Aircraft Factory's staff to investigate the phenomenon. Thus another machine, A4598, was employed in a number of experiments into lateral control, being first fitted with new ailerons with a pronounced 'wash-out' to the tips. Later, ailerons whose chord had been reduced to 16in (40cm) from the usual 24in (60cm) were substituted, followed by surfaces which tapered from a chord of 24in (60cm) at the root to only 8in (20cm) at the tip.

In October 1917, B738 was fitted with an RAF4d, a standard unit whose output had been uprated by the provision of a Rateau-type supercharger. Initial overheating problems were overcome, at least partially, by the provision of a greatly enlarged air scoop. An experimental variable pitch propeller was also tested, although it is not known whether this was still in place when an error in control settings led to overspeeding of the supercharger at 28,000rpm before it failed, the machine managing to glide down to a safe landing from 13,700ft (4,175m).

Although in its early form the RAF4a had proved somewhat unreliable, largely due to lubrication problems which were later resolved, it was an attempt to improve performance rather than to circumvent this problem which led to proposals to replace this engine with the 200hp Hispano-Suiza. Indeed, the Farnborough drawing office was at work on the idea as early as October 1916, long before the R.E.8 entered service. When thus powered, the aircraft was to be given the designation R.E.8a. The actual installation was made in A95, one of the batch of production machines built by the Royal Aircraft Factory, and was completed by December 1916. It had a flat frontal, car-type radiator, but retained the standard T.6296 propeller, usually employed with the RAF engine. The pilot's Vickers gun was mounted on top of the forward fuselage, slightly offset to port, as on the S.E.5, thereby greatly facilitating the clearing of jams, although it is not known what type of synchronizing gear was fitted. Despite the rather inadequate propeller, performance was clearly improved, but the Hispano-Suiza engine and its derivatives were never available in sufficient numbers even for those designs for which no alternative powerplant was possible, and no further examples of the R.E.8a were built.

In October 1917, Messrs D. Napier & Sons was awarded contract No.AS28127 for seventy-five R.E.8s (D4811–D4885), for which the Rolls-Royce 'Eagle' was the specified engine. However, as with the Hispano-Suiza, supplies of the 'Eagle' never even began to approach parity with demand, and Napiers eventually completed the batch as standard R.E.8s using the RAF4a engine.

It appears that complaints that the R.E.8's upper wing extensions were structurally unsound were taken seriously by the designers at the Royal Aircraft Factory, for on 9 June 1917 A4600 made its first flight fitted with what were described as B.E.2d wings. Since the R.E.8's wings had been inherited from the B.E.2e, wings from other B.E.2 variants would presumably have fitted without modification. However, since the wings of the B.E.2c and 2d were identical, save for an external gravity tank which was not fitted to A4600, the use of the '2d designation, rather than the more common '2c, can only suggest that the donor was indeed a machine of that type, although its identity is not known. In addition to the two bay wings, A4600 was the first aircraft to have the all wood undercarriage introduced for later production R.E.8s and, by 8 August, had been fitted with elevators of reduced area. On 14 September it was listed, on the Farnborough strength, as an R.E.9, although drawings A17249 and A17250, which are dated November 1917, depict that type rather differently.

Six aircraft were converted to the new design, these being A3909–3912 from a batch of twenty-five built by the Royal Aircraft Factory; A3452 and A3561 were both built by Daimler. Fitted to the R.E.8 fuselages, which were retained unaltered, were new two bay wings with blunt tips and narrow chord ailerons hinged from a false rear spar a few inches to the rear of the structural member. The R.E.9's designer, H.P. Folland, clearly intended that the new machine would never be subjected to the same criticisms that affected the R.E.8 for, in addition to the new wings, it was fitted with a fin of generous area as well as an aerodynamically balanced rudder.

The first example, A3909, was presented for AID inspection on 9 October 1917,

Specification – R.E.8

Powerplant:	140hp RAF4a
Weights:	Empty 1,803lb (818kg); loaded 2,678lb (1,215kg)
Dimensions:	Upper span 42ft 7in (12.99m); lower span 32ft 7½in (9.95m); chord 5ft 6in (1.68m); gap 6ft 3½in (1.92m); wing area 377½sq ft (31.34sq m); dihedral 3½ degrees; stagger 24in (0.61m)
	Length 27ft 10½in (8.50m); height 11ft 4½in (3.47m); rudder area 9½sq ft (0.88sq m); fin area (early) 5sq ft (0.47sq m); fin area (late) 6¾sq ft (0.63sq m)
Performance:	Speed at sea level 103mph (166km/h); speed at 6,500ft 98mph (158km/h); climb to 5,000ft 11min 15sec; climb to 10,000ft 29min 30sec; service ceiling 13,500ft (4,115m); endurance 4¼hr

Developed from the R.E.8/9, the Siddeley R.T.1 showed little advance over existing types and was not adopted. Author's collection

the remainder all being completed and inspected by 2 November. The comparatively large number of prototypes demonstrates confidence that the new type would find favour, but expectations were too high, or memories too short, for just as the performance of the single bay B.E.2e had shown an improvement over that of the B.E.2c/d, so did that of the original single bay R.E.8 over the new R.E.9. The speed of the two types was very similar, but the old design could comfortably out-climb the new, and so, despite it greater strength, the R.E.9 was not adopted for production. The prototypes were therefore retained at Farnborough for development work, in the hope that their performance might yet be sufficiently improved to warrant production. A3909 was tested with the various different styles of ailerons that had previously been tried out on R.E.8 A4598, and also with what has been described as 'variable Centre of Gravity', although there appears to be no record of how this was achieved. A3542 was re-rigged to reduce its dihedral angle, presumably because it was thought that any reduction in inherent stability might bring about a corresponding increase in manoeuvrability. In September 1919 it was fitted with the supercharged RAF4d engine.

By 9 November, A3911 had been tested with ailerons of reduced span, then was fitted with a fully enclosed cockpit canopy and tested in flight on 13 March 1918. Since it was to be almost twenty years before any aircraft fitted with an enclosed cockpit entered service, it seems safe to say that the experiment was not generally considered to have been successful. June 1918 saw A3561 tested with a 265hp Sunbeam Maori engine, but the installation proved as unreliable as it was ugly.

The R.E.8 also served as the basis for the Siddeley R.T.1., the design being produced by private industry albeit under the direction of F.M. Green, who had, by that time, left Farnborough to join the Siddeley-Deasey Motor Car Co. The R.T.1's fuselage was basically similar to that of the R.E.8, but with the addition of a deeper top decking. However, the wing structure was entirely new, the upper wing being of much broader chord than the lower, with the gap reduced to only 56½in (144cm).

Six prototypes were built, the serial numbers allotted to them (B6625–B6630) being the last of a batch of aircraft originally ordered as R.E.8s. The first machine, powered by a 200hp Hispano-Suiza, was at Farnborough for inspection by 11 October 1917, and at No.1 Aircraft Depot, St Omer, by the following month.

Whatever Service pilots might have thought of it, Trenchard made it clear that the aircraft would not be required by the RFC. Nonetheless, the remaining prototypes were completed, B6626 and 6627 being fitted with the RAF4a, and B6630 having an underslung radiator in lieu of the frontal type fitted to B6625. B6630 was sent to the Aeroplane and Armament Experimental Establishment at Martlesham Heath for testing, and was still there at the end of the war, not returning to Farnborough until February 1919. B6627 was written off in a crash on the Isle of Grain on 9 May 1918, at which time it may have been fitted with the supercharged RAF4d. B6625 survived at Farnborough until the end of the war, but its eventual fate, like that of the others, is unknown.

Specification – R.E.9

Powerplant:	140hp RAF4a
Weights:	Empty not known; loaded 2,800lb (1,270kg)
Dimensions:	Span 38ft 6in (11.74m); chord 5ft 6in (1.68m); wing area 382sq ft (35.53sq m); dihedral 3½ degrees; stagger 24in (0.61m)
	Length 27ft 10½in (8.50m); height 10ft 5in (3.18m); rudder area 9½sq ft (0.88sq m); fin area 6¾sq ft (0.63)
Performance:	Speed not known; climb to 5,000ft 11min 20sec; climb to 10,000ft 35min 40sec; service ceiling 13,000ft (3,962m)

Specification – R.T.1

Powerplant:	140hp RAF4a
Weights:	Empty 1,773lb (804kg); loaded 2,590lb (1,175kg)
Dimensions:	Span 41ft 9in (12.73m); chord (upper) 6ft 6in (1.98m); chord (lower) 4ft 9in (1.45m); gap 4ft 8½in (1.44m); wing area 420sq ft (39.06sq m); dihedral 3½ degrees; stagger 29½in (9m)
	Length 27ft 8in (8.44m); height 11ft 7in (3.53m); rudder area 11sq ft (1.02sq m)
Performance:	Speed not known; climb to 5,000ft 7min 45sec; climb to 10,000ft 19min 10sec; service ceiling 16,000ft (4,877m)

The R.E.8 Post-War

With the coming of peace, there was no real place in the RAF, now dramatically reduced in size, for a machine like the R.E.8, which had been specifically designed for a particular war situation. However, in addition to those serving as flying test-beds at Farnborough, a few remained in service in areas such as Russia and the Middle East where the RAF was still flying operational sorties, but by the end of 1920 even these had joined the majority in being either scrapped or sold off.

Few, if any, joined the civil register, and today one RAF machine survives, on public display with the Imperial War Museum's extensive collection at Duxford in Cambridgeshire.

Preserved Examples

Only two complete aircraft survive, although fortunately both are on public display. These are:

F3556 –	Imperial War Museum, Duxford, Cambridgeshire, CB2 4OR. England.
326 (ex A4719) –	Musée Royal de l'Armée, Parc du Cinquantenaire, B1040, Brussels, Belgium (Hispano-Suiza engine).

In addition, various components are displayed in museums, most notably the Midland Air Museum in Coventry, the city where the majority of R.E.8s were originally built.

CHAPTER FOUR

The F.E.2 Series

Whilst it is true that no aeroplane ever flies straight off the drawing board without the need for any development or modification, it is equally true that, more than any other Royal Aircraft Factory type, the F.E.2 was created by a process of empirical stumbling, rather than by the reasoned development of a single basic design. It had its roots in the first successful aircraft designed and built by Geoffrey de Havilland, which the Army Aircraft Factory (as it then was) bought for £400 when its creator joined the Farnborough staff as designer and test pilot towards the end of 1910. It was a condition of the purchase that de Havilland should demonstrate the machine's ability to fly for one hour without adjustment; this he did on 14 January 1911, although due to the extremely cold weather he was allowed to land twice in order to warm up.

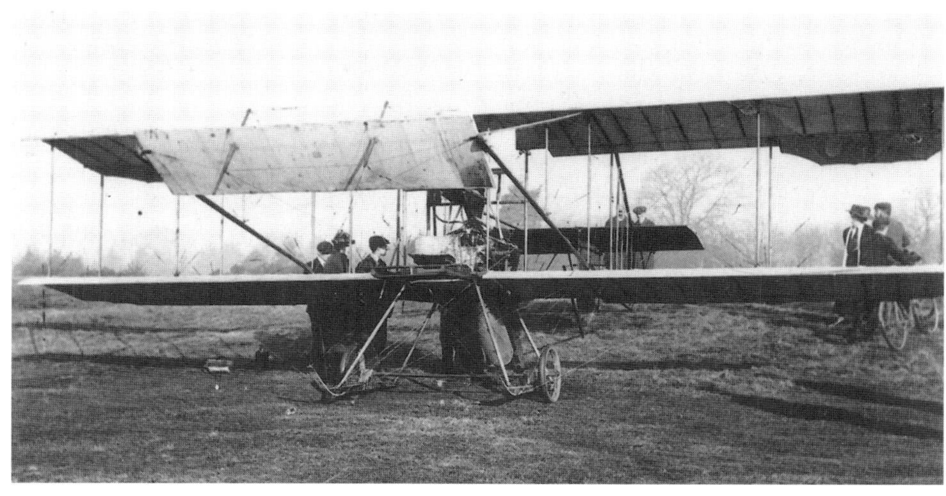

The de Havilland pusher biplane which became the F.E.1. Author's collection

As originally built, the machine was a conventional forward elevator pusher biplane, and was powered by a 45hp horizontally opposed four-cylinder engine, which had also been designed by de Havilland, and built for him by the Iris Motor Co. In general configuration it differed from the Farman, after which O'Gorman's 'F' class was named, only in that it had a monoplane tail, and so was, almost inevitably, given the Factory designation F.E.1.

Once at Farnborough, it was fitted with new interplane struts of improved streamlined form as part of a general aerodynamic clean up, its modest top speed showing some measurable improvement as a result. Initially, it proved to be unstable in the pitching plain, and during March 1911 it was fitted with new, larger, horizontal tail surfaces, which were tested in flight on the 31st, de Havilland's log recording that the machine was now 'steady fore and aft'.

On 11 April it was flown with extensions fitted to the upper wing, increasing its span to 65ft (20m). These afforded a considerable increase in lift, but also added to the yawing moment required to turn the machine, rendering the existing rudder too small. Comparative trials were made, early in May, with the extensions removed then refitted, and by the 26th of that month a new rudder, which extended above the tailplane, had been fitted, de Havilland recording that it gave 'better control and to a certain degree better lateral balance'.

Throughout June, the Farnborough staff's attention was largely directed towards the development of the S.E.1, for which O'Gorman had great hopes, but on the afternoon of the 12th de Havilland flew a few circuits in the F.E.1, landing now and then for adjustments to the tailplane. Then on 3 July he took it up with the front elevator removed entirely, finding it stable but in need of some adjustment. It was therefore re-rigged, moving the upper wing back to take some load off the tailplane, and test flown again the following day, this time to de Havilland's satisfaction. A barograph test, conducted on 27 July, appears to have indicated that its ceiling was 920ft (280m), with the wing extensions fitted, although it did rather better later. The following evening was spent giving air experience flights to NCOs and men of the London Balloon Company. Thereafter, Lt Theodore J. Ridge, the Factory's Assistant Superintendent, who had just taken his ticket, began to fly the machine, making his first circuit on 31 July. Unfortunately, on 15 August he suffered a smash, breaking one undercarriage skid, one spar and some other minor components. It is also recorded that an engine bolt broke, allowing two cylinders to come loose, with considerable

Specification – F.E.1	
Powerplant:	45hp Iris
Weights:	Empty not known; loaded 1,100lb (499kg)
Dimensions:	Span 33ft (10.07m); wing area 340sq ft (31.62sq m); length 40ft (12.2m)
Performance:	Speed at sea level 37mph (59km/h); endurance 1hr 20min

damage to the engine, but it is not clear whether this was the cause of Ridge's crash, or the result of it.

In accordance with the Army Aircraft Factory's well-known 'reconstruction' ploy, it was suggested then, and has often been repeated since, that the wrecked F.E.1 was rebuilt as the F.E.2. If that is so, the Factory's workshops must have worked with commendable efficiency, for de Havilland took the new machine out for its first flight at 4.30pm the following day, immediately upon his return from his annual holiday.

The first (1911) F.E.2 at Larkhill in August 1912 with a machine-gun mounted on its nose. Author's collection

The new machine resembled its alleged parent in its overall dimensions and general configuration, but with numerous detail changes. Although the rudder was virtually identical to that of the earlier design, the tailplane tips were more rounded. The wings were of similar span and chord, but with ailerons of higher aspect ratio. The undercarriage again employed four vertical struts and twin skids, to which the axle was secured with rubber shock cord. A rudimentary nacelle was provided to house the crew of two, the pilot being placed in the rear cockpit, with a gravity tank at his back feeding fuel to the 50hp Gnome rotary engine. This latter item proved to be remarkably unreliable, even for those days, the first take-off having to be aborted after only 50yd (45m) when the top of a piston came through the exhaust valve in pieces. A second attempt at 6.30am on 18 August proved more successful, with de Havilland able to fly four circuits of Laffans Plain before landing with the engine misfiring. The ailerons proved effective, the side balance being good despite the gusty breeze, although gliding was difficult as the machine turned out to be tail heavy. An attempt made to rectify this by 50lb (23kg) of lead being hurriedly tied to the nose, and a second flight made, but the balance was not entirely corrected, and it was decided that the machine would have to be modified. However, later the same day T.J. Ridge suffered his fatal crash in the S.E.1, which naturally upset the Farnborough staff quite considerably, and it was not until the 30th that de Havilland was able to take the F.E.2 out again. His logbook for that day states that the machine was now flying well after the alterations, but, uncharacteristically, he gave no indication as to what these alterations might have been. However, since it is recorded, some three weeks later, that the extra tailplane was removed, it seems entirely probable that the fitting of this surface, to carry some of the load on the tail, was the alteration referred to by the logbook.

The following day, the rudder controls were adjusted to give more movement, but a test flight on 1 September was cut short after a single circuit when an inlet valve broke, although the aircraft was able to land safely. Throughout September test flying was hindered by continual engine problems, with first the petrol feed, then the plugs, then the valves all giving trouble. Even the propeller went out of balance, presumably due to warping, and

Specification – F.E.2 (50hp)

Powerplant:	50hp Gnome
Weights:	Empty not known; loaded 1,200lb (5449kg)
Dimensions:	Span 33ft (10.07m); wing area 340sq ft (31.62sq m); length 28ft (8.54m)
Performance:	Speed at sea level 48mph (77km/h); climb 140ft/min (42.7m/min)

several others had to be tried before the engine would pull satisfactorily. Nonetheless de Havilland did manage to take up a number of passengers, including Capt Maitland on 5 September, Mr F.M. Green and Capt Brooke-Popham on the 7th, and Mr Seaman on the 22nd. The machine was then returned to the workshops so that its fabric could be treated with 'Emaillite', a proprietary 'dope' which was rapidly taking over from the concoctions such as varnish, size and even sago pudding that were used by the early pioneers.

During October, with the engine finally running satisfactorily, the F.E.2 was put through a number of performance trials which measured its top speed as 46mph (74km/h), and its rate of climb with a passenger, and with small wing extensions fitted, as 116ft (35m) per minute. A later trial, with a 12 stone (76kg) passenger, achieved 140ft (43m) per minute. de Havilland's log of these trials notes his own weight as precisely 150.5lb (68kg), but fails to state whether this included his clothes.

On Monday 16 October it was fitted with an air speed indicator and, during the early part of November, with dual controls. These enabled de Havilland to give some flying instruction, his pupil being a Mr Bear. However, Bear left the Factory staff early in December, and seems to have lost interest in aviation, for there is no record of his qualifying for a pilot's certificate. Geoffrey de Havilland, on the other hand, was only the fourth aviator to be awarded the 'Superior Aviator's Certificate', which involved rather more exacting trials than the basic one, undertaking the necessary tests during the first weeks of December 1911, flying the F.E.2. Thus, on Wednesday 6 December he took off from Farnborough at 11.14a.m and flew to Larkhill on Salisbury Plain, arriving at 12.54. From there he flew to Shrewton and back, then returned to Farnborough, covering a total distance in excess of 100 miles (160km) in 2¾ hours. This flight appears to have been made not to test the aeroplane, but as part of the qualifying tests for de Havilland's 'Superior Aviator's Certificate'. A climb to over 1,900ft (580m), made on 23 December, also appears to have been part of these tests.

Development of the F.E.2 was now considered to be complete, and with de Havilland, in his role as Farnborough's chief test pilot, now giving his attention to the newly built B.E. machines, Mr E.W.C. Perry took over as its pilot for routine flights.

Towards the end of April the F.E.2's ever troublesome Gnome engine was finally replaced, the new 70hp unit being flight tested on the 26th, de Havilland again taking the controls. The following day it was flown over to nearby Fleet Pond so that it could be fitted with floats, and two days later was tested both solo, and with F.M. Green as a passenger, the take-off from the rather small and shallow body of water being made fairly easily even though adjustments were still needed to the floats.

E.W. Copland Perry (1890–1914)

The son of a distinguished archaeologist, Evelyn Walter Copland Perry was educated at Repton and Trinity College, Cambridge. He joined the staff of the Army Aircraft Factory in February 1911, and in the summer of that year learned to fly at the Aeronautical Syndicate School at Hendon, taking his ticket (No.130) on 31 August. At Farnborough he did a great deal of flying on early B.E.s and on the F.E.2.

In July 1912 he left Farnborough to join the Sopwith School at Brooklands, quickly making a name for himself as an exhibition pilot and an instructor, his most distinguished pupil being Hugh Trenchard.

After a brief period with Avro, Perry joined forces with another ex-Factory employee, F. Beadle, to form their own aircraft company, specializing in seaplanes.

On 21 March 1913 he was gazetted Second Lieutenant in the RFC Special Reserve, having volunteered in response to an appeal from Lord Roberts for more men to join the reserve forces. With the coming of war in August 1914 he was ordered to report to Netheravon where he joined No.3 Squadron. With that unit he flew to Dover on 12 August, and the following day crossed to France, flying one of the first 42 RFC machines to go to war.

On 16 August 1914 he was flying B.E.8 No.625, with Air Mechanic H.E. Parfitt in the front cockpit, when the machine stalled at 150ft (46m), crashed and burned, killing both its occupants. Perry was buried next day at La Cimetière de St Acheul, the first British officer to die on active service in the First World War.

The F.E.2's float undercarriage being tested on Fleet Pond, with the crowd of schoolboy onlookers any such event seemed to attract. J.M. Bruce/G.S. Leslie Collection

Initially, the new installation comprised only a broad single central plywood float attached to the undercarriage skids, and a tail float, with wing-tip floats being added later. At the conclusion of the float trials the F.E.2 returned to its wheeled undercarriage.

Its next experimental installation was more significant for by the summer of 1912 it had become one of the very first aircraft to be fitted with a machine-gun. The gun, a .303 calibre belt-fed Maxim, was fitted at the front of the forward cockpit, and was mounted in a fork-shaped bracket, its muzzle secured to the cockpit's front rim with a length of rope. Unfortunately, there is no record of whether the gun was tested in flight, nor of how it was to be cooled, and, considering the additional load it must have placed on the machine's already sluggish climbing abilities, it is possible that the experiment was not considered a total success. Nonetheless the F.E.2 did fly down to Larkhill, with the gun in place, during the Military Aeroplane Competition held there in August.

Specification – F.E.2 (70hp)

Powerplant:	70hp Renault
Weights:	Empty not known; loaded 1,865lb (846kg)
Dimensions:	Span 42ft (12.81m); chord 6ft 4in (1.93m); gap 6ft 3½in (1.92m); wing area 425sq ft (39.52sq m); length 30ft (9.15m)
Performance:	Speed at sea level 67mph (107km/h); climb 330ft/min (101m/min); ceiling 5,500ft (1,678m)

The 1911 F.E.2 photographed in January 1912. As with all rotary engines, its Gnome evidently dripped oil. Crown copyright – DERA

The F.E.2 Reborn

During the summer of 1913 a new F.E.2 emerged from the Farnborough workshops, allegedly rebuilt from its predecessor, but in reality it was an almost entirely new design. The steel tube framework of its nacelle was now enclosed within neatly streamlined fairings, which swept up in pleasantly curved contours to provide deep, well protected cockpits. In this version, power was provided by an air-cooled V8 Renault engine rated at 70hp and driving a four-bladed pusher propeller. Fuel was carried in a cylindrical tank within the decking behind the pilot's shoulders, and fed to the carburettor by gravity. The outer wing panels were similar in plan and section to those of the B.E.2a, but of slightly greater span, and with some minor structural modifications necessary to provide attachments for the tubular tailbooms. The horizontal tail surfaces were positioned above the upper tailbooms, and the rudder resembled an elongated version of the B.E.'s surface. The swivelling tail-skid was fixed to the bottom of the rudder post, and the undercarriage again employed the twin skids typical of the period. It was eventually allotted the serial number 604.

It appears that some of the Factory's staff believed that the F.E. designation stood for 'Fighting' rather than 'Farman' and planned accordingly, for the original side elevation drawing, No.A3501, also shows provision for mounting a one-pounder Coventry Ordnance Works 'pom-pom' gun on the prow of the nacelle. However, no gun was ever fitted to this reconstructed F.E.2 for, on 23 March 1914, it spun and crashed near Wittering whilst performing stall trials, the crash almost certainly being due to the machine's lack of any sort of fin area, a deficiency common in aircraft of that period. The pilot, Roland Kemp, survived the crash, although with a broken leg, but his passenger, Ewart T. Haynes, was killed outright.

Although this version of the F.E.2 had remained unarmed, a further development of the pusher formula was designed by S.J. Waters and Henry Folland specifically to carry the Coventry Ordnance Works gun. This was the F.E.3, also known as the A.E.1, or Armed Experimental. It employed the wings and undercarriage of the 1913 F.E.2, but its nacelle was entirely new, with a 100hp six-cylinder Chenu engine mounted near to the front, where it was less likely to cause injury to the pilot in the event of a crash, cooling air being admitted via a circular hole in the nose. This engine turned a shaft passing under the pilot's seat,

The uncovered nacelle of the second (1913) F.E.2 inside the Factory's workshops awaiting covering, its Renault engine already installed but lacking a propeller. Author's collection

The second F.E.2 completed. Author's collection

the propeller being driven via chains. Its most innovative feature was the tail support, for instead of the four tailbooms common to pusher designs the tail surfaces were carried on a single boom, mounted on the propeller boss and braced by wires running to the upper wings and undercarriage. However, test flights, by both Geoffrey de Havilland and Roland Kemp, revealed that this tail assembly lacked sufficient rigidity and so, in mid-1914, the Factory's design staff returned to development of the basic F.E.2, again with the express intention that it should be armed. In this manifestation the two-seat pusher was again a completely new aircraft, and was given the distinguishing designation F.E.2a. Much of the initial design work was carried out by Henry Folland, whose preliminary sketches are unequivocably captioned 'F.E.2A GUN CARRIER'. The gun installation was evidently intended to again be a one-pounder C.O.W. gun, or something equally impressive, for Folland's original estimation of the new machine's weight includes, in addition to 160lb (73kg) each for the pilot and gunner, 130lb (60kg) for the gun, 70lb (32kg) for ammunition and 100lb (45kg) for a 'gun pivot, frame and fairing'. However, when the machine was finally built the armament fitted to it was rather more modest, a single Lewis gun on a simple swivel mounting.

The unsuccessful F.E.3, designed to carry the C.O.W. Gun, a cannon developed by the Coventry Ordnance Works. The F.E.2a was developed instead. Author's collection

The F.E.2a's outer wing panels were again copied from those of the contemporary B.E., in this case the 2c, and were fitted to a broad centre section giving a total span of almost 50ft (15m), with three bay bracing. The centre section had no dihedral, whilst the outer panels maintained the angle inherited from the B.E.2. The whole trailing edge of the upper centre section was

An F.E.2a outside the Factory site. Note how its 100hp Green engine is closely cowled. Author's collection

hinged so that it could be used as an airbrake in order to shorten the landing run. The nacelle was again built upon a framework of steel tube and clad in curved alloy panels. The pilot's cockpit was well protected from the elements, and mounted higher than that for the gunner, giving the pilot a clear view forward above his passenger's head. The forward cockpit was less well protected, the gunner's field of fire clearly being considered more important than his comfort. Power was to be provided by a six-cylinder in-line, water-cooled Green engine mounted at the rear of the nacelle, and closely cowled. Its radiator was positioned ahead of the engine, behind the pilot's seat, with small scoops on each side of the nacelle to provide the necessary air flow. The undercarriage was similar in design to one experimentally installed upon a B.E.2c, incorporating sturdy Oleo legs and a small nosewheel. This latter was intended only to help prevent the aircraft tipping onto its nose in a bad landing, a conventional swivelling tail-skid being provided for normal use. The tubular tailbooms, or outriggers as Folland referred to them, were separated by streamlined wooden struts and cross-braced with wire, the monoplane tail-surfaces being mounted above them. An 'inverted vee' kingpost not only provided an attachment for the tailplane's bracing wires but, fitted with two ribs and fabric-covered, provided the fin area that earlier models had so tragically lacked. Additional fin area was created by the simple expedient of increasing the chord of the rearmost pair of vertical struts, thus also ensuring that their strength was adequate to meet the landing shocks of the tail-skid mounted immediately beneath them. The rudder was built on a framework of steel tube, and was hinged a short distance aft of its leading edge, thereby being aerodynamically balanced.

The idea of fitting the C.O.W. gun to the F.E. seems to have persisted, and in mid-1914 a larger version of the F.E.3/A.E.1 formula, the F.E.6, was built, utilizing the wing structure of the F.E.2a. The single tailboom, mounted on the propeller hub, was again employed, but in this version it was a fully cantilevered structure, all bracing wires being eliminated. The machine was built, but was damaged in a heavy landing early in its flight trials and was not rebuilt, which suggests that it did not meet its designers' expectations.

Specification – F.E.2a

Powerplant:	100hp Green
Weights:	Empty 1,993lb (904kg); loaded 2,690lb (1,220kg)
Dimensions:	Span 47ft 9in (14.56m); chord 5ft 6in (1.68m); gap 6ft 3½in (1.92m); wing area 494sq ft (45.94sq m)
	Length 32ft 3in (9.84m); height 12ft 7½in (3.85m); tailplane span 16ft 11in (5.16m)
Performance:	Speed at sea level 75mph (120km/h); climb 8min 25sec to 3,000ft (915m); ceiling 6,000ft (1,830m)

The F.E.2 Enters Production

Meanwhile, with the war now in progress, the War Office placed an order for twelve production F.E.2as, without waiting for any prototype to be built. The first of these was completed, ready for AID inspection on 22 January 1915, and made its first flight four days later, with Frank Goodden at the controls. The only criticism seems to have been of its engine, whose power-to-weight ratio was poor even by the standards of the day. A replacement engine was fitted, and the aircraft flown again on the 29th, but it remained seriously underpowered. A hasty decision was therefore made to substitute the 120hp Austro-Daimler, which was dimensionally similar to the Green, and which was being manufactured by Wm. Beardmore Ltd. This engine, later known as the 120hp Beardmore, was less closely cowled than the Green, and necessitated larger air scoops to cool its radiator. A fully streamlined gravity tank was added under the upper centre section. The first installation was made in the third production machine, No.2864, which was flown to the CFS Experimental Flight at Upavon for evaluation on 30 March 1915, where it was favourably received, being considered easy to fly and very easy to land.

The first two examples, 4227 and 4228, were then converted to the new engine, being inspected by AID on 17 April and 5 May respectively, before going to France where they joined 6 Squadron on 14 May 1915, the latter machine only surviving for two days.

However, the Beardmore-built engine, which also powered the R.E.5, was in short supply until other contractors began to produce it, so completion of the twelve machines was achieved in a rather leisurely fashion. The next example was completed on 13 May, with others following on 10 June, 13, 19 and 28 August, and 7, 13 and 23 September. The tenth example, 5647, was assigned to 16 Squadron on 26 October 1915, the remainder all going to join 4227 at 6 Squadron, one of them, 5642, later transferring to 20 Squadron. A number of this batch of F.E.2as were presentation aircraft, with 5642 and 5645 becoming 'Montreal' No.1 and No.2 respectively, whilst 5646 bore the name of its sponsor, 'Nova Scotia'.

The eleventh F.E.2a, 5647, was modified to have a simple 'vee' undercarriage, and to eliminate the airbrake from the upper centre section. These modifications, most of which would be incorporated into the next variant, delayed its completion, making it the last example to be finished. It was inspected on 5 October 1915, before joining the remainder in France. It too became a presentation machine, 'Bombay No.2'

Fighter Mark 1

Before the first F.E.2a even arrived in France, the big pusher's utility was already appreciated, for even before the advent of the enemy Fokker the need for an effectively armed aircraft was clearly apparent. An order for 200 was therefore placed with G. & J. Weir Ltd of Glasgow, together with an order, initially for fifty but later increased to 200, from Boulton & Paul of Norwich. In addition, a further fifty were to be built by the Royal Aircraft Factory. Other orders were placed later, a total of eight companies eventually manufacturing the type. These new batches of aircraft incorporated a number of modifications which were intended to speed up production: the airbrake had been deleted from the upper centre section, and the shape of

The eleventh F.E.2a, 5647, fitted with a 'vee' undercarriage. The windscreens are unusual and must have prevented the observer from making much use of his gun. The aircraft in the background is an R.E.5. Crown Copyright – DERA

F.E.2b, 6975, fitted with the No.2, Mk1 gun mounting which allowed the gunner to both elevate and traverse his Lewis gun, although through limited arcs. J.M. Bruce/G.S. Leslie Collection

Boulton and Paul were one of many companies who turned from other industries – in their case the manufacture of agricultural machinery – to meet the needs of war. As this advertisement from The Aeroplane **of 13 June 1917 shows, their commitment to this role was wholehearted and irrevocable. Note the telegraphic address.**

the gravity tank simplified. The armour plate which had been designed to protect the underside of the nacelle against small arms fire from the ground was considered superfluous, and was deleted. Although the Royal Aircraft Factory's drawings gave the new variant the designation F.E.2b, a memo from Lt Col D.S. MacInnes, Assistant Director of Military Aeronautics to the Administrative Wing of the RFC, instructed that in official nomenclature it was to be referred to as 'Fighter Mark 1'. However, like many of the whims of officialdom, this name was short-lived, and by the time it entered service the Factory's designation had entirely superseded the machine's official title. In signals the type thus became the 'Fetubi', and was generally referred to, not without affection, simply as the 'Fee'.

The Beardmore engine's production problems were clearly resolved well before the end of 1915, for the first F.E.2b completed, No.5201, was presented for inspection on 2 October 1915, ahead of the last of the twelve F.E.2as. Being the first of a new type, as well as the first aircraft built by Boulton & Paul, it was subjected to fairly exhaustive testing before being released for active service. Thus it was not until 30 October that it joined 16 Squadron in France, although others quickly followed, the first squadron to be fully equipped with the type being No.20 on 23 January 1916.

It proved popular with pilots, who regarded it as easy to fly, and with ground crews, who found the Beardmore engine easy to start, especially since a vigorous cranking of the starter magneto would frequently bring it to life without any need to swing the propeller. Being largely uncowled, the engine was also relatively easy to work on, with many mechanics taking a particular pride in keeping its copper water jackets polished to a high shine.

It was perhaps less popular with those who occupied its front cockpit, many of them ordinary soldiers who had chosen to swap the squalor of the trenches for a cleaner, if more dangerous, war in the skies. They were not trained observers, merely aerial gunners, and as such were required to put in a minimum of fifty hours of flying over the lines before they were

Specification – F.E.2b (120hp)

Powerplant:	120hp Beardmore
Weights:	Empty 2,105lb (955kg); loaded 2,967lb (1,386kg)
Dimensions:	Span 47ft 9in (14.56m); chord 5ft 6in (1.68m); gap 6ft 3½in (1.92m); wing area 494sq ft (45.94sq m)
	Length 32ft 3in (9.84m); height 12ft 7½in (3.85m); tailplane span 16ft 11in (5.16m)
Performance:	Speed at sea level 80mph (128km/h); climb 19min 30sec to 6,500ft (1,983m); ceiling 9,000ft (2,745m); endurance 3½ hr

'Care & Maintenance of Beardmore Engines'

When the engine is first started up, it should be run slowly for at least two minutes before being run full out, to allow the water to become warm for the purpose of warming the carburettors. If this is not done and the engine is opened too quickly, it will almost invariably pop back and run very erratically.

The engine should not be run full out on the ground, but just long enough to see that it is giving the requisite number of revs. The 160hp Beardmore will develop 1,275 to 1,375 when flying level, but it has been proved by previous experience of pilots with these engines that in almost every case 1,250 revs is the best to run at. At this speed the engine runs very smoothly and keeps moderately cool. If allowed to run at over 1,250 overheating will ensue and the engine will give a lot of trouble.

The best temperature for an engine to run at is 75 deg. C, but it is quite safe, when climbing hard, even if 90 deg. is registered: it will soon drop if the engine is eased down a little when flying level. The engine should always be run with both magnetos switched on, otherwise one set of plugs will get 'oiled up'.

Always try each magneto separately before leaving the ground, and make sure the self-starter is switched off. Trouble has arisen through the switch being left on, in that difficulty has been experienced in starting when the machine is taken out again.

Engine must be carefully examined after each flight and all sparking plugs taken out and cleaned and all greasers filled up. Old grease should be cleaned off the valve stems and fresh grease put on. Note carefully that the valves move freely in the guides. Graphite and grease is to be commended as it adheres to the valve stems better than any other preparation and does not blow off when the engine gets warm.

Rain water should be used whenever possible. If the water used is very dirty or hard, the entire engine and radiator should be frequently cleansed, either with hot soda or a mixture of paraffin and water.

Pilots' Opinions

'In those days [July 1916] the F.E. with the 250 Rolls-Royce was a very good and powerful machine, and the enemy very much respected it.

... the way our observers and pilots used to climb round the capacious nacelle was most amusing. In fact, on patrol up high, I sometimes stood on my seat and looked over the tail, the machine was so steady and stable.'

Sgt J. McCudden, RFC.

'These F.E.s were slow and clumsy.'

Lt Oliver Stewart, RFC.

'It was a fine machine, slow but very sturdy ... they soon had the respect of the Huns, who would never risk attacking unless they outnumbered them by two to one, and did wonderful work right through 1916 and on until 1917, when the DH4s and Bristol Fighters took their place.

But at this time [mid 1916] *the F.E. was the last word in aircraft ... we should any of us be lucky to be posted to an F.E. Squadron.'*

2nd Lt Cecil Lewis, RFC.

grudgingly allowed to wear an observer's half wing. Their front cockpit was cold and exposed, its shallow sides offering little protection unless the occupant were to crouch on the floor. In practice, most chose to sit on the only seat available, the top of the ammunition locker at the rear of their cockpit, although a brave few elected instead to perch precariously on the cockpit rim.

One volunteer, newly transferred from the trenches, recalled his pilot giving him instruction regarding his future duties as a 'Fee' gunner thus: [Arch Whitehouse; *The Fledgling* London 1964];

> 'It's simple,' he said in much the same manner he would use to wish me a pleasant afternoon. 'You can sit on the floor until we get up near the line. After that I want you to stand up, move about, and familiarize yourself with the gun mounting. You can scotch on the locker, or better still on the edge of the nacelle.'
>
> He actually said that. He expected me to stand up in that three-ply canoe when we got up in the air.

Armament

The F.E.2 was conceived when aerial warfare was still far in the future, when it was thought that the gunner would need to pivot his gun to bring it to bear on any target which might present itself, and that aeroplanes would fly alongside an opponent, firing broadsides like Nelson's men o'war. Indeed, just as the Navy's fighting ships were 'battleships', it was not uncommon for the 'Fees' to be referred to as 'battleplanes'. Thus the F.E.2b had a superb field of fire forwards and to the sides, but, designed for attack, it had little defence against attack from the rear. However, the advent of the fighter, with its fixed, forward-firing machine-gun, led to such attacks becoming commonplace, making defence against them essential. The presence of the pusher propeller prevented any arrangements similar to those adopted for the B.E.2 series, and the eventual solution was for the gunner to stand up and fire backwards over the upper wing, clear of the propeller. This was obviously a far from ideal arrangement, yet one which the gunners accepted with the fortitude typical of that generation.

The offensive armament of the F.E.2a had comprised a Lewis gun mounted on a swivelling pillar fixed to the cockpit floor inherited from the original F.E.2. This was superseded in the early F.E.2bs by the No.2 Mark I mounting, which comprised a horizontal bar between two 'inverted vees' of steel tube fixed to the framework of the nacelle. This brought the Lewis gun well above the cockpit rim, thus allowing the gun to pivot and giving a reasonable range of elevation, although with limited traverse. A Mark II version, giving increased movement, was introduced before the whole thing was superseded by the introduction in April 1916 of the No.4 Mark I mounting, a simple pillar mounting at the front of the gunner's cockpit. Later came the Mark III version, a rocking pillar, fixed to the cockpit floor, which was capable of being swung to either side of the cockpit to allow the gunner to fire downwards, as well as up and to the front. The Mark IV, or Clark mounting, introduced a further refinement in the form of a universal joint which allowed the pillar to be swung to any position, forks of spring steel being fixed at several points on the cockpit rim to hold the pillar steady whilst in use.

The use of the No.4 Mounting is here demonstrated. The Lewis has a Norman vane foresight and a bag to collect spent cartridge cases, but lacks an ammunition drum.
J.M. Bruce/G.S. Leslie Collection

In addition, socket mountings were frequently fixed at each side of the nacelle,

This well-known view of the F.E.2b nacelle shows the No4. MkIV gun mounting, its spring forks visible at points around the cockpit rim. There is an Anderson arch mounting at the rear of the front cockpit and swivel mounts at each side, that to port has the gun clamp still attached. These swivel mountings could be used by either crew member. Author's collection

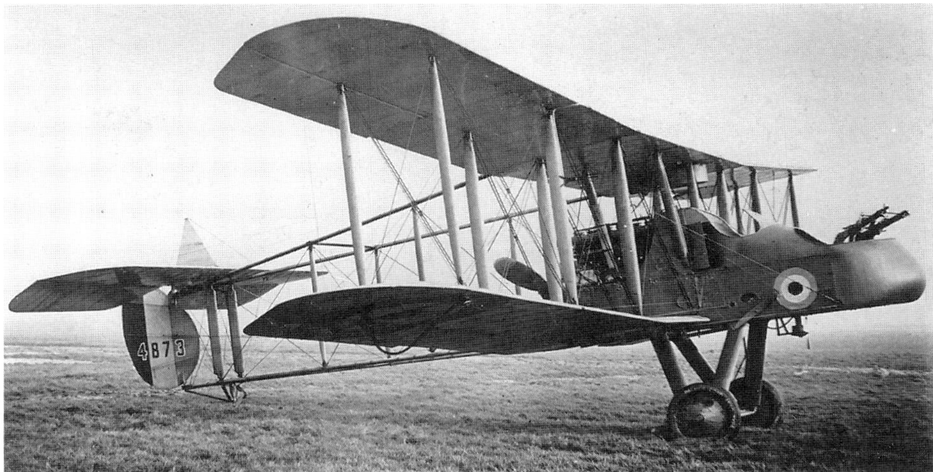

Photographed at the Armament Experimental Station at Orfordness, 4873 boasts an unusual armament of twin Lewis guns yoked together. J.M. Bruce/G.S. Leslie Collection

In a carefully posed shot the observer of 25 Squadron's A5478 demonstrates how he might attack targets on the ground using a Lewis gun on a rocking pillar. The courage required to do this in flight, during combat manoeuvres, is better imagined than described. Note that this F.E.2b has the 'vee' undercarriage, with a bomb rack immediately behind it. Author's collection

allowing either the pilot to fire obliquely forwards or the gunner to fire at a similar angle to the rear, using the same mounting. However, since only one gun was normally carried it was, of course, necessary to transfer the gun from one mounting to another before it could be brought into action in a different mode. Leather pouches were usually attached to the ejector slots of the Lewis guns to collect the spent cartridge cases, so preventing them from flying backwards in the slipstream with a consequent risk of damage to the pusher propeller.

Defence against attack from the rear was initially catered for by *ad hoc* 'goalpost' mountings similar in design to those frequently fitted to the B.E.2 series. These were soon superseded by the No.10 Mark I mounting, which comprised a telescopic, cranked, swivelling pillar attached to an 'Anderson arch' which was built into the rear of the gunner's cockpit to provide the necessary support, the decking separating the cockpits being too flimsy to take the weight of the gun. However, in order to make use of this mounting, the gunner was obliged to stand up on the ammunition locker, or even on the cockpit rim, facing backwards, wholly exposed to the force of the slipstream, whilst the pilot carried out whatever manoeuvres he felt were appropriate to the situation. A waist strap with a steel cable attached to it, its other end fixed to the nacelle's floor, was later introduced to give at least some sense of security, for there were no parachutes.

The F.E. gunner's vulnerability was demonstrated on 22 October 1916 when an 18 Squadron aircraft on escort duty was attacked by a number of enemy fighters. The observer, Lt F.S. Rankin, sprung into action, and succeeded in bringing one down before he was shot in the head, causing him to lose his footing. The pilot, 2nd Lt F.L. Barnard, tried to catch hold of his coat but was unable to drag him back on board. He therefore climbed into the front cockpit, pulled Rankin aboard, and then clambered back into his own cockpit. He managed to land his badly damaged aircraft, and was rightly decorated for his bravery, although Rankin's wound proved fatal.

Although individual F.E.2's had to rely on the courage and agility of their gunners for defence against attack from behind, groups of machines quickly adopted a tactic known as the 'defensive circle', in which, by literally flying around in circles, each gunner was able to cover the tail of the aircraft in front. However, this manoeuvre could not be used for long, particularly if the wind was blowing strongly from the west, lest the whole formation should drift too far over enemy lines, making their return home impossible.

In Combat

Initially, at least, the F.E.2b was easily able to hold its own in combat and, although losses were, of course, inevitable, it achieved significant victories too.

In the afternoon of 18 June 1916, three aircraft from 25 Squadron were attacked by seven Fokkers, led by Oberleutnant Max Immelmann. One of the F.E.s was shot down almost immediately, but the other two, piloted by Capt W.A. Grattan-Bellew and 2nd Lt J.L. Armstrong, each brought down one of their attackers, the remainder breaking off the engagement. At nine o'clock in the evening of the same day two more F.E.s from 25 Squadron were on patrol at 8,000ft (2,438m) over Annay when they spotted three Fokkers below them. Such was their confidence in their mounts that, despite being outnumbered, they dived to attack. In the ensuing combat one of the British machines, flown by Lt J.R. Savage and A/M T. Robinson, was shot down; the other, 4272, flown by 2nd Lt G.R. McCubbin and Cpl J.H. Waller, brought down the enemy leader, thus ending Immelmann's career. Just a few days later Grattan-Bellew was leading a flight of five F.E.s when they were attacked by eight enemy fighters. Two fell victim to the British gunners, and the rest retreated.

On 17 September 1916 a group of F.E.2bs of 11 Squadron were escorting some B.E.2s on a raid to bomb Marcoing railway station when they were attacked by the *Jasta* Boelcke; two B.E.s and four of the F.E.s were brought down. F.E.2b 7018 had the dubious distinction of being shot down by Manfred von Richtofen and so becoming his first confirmed victory. Its crew, 2nd Lt L.B.F. Morris and Lt T. Rees, were both killed. Although a total of eleven more F.E.s were to fall to victim to the legendary 'Red Baron' before he was himself brought down in April 1918, they were never 'easy meat', especially when flown by a determined crew.

Development

Even before any production F.E.2b could be completed the Royal Aircraft Factory's design staff were at work on a new variant of the big pusher, the F.E.2c, drawings for which were completed by October 1915. The crew positions were reversed, the pilot now occupying the front cockpit, ahead of the gunner, and the nose contours were amended to afford better protection from the elements whilst at the same time improving streamlining. The armament included a forward-firing Lewis gun for the pilot's use, linked to a sighting bar in a manner very similar to that adopted for the prototype F.E.8, which was then under construction. The observer's Lewis gun was attached to a swivel on top of an Anderson arch-type mounting at the front of his cockpit.

One of the F.E.2as (possibly either 5644 or 5646) was converted to form the prototype '2c, and two aircraft from the Royal Aircraft Factory's batch of F.E.2bs were also converted to the new layout. The first of these, 6370, was inspected on 19 April 1916, and was retained at Farnborough for experiment, being finally written off after a crash on 9 May 1917. The second machine, 6371, was sent to France sometime in April, apparently in mistake for an F.E.2b, and was assigned to 22 Squadron, transferring to 25 Squadron in June. On 17 July 1916 it crashed, and was struck off charge. The type was not adopted for production, for it showed no advantage over the original layout, and lacked the protection against attack from the rear which recent experience had shown to be vital in a Service aircraft.

An F.E.2c, with crew positions reversed and the nose contours modified.
J.M. Bruce/G.S. Leslie collection

Almost immediately upon the F.E.2b's arrival in France, one operational difficulty became apparent: its endurance was only 2½ hours, but that of the reconnaissance aircraft it was tasked to escort and protect was longer, and 3-hour patrols had already become the norm. Brooke-Popham criticized this aspect of an otherwise splendid machine as early as 2 January 1916, and on 1 March Trenchard himself wrote to Lt Col MacInnes, Assistant Director of Military Aeronautics at the War Office, requesting that the F.E.2's fuel tank capacity should be increased by 8 gallons (36 litres) in order to give the endurance required. The Factory's response was to provide an additional 16 gallons (72 litres), to be stored in a pressure tank under the pilot's seat, the revised drawings being issued so that the modification could be incorporated into current production as soon as possible. The extra 8 gallons, in excess of Trenchard's request, were provided in anticipation of the increase in fuel consumption that would occur when a more powerful engine was fitted, a development which was, at that time, already well in hand.

The new engine was to be an uprated version of the six-cylinder in-line Beardmore/Austro-Daimler which was the F.E.2b's standard powerplant. The increase in power was brought about by the simple expedient of increasing the cylinder bore from 130 to 142mm (5 to 5½in). This was initially made not by an engine manufacturer but by Frank Halford, then employed by the AID as an inspector, but later to become an engine designer of considerable renown. Although the uprated engine weighed some 77lb (35kg) more than the original, its power output had been increased by one-third, to 160hp. The first aircraft to be fitted with the 160hp Beardmore was 6357, which made its first flight on 2 February 1916, piloted by the pre-war exhibition flyer B.C. Hucks. Although the increase in power naturally brought about an improvement in maximum speed, ceiling and rate of climb, it was not without penalty, for the uprated engine did not share the original's commendable reliability, and was rather prone to overheating. Nonetheless, with performance being all important, the 160hp. engine was adopted for future production. However, due to production delays it never entirely superseded the smaller version, and the two types frequently served side by side.

A Bigger Brother

In the summer of 1915 S.J. Waters and H. Folland produced a design for a long-range bomber, with a wing span of over 75ft (23m) and an endurance of 8 hours, which, although it had a conventional fuselage and tailplane, had its twin engines arranged as pushers, and was therefore given the designation F.E.4. Built in response to a request from Trenchard for such a machine, it was designed to have dual controls in the two forward cockpits, with a third cockpit behind the wings for a gunner. The intended powerplant, the 200hp RAF3, was not yet in production when the prototype, 7993, was nearing completion and so two RAF5s, the pusher version of the 140hp RAF4a, were fitted instead. Completed and ready for inspection by 8 March 1916, it was taken up by Frank Goodden for its maiden flight a few days later. Although stable and comfortable to fly, it was very sluggish, a fact confirmed by its evaluation at CFS, and the second prototype was therefore fitted with Rolls-Royce 'Eagle' engines. However,

Specification – F.E.2d (160hp)	
Powerplant:	160hp Beardmore
Weights:	Empty 2,121lb (962kg); loaded 3,037lb (1,378kg)
Dimensions:	Span 47ft 9in (14.56m); chord 5ft 6in (1.68m); gap 6ft 3½in (1.92m); wing area 494sq ft (45.94sq m)
	Length 32ft 3in (9.84m); height 12ft 7½in (3.85m); tailplane span 16ft 11in (5.16m)
Performance:	Speed at sea level 88mph (141km/h); climb 18min 20sec to 6,500ft (1,983m); ceiling 11,000ft (3,355m); endurance 3hr

The second F.E.4, 7994, with Rolls-Royce 'Eagle' engines. Author's collection

flight trials of this machine revealed that it was not much faster, and an order for 100 machines placed with Daimler was cancelled before any aircraft were completed. Thus long-range bombing remained a dream for the future, and efforts were concentrated on improvements to existing designs, which could be brought into action with the minimum of delay.

By late January 1916, details of the Factory's next development of the F.E.2 were made known to Trenchard, together with a suggestion that it could be in service by April. The new machine was to be powered by an early model of the V12 Rolls-Royce engine, later named the 'Eagle', which was then rated at 250hp and offered such promise that instructions were given to proceed with it. Few modifications were made to the basic airframe apart from those essential for the accommodation of the much larger and heavier engine. A new, uncowled radiator was provided, and the fuel capacity was increased by 12 gallons (55 litres) in order to maintain the same endurance as the lower powered version, the additional capacity being achieved by changing the main fuel tank from cylindrical to rectangular. In addition, a streamlined gravity tank was mounted above the upper centre section. The prototype F.E.2d, as the new variant was designated, was not ready for its first flight until 7 April 1916, after AID inspection three days earlier, with Frank Goodden again taking control. The following day, it returned to the workshops so that the sides of the nacelle could be cut down, presumably to improve the flow of air through the radiator, which was now immediately behind the pilot's back. Later assigned the service serial 7995, it was flown down to Upavon for CFS evaluation on 7 May 1916. No record of Goodden's opinion has survived, but that of the CFS pilots was less than enthusiastic, for they found it to be nose-heavy in the air, making it tiring to fly and tricky to land, especially when compared to the docile handling of the Beardmore-powered version. Doubts were also raised about structural integrity, particularly since it was some 400lb (181kg) heavier than the F.E.2b.

But all this criticism was merely academic, as the design had already been placed in production at Farnborough, and the first machine, A1, was presented for inspection on 12 May 1916. However, on 29 May the Director of Aeronautical Supplies informed Trenchard that the F.E.2b with the 160hp Beardmore had to be judged the better machine, and the Rolls-Royce-powered F.E.2d was to be considered merely as a 'stop-gap' until the preferred design was available in sufficient numbers. The first few F.E.2ds, including A1, were ferried over to France on 1 June

Comparison of Engines Fitted to F.E.2 Series

	Green	*Beardmore*	*Beardmore*	*Rolls-Royce*	*Siddeley 'Puma'*
Nominal hp	100	120	160	250	230
Cylinders	6	6	6	12	6
Type	in-line	in-line	in-line	V	in-line
Bore (mm)	140	130	142	115	145
Stroke (mm)	152	175	175	165	150
Normal R.P.M.	1,250	1,250	1,250	1,800	1,400
Weight (lb)	498	419	502	933	625

An F.E.2d with a square top radiator and the full oleo undercarriage. Crown copyright – DERA

1916, the German Army learning the details of the new machine simultaneously with the British, as one aircraft, A5, landed on the wrong side of the lines. Its crew, 2nd Lt Littlewood and Lt Grant, were inexperienced and mistook a German aerodrome near Lille for their intended destination of St Omer. Although they made a bad landing, the machine ending up on its nose, it was relatively undamaged and gave the enemy a splendid opportunity to study its new opponent.

The weight of the Rolls-Royce engine, combined with its location at the rear of the nacelle, within the 'vee' of the tailbooms, made its removal for maintenance a difficult operation until the Factory designed a portable hoist which allowed it to be lowered to the ground so that the airframe could then be simply wheeled away over it.

The first to be re-equipped with the new type was 20 Squadron, which received its first F.E.2d in mid-June and was fully equipped by the beginning of July, its F.E.2bs being returned to the depot for use as replacements.

These production aircraft had short exhaust stubs in place of the twin stacks fitted to the prototype. Early versions had three individual pillar mountings for forward fire, together with a telescopic pillar for rearward defence, two Lewis guns and up to ten drums of ammunition being the usual armament. Later production aircraft had the No.4 MkIV (Clark) mounting as fitted to the '2b, together with a forward-firing gun for the pilot's use, its mounting being designed by Capt G. Dixon-Spain of 20 Squadron.

Although the radiators fitted to the first production F.E.2ds varied somewhat in style, some having rounded tops and others square, they all had one feature in common in that they provided excessive cooling, often making it difficult to get the engine warm enough for efficient operation, especially on winter days. The provision of shutters, controlled by the pilot, went some way to resolving the problem, although it introduced a further distraction that a combat pilot could well do without. Eventually a more effective solution was found by fitting radiators originally intended for use with the Beardmore engines, but installing them in the position adopted for those they were to replace, where they received the full effect of the airflow. Shutters were still provided, but only to give a faster warm-up on starting, and once in the air the pilots could leave the radiator to get on with its job, whilst giving full attention to their own.

Despite the unfavourable CFS report, the F.E.2d was, initially, quite effective as a fighter, one report stating that the enemy were reluctant to engage it in combat unless numerically superior. However, development was rapid, and production slow, largely due to demands for the Rolls-Royce engine which was also required to power other aircraft, most notably the Airco DH4. In the end, many of the aircraft ordered as F.E.2ds were completed as '2bs with the Beardmore engine.

The newly formed 57 squadron brought its F.E.2ds to France in December 1916, and was joined by 25 Squadron the following April, by which time the aircraft was already well outclassed for daytime combat. Within a few months both these units had had their 'Fees' replaced by DH4s, although 20 Squadron had to soldier on until much later in 1917 before it too received new aircraft.

However, as late as 6 July 1917 the 'Fee' still had a sting, for on that day an F.E.2d, piloted by Capt D.C. Cunnell with Lt A.E. Woodbridge in the front cockpit, got into

Specification – F.E.2d (250hp)

Powerplant:	250hp Rolls-Royce Eagle
Weights:	Empty 2,509lb (1,138kg); loaded 3,469lb (1,574kg)
Dimensions:	Span 47ft 9in (14.56m); chord 5ft 6in (1.68m); gap 6ft 3½in (1.92m); wing area 494sq ft (45.94sq m)
	Length 32ft 3in (9.84m); height 12ft 7½in (3.85m); tailplane span 16ft 11in (5.16m)
Performance:	Speed at sea level 97mph (155km/h); climb 10min to 6,000ft (1,830m); ceiling 16,500ft (5,033m); endurance 3¼hr

This F.E.2d has the No.10. Mk1 cranked pillar mounting for rearward firing attached to an Anderson arch. Both Lewis guns have Norman vane foresights. J.M. Bruce/G.S. Leslie Collection

This F.E.2d is putting the additional power of its 250hp Rolls-Royce engine to good use, for it carries three Lewis guns as well as a bulky camera. Author's collection

a dogfight, during the course of which it succeeded in bringing down Manfred von Richtofen with a head wound that kept him out of action for some time.

The only Victoria Cross awarded to an NCO pilot also went to the pilot of an F.E.2d. On 9 January 1917 Sgt Thomas Mottershead was piloting A39 when it caught fire at an altitude of 9,000ft (2,700m). Although engulfed in flames he succeeded in bringing it down to a crash landing, thus saving the life of his observer Lt W.E. Gower, who escaped from the wreck. Mottershead perished, the medal being awarded posthumously.

Further Developments

The F.E.2b and 2d were designed for production with the same sprung undercarriage, with buffer nose-wheel, that had been fitted to all but one of the F.E.2as. The 'vee' type undercarriage that had been experimentally fitted to 5468, the eleventh F.E.2a, was, initially, not considered a desirable substitute. Although it gave a useful increase in top speed, it was thought that, without the longer travel afforded by the oleo legs, the lower longerons would suffer damage in the heavy landings frequent on the poorly prepared aerodromes common on the Western Front. On arrival in France in November 1915, it was subjected to a deliberate heavy landing and proved its critics wrong, for although the axle and skid were both damaged the longerons were not. Consequently, in January 1916 Brooke-Popham advised the Assistant Director of Military Aeronautics that he was prepared to accept F.E.2bs with 'vee' undercarriages after all. Further comparison tests were carried out at Farnborough during March and April 1916 which confirmed that aircraft fitted with the Vee undercarriage climbed faster, and were more manoeuvrable than those with the oleo version. 'Vee' undercarriages were therefore specified for the next batch of machines ordered, A778–A877, which were to be built by G. & J. Weir. However, in the spring of 1916 Lt Trafford-Jones, a pilot with 20 Squadron, designed a modification of the standard undercarriage which greatly reduced its drag, improved its climb and added several miles per hour to the aircraft's top speed. In this modification, first carried out to Trafford-Jones' own aircraft, 6359, the nose-wheel was removed, together with the two struts supporting it, and the radius rods which guided the axle's movement, and which had previously been attached near the nose-wheel, were, instead, fixed to the attachment points intended for the forward struts. This so simplified the undercarriage, without any significant reduction in its resilience, that the Trafford-Jones modification quickly became the norm, some squadrons insisting that it was carried out immediately that new aeroplanes were received from the depot. Unfortunately, Trafford-Jones never knew how successful his idea was for he, and 6359, were shot down on 16 May 1916, his observer, Capt Forbes, surviving although wounded in the shoulder.

F.E.2b A6389 has the Trafford Jones modification, greatly simplifying its oleo undercarriage. The Anderson arch mounting can be seen at the rear of the gunner's cockpit. Author's collection

On 3 June 1916 Brooke-Popham requested that all oleo undercarriages should be modified before dispatch to France, and on 11 August he advised the Aircraft Depots that such undercarriages should be modified rather than being replaced with the 'vee' type. In August 1916 an experimental installation of the Trafford-Jones undercarriage modification was carried out to the prototype F.E.2d, 7995. The work was carried out by 20 Squadron and proved satisfactory despite the considerable increase in weight, and the modification was therefore made standard for all variants of the 'Fee'.

A number of F.E.2bs were fitted with cameras, usually mounted externally on the starboard side of the nacelle, convenient to the gunner's right hand, although alternative locations were by no means uncommon.

(Above) **This unidentified F.E.2b has bomb rails fitted below the wings, as well as a camera on the side of the nacelle.** J.M. Bruce/G.S. Leslie Collection

An F.E.2b fitted with an RAF5 air-cooled engine, 10 March 1916. Note that the rearmost centre-section struts are asbestos-wrapped to protect them from the heat of the exhaust manifolds.
Crown copyright – DERA

Specification – F.E.2e	
Powerplant:	230hp Puma
Weights:	Empty 2,280lb (1,034kg); loaded 3,355lb (1,522kg)
Dimensions:	Span 47ft 9in (14.56m); chord 5ft 6in (1.68m); gap 6ft 3½in (1.92m); wing area 494sq ft (45.94sq m)
	Length 32ft 3in (9.84m); height 12ft 7½in (3.85m); tailplane span 16ft 11in (5.16m)
Performance:	Speed at sea level 93mph (149km/h); climb 11min 30sec to 6,000ft (1,830m); ceiling 14,000ft (4,270m)

In the spring of 1916 the B.E.2c, with which the F.E.2 series shared its outer wing panels, changed its aerofoil section from RAF6 to the newly developed RAF14, and at the same time a similar change was made to the F.E. For the pusher, however, the change was not entirely beneficial, for whilst its initial rate of climb showed a similar improvement to that of its tractor stablemate, it performance at altitudes above around 9,000ft (2,743m) was reduced, with both rate of climb and service ceiling being adversely affected by the increased angle of attack which became necessary in order to keep climbing.

In an attempt to combine the improved performance of the F.E.2d with the more pleasant handling qualities of the Beardmore-powered variants, whilst conserving the ever limited stocks of Rolls-Royce engines for other designs, a number of other engines were considered. The Royal Aircraft Factory's own 140hp V12 RAF5, a pusher version of the RAF 4a, was experimentally fitted to two machines, 4256 and 6360, the designation F.E.2e being applied to the result. However, despite the air-cooled engine's lighter weight compared to the water-cooled Beardmore, it lacked any performance advantage, and was not proceeded with. The next two variants, the F.E.2f and g, were planned around the 200hp RAF3 and uprated RAF5b, respectively, but these probably only ever existed as design projects. The final variant, the F.E.2h, employed the 230hp Siddeley Puma, a six-cylinder in-line engine generally similar to the Beardmore. The prototype was created by the conversion of A6345, the necessary work being carried out by Ransomes, Sims & Jefferies. Unfortunately, testing at Martlesham Heath demonstrated that its performance was little better than that of the 160hp F.E.2b. However, three further aircraft were similarly converted, these being A6501–3, originally built by Boulton & Paul, the conversion work again being undertaken by Ransomes, Sims & Jefferies, and the machines renumbered E3151–3. None of these aircraft appears to have seen active service, and little more was heard of the F.E.2h, although one was later used in tests with the non-recoiling Davis gun carried out at the Isle of Grain.

New Roles

Once its effectiveness as a front-line fighter began to wane, its performance eclipsed by newer designs, the F.E.2 transferred easily into a new role, for its generous wing area made it readily adaptable for use as a bomber. It served initially as a day bomber, later becoming outclassed even in that role, whereupon it switched to operating at night. Thus the 'Fee' stayed in service, and in production, right up to the end of the war, a number of production contracts being cancelled with the coming of peace. Aircraft adapted for nocturnal use carried less visible markings than standard, the rudder stripes often being deleted, and were usually fitted with Holt flare brackets on each lower wing-tip in order to facilitate night landings. Flame dampers, devised by Capt C.E. Russell of 149 Squadron, were fitted to the exhausts of some machines, rendering them less detectable. From April 1917 the aircraft of 100 Squadron, which operated wholly by night, were painted black all over, except for the upper surface of the top wing which retained its P.C.10 finish. White circles replaced the national markings on the undersurfaces, with standard roundels being carried on the top of the upper wing.

Bomb racks were fitted under the lower wings, close to the root, two 112lb (50kg) bombs or eight 20lb (9kg) Cooper bombs being carried thereon. In addition, many of the F.E.2s used as bombers were fitted with the 'vee' undercarriage in order that a 230lb (104kg) bomb could be carried beneath the nacelle, which the more complex oleo type did not allow. Any doubts regarding potential damage to the lower longerons having been dispelled after September 1916, it was decided that these components should be changed from spruce to ash, which had a higher compressive strength. Some F.E.2s, that were used as bombers were also fitted with the R.L. tube, through which flares and similar objects could be dropped. On 1 November 1917 it was decided that all future F.E.2bs should have the rectangular main fuel tank designed for the Rolls-Royce-powered variant, the additional 12 gallons (54 litres) of fuel giving a useful increase in range and endurance.

Towards the end of 1917 the F.E.2c concept was revived, for its transposed crew positions afforded the pilot a much improved view for landing at night, whilst the observer could perform his duties with equal facility from the rear seat, particularly as the switch to nocturnal operations had removed the threat of attack from behind. Six aircraft, believed to be A5744, B434, B445, B447, B449 and B450, were converted by the Royal Aircraft Factory,

Squadron Service

The F.E.2 is known to have been on the strength of the following units, although not all were fully equipped with the type:

Active Service	Nos 6, 11, 12, 15, 18, 20, 22, 23, 28, 33, 35, 36, 37, 38, 51, 57, 64, 100, 101, 102, 149, 189, 192, 194 and 205 Squadrons
Home Establishment	Central Flying School. 8 TDS, 12 TDS, 13, 19, 46, 68 (Reserve) Squadrons. No.1 School of Navigation. Area Aerial Fighting School, Lympne. Experimental Station, Orfordness.
Foreign Service	American Expeditionary Force (as trainers); Central Flying School, Point Cook, Australia; Risalpur, India.

A852 preparing to take off for a night bombing mission in June 1917. Only the 'vee' undercarriage allowed a 230lb (100kg) bomb to be carried. Author's collection

Experiments with a braking parachute fitted to an F.E.2a, 9 February 1915. Crown Copyright – DERA

and on 28 November 1917 were sent to the RFC in France. Such was their immediate popularity that in February 1918 Brooke-Popham requested that 25 per cent of all future F.E. production should be '2cs. However, it appears that changes could not be quickly incorporated into the mammoth industry that aircraft manufacture had become, and it was not until September that Ransomes, Sims & Jefferies were instructed that twenty-four machines from the batch H9913– 9962 then under production should be completed as F.E.2cs. At the end of the war only eighteen machines had been completed, all F.E.2bs, presumably because these were simpler to build, having been in constant production for almost three years.

On 24 January 1918 one of 100 Squadron's nocturnal F.E.2bs fell victim to an enemy balloon barrage whilst returning from a raid on Treves, when it struck one of the cables and was brought down, although the crew, 2nd Lts L.G. Taylor and F.E. Le

Production

F.E.2a:
2864; 4227–8; 4253; 4295; 5642–8 – Royal Aircraft Factory.

F.E.2b:
6328–77; A8950; A5338–A5437 (cancelled) – Royal Aircraft Factory.
4256–92; 4838–5000; A778–A870; A5500–A5649 – G. & J. Weir.
5201–50; 6928–7027; 7666–7715; A5438–87 – Boulton & Paul.
B401–B500; C9786–C9835; D7037–D7136; D9900–D9999. F3768–F3917 (cancelled) – Ransomes, Sims & Jefferies.
D3776–D3835; E6687–E6736 (cancelled) – Garratt & Sons.
D99081–D9234; F4071–F4170 (cancelled) – Alex Stephen & Sons.
F3468–F3547; J601–J650 (cancelled) J601–J650 (cancelled) – Barclay Curle.
A5650–A5799; D9740–D9799 – Unknown.
A8895; B704; B7779; B7782; B7788; B7794–5; B7800; B7808–9; B7813–16; B7836–41; B7843; B7847–9; B7856; B7872; B9740; F5858–9; F5862; F6071; F6080; F9550; F9566 – Rebuilds.

F.E.2c:
6370–1; A5744; B434; B445; B447; B449–50 – Royal Aircraft Factory.
E7112–3; H9913–H9936 (possibly cancelled) – Ransomes, Sims & Jefferies.

F.E.2d:
7995; A1–40; A1932; A1966; A5143–52 – Royal Aircraft Factory.
A6351–A6600; B1851–1900 (many completed as F.E.2b) – Ransomes, Sims & Jefferies.

F.E.2h:
A6545; E3151–E3153 – Ransomes, Sims & Jefferies.
F9296–F9395 (cancelled) – Garratt & Sons.

The F.E.2b which was deliberately flown into a balloon cable by Roderic Hill. The 'bowsprit' and outrigger struts to which the cable fender wire was attached can be clearly seen. J.M. Bruce/G.S. Leslie Collection

Fevre, survived the crash. This rare occurrence may well have initiated an attempt to equip the F.E.2 with a balloon fender which was made at Orfordness in the spring of 1918. A long spar, resembling the bowsprit of a sailing ship, was mounted beneath the nacelle and projected about 6ft (1.8m) in front of it. A cable ran back from this to each wing-tip, where an additional interplane strut had been fitted. An experiment in which Capt Roderick Hill deliberately flew the machine into a balloon cable was only partially successful, the effect of the impact causing the aircraft to spin. Although Hill was able to regain control and land successfully, the wing-tip was found to be damaged by its impact with the cable, and the idea was discontinued.

One resident of South Australia donated £2,250 to his country's war effort with

F.E.2b 1877 was one of a small batch transferred to the US Air Service in the summer of 1918.
Author's collection

F.E.2b A781 at the edge of Farnborough Common. It is fitted with twin Lewis guns yoked to a small searchlight. The wind-driven generator which provided the necessary power is just visible below the forward edge of the nacelle. Author's collection

the express wish that it should be used to purchase a 'battleplane' for the Australian CFS. Thus A778, bearing the inscription 'Presented by Alfred Muller Simpson, Parkside, SA' arrived at Point Cook in March 1917, where it was given the new identity CFS14. After the war, it found its way on to the Australian civil register as G-AUCX, and was flown by R.J. Parer in an unsuccessful attempt to complete the first round-Australia flight in 1921. It was finally written off in a crash on 7 February 1922.

Another example which travelled far afield was A790, which ended up at Risalpur in India where the climate proved too warm for the original design, resulting in its radiator being raised above the top decking in a manner similar to that of the F.E.2d. Some time in 1920 it was extensively damaged in a landing accident and was scrapped.

A handful of 'Fees' were employed for home defence, although even with the Rolls-Royce engine their ceiling was scarcely sufficient to reach the altitudes at which raiding Zeppelins normally operated, and few real engagements took place. On 13 March 1918 an F.E.2d of 36 Squadron took off from Seaton Carew, piloted by 2nd Lt E.C. Morris, with 2nd Lt R.D. Linford as his observer. Patrolling at 15,000ft (4,572m) over Hartlepool, they spotted a Zeppelin some 5,000ft (1,524m) higher, and climbed towards it to give chase. They were unable to achieve the same height, although they eventually reached some 17,300ft (5,273m), and followed it out to sea for around 40 miles (64km), firing at it whenever they could, until it was finally lost in cloud.

In several experiments, presumably made with home defence in mind, a number of F.E.2s were fitted with searchlights, with wind-driven generators to provide the necessary power. The first of these was the brainchild of Dr. Widdington of the Factory's Instrument and Wireless Department, and was installed on F.E.2b 4928 early in October 1916. The light was mounted just above the nose-wheel of a standard oleo undercarriage, fixed to the forward struts, with the generator in the nose of the front cockpit. The only provision for armament was a No.2 Mk.1 Lewis gun mounting.

Another installation, made to F.E.2b A781 in March 1917, incorporated a French Sautter-Harle light on a swivel mounting at the front of the forward cockpit, with a Lewis gun attached to each side of the light. A wind-driven generator was mounted below the nose of the nacelle and powered four small landing lights as well as the big searchlight. Although A781 was later used by 199 Squadron, there is no record of its taking the searchlight into service.

A number of home defence machines were converted into single-seaters, presumably in the hope that the saving in weight might increase their ceiling. The front cockpit was faired over, and a fixed machine-gun installed for the pilot's use, the tailplane incidence being adjusted to compensate for the altered centre of gravity. A rather more elaborate conversion was made to D9134, a 51 Squadron machine based at Tydd St Mary, near the Wash, in which the pilot's cockpit was moved slightly forward, and two machine-guns fixed internally, firing through ports in the nose.

A proposal for a seaplane version of the F.E.2 was dropped in April 1917 in favour of the Royal Aircraft Factory's only flying boat design, the C.E.1, of which only two were built, (*see* chapter Seven). However, early in 1918 a number of aircraft of No.36 Squadron were transferred from anti-Zeppelin duties to anti-submarine patrols, under the direction of the Admiralty.

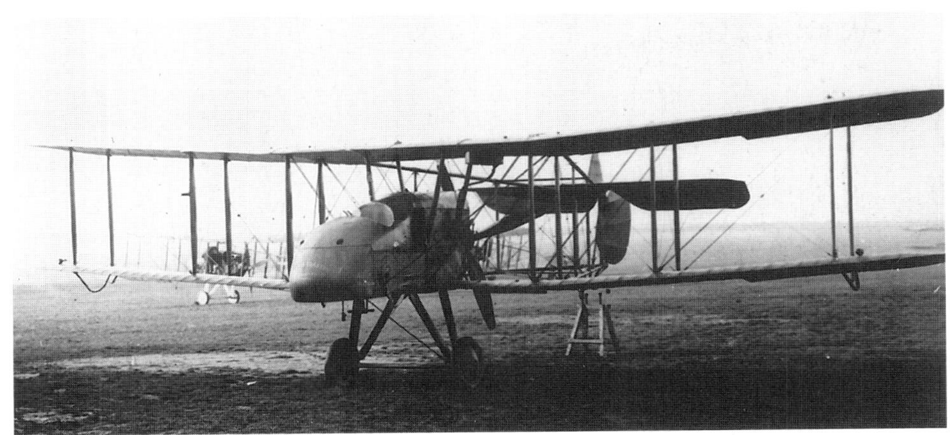

F.E.2b A5549 of 51 (H.D.) squadron. It has been converted into a single seater by fairing over the front cockpit. Author's collection

Flotation trials of F.E.2b 6536 at the Isle of Grain.
Imperial War Museum

The first 'Pom-pom' installation at Orfordness in August 1916. The small searchlight seen here below the much modified nacelle, was not included in later installation.
J.M. Bruce/G.S. Leslie Collection

Possibly as a direct result of this unlikely employment, the RNAS experimental station at the Isle of Grain devised emergency flotation gear for the F.E.2b/d, the actual installation being made on A6536. The undercarriage was replaced by one with twin skids and a hydrovane immediately in front of the forward struts. Large air bags were positioned beneath the roots of the lower wings, with small floats fitted at their tips. Trial ditchings were made on 30 May 1918, and again on 25 June, and were entirely successful, the aircraft being recovered undamaged on each occasion, but the idea was not pursued further, probably because the F.E.2 gave up its coastal patrol duties as soon as more suitable aeroplanes became available. However, on 31 May 1918 a 'Fee' based at Seaton Carew did contribute towards the destruction of one submarine, the UC49, by dropping

Not all C.O.W. gun installations followed the same pattern, this one involving a particularly blunt nose to the nacelle. J.M. Bruce/G.S. Leslie Collection

A third variant of the C.O.W. gun installation. This 100 Squadron 'Fee' also carries two 100lb (45kg) bombs. Author's collection

two 100lb (45kg) bombs onto it, the sinking being completed by a depth charge from the destroyer 'Locust'.

Although the installation of the recoilless Davis gun, tried out on one of the three F.E.2hs proved unsuccessful, the idea of using the 'Fee' in a ground-attack role was clearly worthwhile. A far more effective armament installation turned out to be that of the 'pom-pom' quick-firing gun, fed with a belt of forty one-pound shells, thus resurrecting the armament originally conceived for the type, as well as for the unsuccessful F.E.3 and F.E.6. The gun was first fitted to 6377 in mid-1916, the observer's cockpit being eliminated and the nose contours extensively modified to accommodate it, and was tested at Orfordness in August of that year. Judged as a success, a small number of aircraft were similarly equipped and issued to 51 and 100 Squadrons in March/April 1917. The latter unit had the honour of being the first to employ the weapon in anger on the night of 17/18 April when railway trains were attacked in the Douai area. Although the gun was far from reliable, particularly as jams could not be cleared in the air, such attacks were repeated throughout the remainder of the war, supply trains making good targets since the glow from the locomotive's firebox made it impossible for them to disguise their location.

Another F.E.2b, 7001, was fitted with a 0.45 calibre Maxim gun and this too was tested in August 1916, although neither the intended purpose of the installation nor its effectiveness is now known, but as no other aircraft was so equipped it was, presumably, considered a failure.

Inevitably, as they were replaced in front-line service by newer aircraft, some F.E.2s ended up in training establishments back in England. This was not a role for which they were especially suited, for

F.E.2b A800 fitted with a Scarff ring for air gunner training. Such refinements were never made available for 'Fees' on active service. J.M. Bruce/G.S. Leslie Collection

A 'Five Bob Flip'. F.E.2b D3832 selling joyrides at Bournemouth. Author's collection

Joyriding American style. The nacelle bears the legend 'The Flying Bath tub'.
J.M. Bruce/G.S. Leslie Collection

virtually the only pushers still in service at this stage in the war were the night-bomber 'Fees' themselves. However, they still proved useful in giving air experience and in training gunners, a small number of the aircraft being fitted with Scarff ring gun mountings.

But, however ill-suited the 'Fee' was to training, it was at least still making some contribution to the war effort; the coming of peace left 'Fighter Mark 1' without a purpose. The type was declared fully obsolete early in 1919, and all RAF stocks were disposed of. Only one machine, D3832, found its way onto the civil register where, as G-EAHC, it had a brief career selling joyrides along the south coast. At least one F.E.2b found equally productive employment in the USA, serving for a time as a camera ship for the fast growing movie industry, although its eventual fate is unknown.

The last survivor was probably D9108, which was retained at Farnborough as a flying test bed until November 1924.

CHAPTER FIVE

The F.E.8

The first Farnborough-designed fighter to see active service in France, the F.E.8, was a single-seat pusher biplane armed with a single Lewis machine-gun. It was, however, beaten into action by a rival type of broadly similar layout, the Aircraft Manufacturing Company's DH2, designed by Geoffrey De Havilland, and was therefore dismissed by the ever-critical aviation press as being no more than a copy of the privately produced design and has, in consequence, never received the recognition it really deserves.

By the spring of 1915 it was becoming clear that reconnaissance machines would not be left to do their work unmolested, and that in order to afford them some protection some kind of armed machine would be required. If it was to be both quick and agile, it would clearly need to be small and, for its day, powerful, which ruled out earlier designs such as the F.E.2, which had first been fitted with a machine-gun way back in 1912. So in May 1915 a design team, headed by John Kenworthy, the Factory's Chief Draughtsman, started work on what was to become the F.E.8. The Airco DH2 was not unveiled, fully completed, until several months later, and rather than being copies, one of the other, the rival designs were no more than similar solutions to a common problem.

No workable synchronization gear then existed, and so the machine was designed as a pusher, giving its gun a superb forward field of fire, albeit at the expense of the additional drag inherent in the pusher layout. The centre-boom tail support employed in the earlier F.E.3 and F.E.6 had not proved entirely satisfactory, for although its drag was lower, its structural integrity remained unproven. The F.E.8 therefore reverted to the nacelle and tailboom arrangement of the F.E.2, but with the steel tube booms meeting, not at the rudder post, but at the tailplane spar, thus forming a 'vee' in elevation rather than in plan. The design incorporated a number of other innovative features. The nacelle was built around a framework of triangulated

Female workers stringing the wing panel of an F.E.8. By October 1916, when this photograph was taken, around twenty-five per cent of the Royal Aircraft Factory's workforce were women, the number growing greater as the war progressed.
Crown copyright – DERA

steel tubes which, once assembled, needed no further truing up in service. This was covered with pre-formed aluminium panels fixed to wooden formers. The panel covering the petrol tank was laced on in the same manner used for fabric, to facilitate access, the tank itself being shaped to match the profile of the nacelle. There was even provision for a small piece of armour plate to afford the pilot some protection from shell splinters and small arms fire. The wings were of conventional construction, with wooden spars and ribs, fabric-covered, with a small riblet between each pair of ribs to maintain the leading edge profile. The broad centre section had no dihedral, and the outer panels were a generous five degrees, each panel incorporating an aileron running the full span from the tailboom attachment point to the tip. These big, high-aspect ratio ailerons had no spanwise balance cables, with rubber bungees instead being provided to return them to their normal position, as in the early F.E.2. Unusually for the time, the tailplane, elevators and rudder had ribs of pressed duralamin, fixed to wooden spars, the outer frames being of steel tube. Tailplane incidence could be adjusted, on the ground, the strut between the tailbooms immediately ahead of the elevator's leading edge being drilled with a series of holes into which the fixing bolts were placed, the hole being chosen in order to obtain the angle required. The tailskid was attached directly to the bottom of the rudder, which had internal springing to absorb landing shocks, an arrangement which was occasionally criticized, although there is no record of this giving any difficulty in service.

Armament comprised a single Lewis gun on a swivel mounting, its muzzle projecting from a small dish-shaped recess at the point of the nose and its breech level with the pilot's shins. It was controlled, through a linkage, by a spade grip convenient to the pilot's hand, and sighted by a small ring-and-bead sight attached to the linkage so that it would move in parallel with the gun. Whilst this arrangement was to prove inconvenient it must be remembered that aerial fighting was still very much in its infancy, and the idea that the gun should be fixed so that the pilot could aim the whole aeroplane at his target had yet to be fully appreciated, although the mounting did allow this to be done if the pilot so wished.

The instrumentation provided was typical of the spartan standards of the period: an engine rev counter, fuel tank pressure gauge, altimeter air speed indicator, compass, 'bubble' inclinometer, and a watch. Power was provided by a 100hp nine-cylinder Gnome Monosoupape rotary engine and, as was common for Royal Aircraft Factory designs, a four-bladed propeller was employed, the original design including a large, but wholly unnecessary, streamlined spinner.

Two prototypes were built, and were given the serial numbers 7456 and 7457. The first of these was ready for final inspection on 6 October 1915. The first flight was made at 11.40a.m. on 15 October, after a pre-flight inspection an hour earlier, with Frank Goodden at the controls. This flight lasted ten minutes, and presumably revealed no defects, for there is no record of any subsequent modifications.

> requires careful handling, especially of the rudder. The seating accommodation is comfortable, but rather too much lying back. Pilot would be more comfortable sitting straighter. Machine gun, as now fitted, is rather low and difficult to reload and use. It is suggested that the gun mounting should be raised at least six inches, the pistol grip then being in line with the top of the control lever. More than one gun, with the present size of fuselage, would rather cramp the available room for handling, etc. The machine is in every other respect highly satisfactory, and very handy and controllable and extremely easy to land. Variation of speed and view obtained by pilot are highly satisfactory. Wind screen fitted is efficient and goggles can be dispensed with. Controllability on the ground is good.

The prototype F.E.8, with Frank Goodden in the cockpit. The sighting bar for the nose-mounted Lewis gun can just be seen projecting through the windscreen.
Author's collection

The machine's next recorded flight, a few days later, lasted an hour and a half, allowing Goodden to explore fully the fighter's potential. These initial trials were made with no armament fitted, but this was installed around the end of October. By 8 November, with well over 5 hours of flight trials completed, it was flown to the Central Flying School at Upavon for initial service trials. Pilots at CFS found it pleasant to fly, being in no way tiring, and noted that it was very easy to land, an admirable quality given the rough and ready nature of many of the aerodromes in France. The following suggestions were made regarding possible improvement to the design:

> Machine is very satisfactory and easy to fly. Being small and high powered it naturally

The CFS test flight also noted that its top speed was 94.5mph (152km/h), that the take-off run was 60yd (55m), and the landing run 90yd (82m).

On 15 November it was flown back to Farnborough by the well-known pre-war exhibition pilot B.C. Hucks who, for some inexplicable reason, had the misfortune to crash rather badly on landing, and the machine was effectively written off. Construction of the second prototype, 7457, was fortunately fairly well advanced, and it was made ready for its final inspection on 3 December 1916, fitted with the same engine that had powered 7456. Flight trials, again at the hands of Frank Goodden, commenced on 6 December, this machine proving almost 3mph (4.8km/h) faster than its predecessor, at 97.4mph.

Service Trials

On 19 December, a month later than might have been had the original machine not crashed, this second prototype was flown over to France by Goodden for evaluation by front-line pilots. Since it was powered by a Gnome Monosoupape, which was considered a rather 'tricky' engine, it was sent to 5 Squadron at Abeele as they were equipped with the similarly powered two-seat Vickers FB5 'Gunbus'. At the time, 5 Squadron also had on its strength one single DH2 which was usually flown by its 'scout' pilot, Lt Frederick J. Powell, and so it was Powell who was given the job of evaluating the F.E.8, thus placing him in a unique position to compare the two machines, whose performance he eventually decided was 'about equal'. Powell was immediately impressed with the Factory's machine, and later called it 'a very beautiful design'. He was equally impressed by the workmanship of the Farnborough-built prototype, and said of it: 'every detail of the F.E.8 was so far advanced from the rather Heath-Robinson DH2.'

Fredrick J. Powell

Soon after the outbreak of the war, F.J. Powell, then a volunteer in the Duke of Lancaster's Yeomanry, transferred first to the Manchester Regiment, then to the Royal Flying Corps in a frantic effort to get out to France and play his part in the great adventure which everybody believed would be over by Christmas. On joining the RFC he soon found that they had a surfeit of observers, and so requested pilot training purely as a way of getting into the war. After basic flying instruction at Farnborough, followed by more advanced training at Upavon he was posted to 5 Squadron at Abeele to fly Vickers FB5 fighters.

Having emerged victorious from a couple of aerial combats in the two-seater Vickers he was rewarded by being appointed the Squadron's 'scout', flying the unit's only single-seater, a DH2, which was later replaced with the prototype F.E.8.

Following a brief posting to Home Establishment, during which he broke his ankle in a crash which resulted from a failed attempt to become the first man to loop straight after take-off, he returned to France as a Flight Commander with 40 Squadron, sharing his experience on the F.E.8 with newer pilots.

He later commanded 41 Squadron, which had just re-equipped with the DH5, and was shot down and captured whilst leading a patrol designed to ensure that newer pilots would experience a fight in the air.

He was interviewed by the author during 1990.

However, his report was not all praise, for he criticized the gun sight as inaccurate, and was just as unhappy with the gun mounting as the pilots at CFS had been. He thought that the propeller spinner was unsafe as it frequently set up a significant vibration, particularly if fitted even slightly off-centre, and eventually had it removed. Being most familiar with the Vickers FB5, which lacked any dihedral at all, Powell was also critical both of the five-degree dihedral given, in the interests of lateral stability, to the F.E.8's outer wing panels and of the generous aileron area thought necessary to overcome it, and so provide the manoeuvrability the B.E.2c was so heavily criticized for lacking.

The commander of the RFC in France, Maj Gen Hugh Trenchard, thought that the endurance of 2¼ hours was insufficient, and requested it be increased to 3 hours. However, this required that the petrol tank capacity should be increased from 25 gallons (114 litres) to 32 gallons (145 litres), which could not be achieved without a major redesign of the fuselage nacelle, and so a compromise increase to 29 gallons (132 litres), which gave an

This side view of the Airco DH2 shows that, whilst it and the F.E.8 were broadly similar in concept, they differed considerably in detail. Author's collection

endurance of 2¾ hours, was eventually implemented.

His suggestion, later adopted, that the gun mounting should allow the gun to be fired vertically upwards arose from an occasion when Powell, whilst flying 7457 over the lines, managed to get under the tail of an enemy Aviatik two-seater before realizing that he was too close to use the gun without raising the nose of the F.E. so much that he risked colliding with his opponent. With the German machine heading east, he could not remain beneath its tail for long and so made a break for home. As he did so, the enemy observer got in a good burst which riddled the petrol tank, leaving Powell with an anxious glide home with a dead engine. The machine was recovered from the field in which it landed, fortunately on the right side of the lines, and the petrol tank from the wreckage of 7456 was shipped over as a replacement.

Trenchard accepted Powell's criticisms of both the gun mounting and the spinner, and requested that the Factory should send 'a good man such as Captain Green, or Mr Heckstall-Smith' out to Abeele to discuss the machine's defects. It would seem that neither of the two gentlemen named was available and, although Powell later recalled that the Factory Superintendent, Mervyn O'Gorman, went out to France himself, it seems likely that he was mistaken, and that it was S.W. Hiscock who made the journey, for he was certainly in France on 31 January. But whoever it was who met with Trenchard and Powell, the Servicemen had their way and the gun mounting was changed for that already in use on the DH2, the circular hole thus left in the nose of 7457 being rather crudely covered with a metal disc. In addition, racks for spare ammunition drums were added on each side of the cockpit, although I have been unable to ascertain what effect, if any, this had on the machine's overall performance.

This head-on shot of a 40 Squadron F.E.8 shows clearly that only the outer wing panels had dihedral. Author's collection

Production

As with all Royal Aircraft Factory types, fully detailed drawings were prepared during the design process, and were therefore available for distribution to contractors as soon as the type was adopted for production. In the F.E.8's case this appears to have happened before the initial prototype's first recorded flight, since serial numbers 6378–6477 were allotted on 11 October 1915 for 100 F.E.8s to be built under contract No.87A/179 by the Darracq Motor

Production F.E.8 6390. The rubber 'bungees' which returned the ailerons to their normal position can clearly be seen above the upper wing. J.M. Bruce/G.S. Leslie Collection

Engineering Co. Ltd of Fulham in West London at a cost, less engine and instruments, of £680 each. The Darracq Co., as their name suggests, had previously built only motor cars, this being their first step into aircraft production.

Whilst the drawings were amended after this order had been placed, so as to incorporate the modifications brought about as a result of the service trials, this did not necessitate any revision to the aeroplane's basic structure, and it therefore seems probable that Darracq's initial slow progress was caused by inexperience in aircraft production, and the consequent need to rearrange their workshop facilities in order to facilitate the change from cars to aeroplanes. But whatever the cause of the delay, on 7 February 1916 contract 87A/339 for fifty F.E.8s (serial numbers 7595–7644) was placed with Messrs Vickers Ltd, whose aircraft building ability was already well proven, so as to get the F.E.8 into service as quickly as possible to counter the growing threat from the Fokker monoplane. The War Office also placed an order for a batch of twenty-five F.E.8s to be built by the Royal Aircraft Factory itself. The serial numbers A41 to A65 were allotted to these machines, yet none was ever completed, and it seems unlikely that manufacture even started. Although there is no evidence that the order was ever formally cancelled it seems probable that the matter was left in abeyance pending the result of the enquiry which followed Noel Pemberton-Billing's accusation against the Factory, made on 22 March, following which the factory's role was greatly re-defined.

Into Service

The prototype, 7457, which had gone to France for service trials, stayed on with 5 Squadron once these were completed despite the almost total lack of any spares for it. When the engine needed to be replaced, a British-made Gnome Monosoupape was 'borrowed' from a Vickers FB5 in order to keep the F.E. flying, as French-built engines were not interchangeable with British ones. Powell still regarded it more highly than the DH2 and, when told that he clearly could not keep both, happily gave up the Airco machine, which was then used by the Commander of 'C' flight, Capt Robert Loraine, the 'actor/airman'. Indeed so fond was he of it that he refused a week's leave when his CO could not promise that it would not be flown by any other pilot (in particular Loraine, who had a reputation for being somewhat ham-handed) whilst he was away.

With the need for fighters growing ever more urgent, production F.E.8s were sent to the Western Front as soon as they were available. The first two were assigned to 29 Squadron on 15 June, although one of these, 6378, was shot down just seven days later. In all, a total of five F.E.8s (6378, 6380, 6381, 6383 and 6385) served with 29 Squadron. These machines had been made by Darracq, the first Vickers-built F.E.8., No.7595, not being delivered until 1 July, and were delivered fitted with propeller spinners, which were removed at the Depot before they were sent on to their squadrons. Flying Corps Headquarters promptly requested that further examples were sent 'without nose pieces for the propellers' and the spinner which had so concerned F.J. Powell was seen no more.

The first squadron to be equipped exclusively with the F.E.8 was the recently

A 40 Squadron F.E.8 photographed at Treizennes. via David Gunby

'A' flight, 40 Squadron. via David Gunby

Robert Loraine DSO, MC

Described in 1902 as Broadway's 'Most Beautiful Man', Robert Loraine was a man of many facets.

Born in Merseyside in 1876, he left school at 13 to join a touring theatre group and then, just as his name was becoming known as a West End 'Star', he left to fight as a trooper in the Boer War. Invalided home with enteric fever he soon travelled to America to play on Broadway. He made his name and a great deal of money performing, both in England and America, in plays by George Bernard Shaw with whom he became good friends.

In 1910 he took up flying and soon became widely known as the 'Actor/Airman'. Whilst competing at the Bournemouth Aviation Meeting in July he became the first man to land an aeroplane on the Isle of Wight. The following month he took part in the Aviation meeting at Blackpool before becoming the first man to fly the Irish Sea. However, this latter record is contested by some as his machine came down some 100yd (91m) short of his target and he was obliged to swim ashore.

At the outbreak of World War I, although aged 38, he again volunteered for military service, this time as a pilot, serving with Nos 2, 14 and 5 squadrons, before assuming command of the newly formed 40 Squadron, and so bringing the first complete squadron of F.E.8s to France. Promoted to command the 23rd Wing, a training unit, he accepted a reduction in rank to return to active service as CO of 211 Squadron, and in July 1918 was invalided home with a bullet through the knee.

After the war he resumed his stage career once again, playing many great roles. He also appeared in a number of films before his death in 1935.

formed No.40 under the command of Maj Robert Loraine. The Squadron formed up at Gosport, with F.J. Powell joining it as a Flight Commander after a brief period of 'rest' as an instructor, arriving on crutches having broken his ankle in a crash resulting from an unsuccessful attempt to loop a Bristol 'Bullet' straight after take-off. Since the Battle of the Somme was at its height, and 40 Squadron's services were badly needed, it was not allowed to wait until it received its full complement of eighteen aeroplanes, but was instead sent over to France by Flights. First to leave was 'A' flight on 2 August, flying to its base near Aire via Folkestone and St Omer. It quickly settled into its new home, flying its first patrol on the 4th. 'B' and 'C' Flights were not able to fly out until the 25th.

Once in France, squadron pilots, many of whom had received only the most basic flying training, reported that the machine seemed prone to spinning, recovery from which was not then regularly taught, and as a result several accidents occurred. For example, 40 Squadron lost one pilot, 2nd Lt Dawes, and his machine, 7595, in a crash on 5 August, just three days after its arrival.

Concerned lest the type should have some inherent fault, on 23 August 1916 Frank Goodden carried out a series of deliberate spins, to both left and right, recovering successfully each time. His report of these trials, describing the recovery method employed, seems to have restored confidence, and no further complaints were made.

Once the Squadron settled down to its routine, and the rather exacting demands of its CO, the F.E.8s were flown to good account, with their first combat victory being scored on 22 September by Capt D.O. Mulholland who, flying 6384, brought down a Fokker which he surprised whilst it was attacking an F.E.2b. On the same day, 2nd Lt Hay engaged in combat with a Roland, which he was sure he had hit but was forced to break off when his own engine began to misfire.

Further victories followed, with Mulholland scoring again on 20 October, this time bringing down two Fokkers, and Lt E.L. Benbow and 2nd Lt S.A. Sharpe each downing a Roland, a two-seater then regarded as being a more formidable enemy than the Fokker. Lt Benbow went on to score eight victories whilst flying with the Squadron. On 21 October five enemy aircraft were brought down, an achievement which earned a congratulatory signal from Maj-Gen Trenchard, in which he said 'Please congratulate all pilots concerned. It is good work.' On 26 October Trenchard paid a personal visit to the Squadron and reported:

> I visited 40 Squadron yesterday, and was much struck by the extraordinarily fine organization in the Squadron, also by the excellent method and cleanliness in regard to machines, workshops, transport and sheds.

Development

Meanwhile, back at Farnborough, initial prototype 7456 which had crashed on 15 November 1915 was rebuilt, even though the type was already in production, in order to use it for experimental purposes. Three ailerons, the fin and horizontal tail surfaces had survived the crash and were incorporated into the rebuilt machine, as were

R & M 168

Maj F.W. Goodden's Report on tests of Spinning of F.E.8.

'In view of the recent accidents on F.E.8 aeroplanes, I carried out on 23/8/16 a series of tests to investigate the cause. The tests were made on an F.E.8 aeroplane with a 100 h.p. monosoupape Gnome engine.

At a height of about 3,500 feet I put on gradually all right rudder, and at the same time gradually pulled the control stick over to the left. In this way the aeroplane was turned to the right without any bank. When I had turned the machine in this manner for about 180 degrees the speed had dropped, due to the turn and the resistance of the fully-over rudder, and flaps [ailerons] to nearly the stalling speed. I next pulled back the control stick and this increased the turning speed, and when I had completed 300 degrees turn spinning suddenly started.

I kept the control stick in the position described above, and the spinning continued and gradually got steeper. The whole aeroplane was then turning about a point midway between the right-hand wing tip and the body.

In this way I tried three spinning tests to the left and three to the right and whereas spinning starts after about 300 degrees on the right-hand turn with control as described above, spinning to the left does not take place until a turn and a half have been completed.

In bumpy and disturbed air a turn attempted with the controls set in the manner described would undoubtedly start the aeroplane spinning much earlier in the turn.

The following was the procedure adopted to get the aeroplane out of the spin:

1. *Switch off motor.*
2. *Control stick put central and pushed forward.*
3. *Rudder put in centre.*

This resulted in a nose dive, from which the aeroplane, having once got up speed, can easily be pulled out with the control stick pulled back slightly.

If the aeroplane is dived to bring it vertically downwards, spinning cannot continue, provided all the controls are central.

This aeroplane is perfectly stable, and as safe from spinning as any aeroplane I have flown. There are large elevator, rudder and wing flap surfaces, and the controllability of the aeroplane is consequently very great. This controllability, which is so desirable in any aeroplane, and particularly in a fighting machine of this type, should it be misused, must result in upsetting the whole stability of the aeroplane. Similarly, if the aeroplane is allowed to get out of control, then, if care is taken to make the correct movements required by the particular conditions, these powerful controls will enable the aeroplane to be readily brought under control again.

I could only succeed in making the aeroplane spin by the misuse of the controls I have described, and from reports I have of the spinning accidents to F.E.8 aeroplanes this seems to have been the cause.'

some metal fittings and a few instruments. Other salvageable parts, including the engine and fuel tank, had already been fitted to 7457. However, the job seems not to have had a very high priority as the rebuilt machine was not ready for pre-flight inspection until 6 April 1916. It was finished to production standard, including the modified gun mounting and external ammunition racks, and was flown, fitted with a Gnome Monosoupape engine, on 9 April, with Frank Goodden at the controls. Later that month it was tested with a 110hp Le Rhone and by 18 May was fitted with a Clerget, also of 110hp, although this installation seems to have been less straightforward and the machine's visit to CFS for evaluation included longer periods in the workshops than on the flight line. From this, it is clear that every possible alternative to the Gnome Monosoupape was being considered, as supplies of that powerplant seem to have been in doubt. However, a sufficient number of Gnomes was eventually received, and all production F.E.8s were so equipped.

The F.E. was designed to have wheels of 700 × 75mm (27 × 3in) but, following early experiences with the poorly prepared French aerodromes, the larger 700 × 100mm (27 × 4in) wheel was adopted as standard.

The rubber bungees, which were intended to return the ailerons to their normal position, broke frequently as the rubber perished rapidly in sunlight, and on 30 August 1916 an order was issued that these should be replaced on all F.E.8s by a spanwise balance cable. This was a fairly simple operation, and those machines already in service were modified in the field.

Pilots descending to land after a 2-hour patrol with near empty tanks frequently found that the fuel-feed system could not maintain sufficient tank pressure, unless they used the hand pump throughout the descent, and consequently their engines cut if the throttle was opened. The introduction of a gravity tank was therefore requested. 40 Squadron experimented by fitting an external gravity tank taken from a DH2 to F.E.8 No.6426, but found that, whilst it solved the fuel pressure problem, its drag reduced the machine's top speed by 4mph (6.4km/h) and added a minute to the time needed to climb just 3,000ft (915m). Sgt Ridley, a Squadron fitter, therefore fabricated a tank from 22-gauge sheet copper which would fit within the centre section, between the spars, and thus have no adverse effect upon the machine's performance. On 28 October Maj Loraine, 40 Squadron's CO reported the results of these experiments to Brooke-Popham, who decided that Ridley's tank should be adopted and, despite some initial objections from the AID, an order was placed with a contractor in England for sufficient tanks to equip all the machines in service.

Towards the end of 1916, when some F.E.8s had been in service for three or four months, it was discovered that the duralamin elevator ribs had begun to corrode, and in some cases had become detached from the steel outer frame. On 8 November Brooke-Popham instructed No.1 Aircraft Depot at St. Omer to replace the duralamin ribs in the tail-surfaces of all F.E.8s with wooden components. He then had an even better idea and suggested that DH2 elevators, which had a similar span, should have their hinge positions modified so that they could be fitted in place of the defective components. Tests carried out by the Chemistry Department of the Regent Street Polytechnic, under the direction of Mr F. Western, established that the cause of the deterioration was electrolytic corrosion brought about by having dissimilar metals in contact.

At Farnborough, No.7456 was test-flown fitted with DH2 elevators, which then became the temporary fitting for service F.E.8s until new elevators, manufactured to the original design but with ribs of steel rather than duralamin could be shipped out to replace them. New rudders were also made, also with steel ribs. These replacements, which had the words 'steel ribs' stencilled onto their fabric covering to avoid any confusion, began to arrive in France before the year was out. Thus the existence of F.E.8s fitted with DH2 elevators was a fairly short-lived phenomenon.

A few F.E.8s were fitted with modified tail-skids, in which a long skid was fitted into a swivel mounted at the bottom of the rudder post, with a spring attached to the forward end of the skid to absorb landing shocks. The reason for this modification is not now known.

On the Western Front

On 15 October 1916 a second F.E.8 squadron, No. 41, arrived in France, its formation delayed by the need to use early production machines to make good losses sustained by other units. With Germany already introducing its new model Albatros

How They Compared

	Max. Speed	*Ceiling (min. 305m)*	*Climb (to 10,000 ft)*	*Endurance*
F.E.8	94mph (151km/h)	15,000ft (4,572m)	23¾	2¾hr
DH2	93mph (150km/h)	14,000ft (4,267m)	24¾	2¾hr
Sopwith Pup	108mph (174km/h)	17,500ft (5,334m)	16¼	3hr
Nieuport 17	103mph (166km/h)	17,500ft (5,334m)	12½	1¾
DH5	110mph (177km/h)	16,000ft (4,877m)	12½	2¾
Fokker EIII	88mph (142km/h)	11,500ft (3,505m)	30	1½
Albatros DII	109mph (175km/h)	17,000ft (5,182m)	22	1½
Halberstadt DIII	90mph (145km/h)	19,600ft (5,974m)	15	unknown

41 Squadron's 7616 photographed in flight. It has leader's streamers attached to the rear interplane struts. Author's collection

fighter, now with two guns and an improved performance, pilots of the now obsolete pusher would need to work harder to carry out their duty. As ever, they rose readily to meet the challenge.

On 9 November 1916 Cap Tom Mapplebeck, a flight commander with 40 Squadron, was forced down behind the German lines during a combat with pilots from *Jasta* 8, and was captured. His machine, 7624, was also captured, intact, and was later test-flown with Black crosses painted over its British markings (although its captors remained convinced that it was a DH2). That same day, another pilot with 40 Squadron, Sgt Darvell, was changing ammunition drums after shooting down an enemy two-seater when the empty drum slipped from his grasp in the slipstream, striking the propeller and damaging one of the tailbooms. He was forced to land hurriedly, fortunately just behind the British lines. Just four days later he was injured in a take-off crash. 41 Squadron had a pilot, 2nd Lt Deare, shot down and captured on 13 November, his machine, 6454, being badly damaged. And so it continued, with combat victories becoming less frequent, and each one offset by mounting losses as the enemy formations grew stronger. Things took a turn for the worse when *Jasta* 11, commanded by Manfred von Richtofen, moved to the same section of the front as 40 Squadron. First contact was made on 23 January 1917, with Lt Hay being shot down in the ensuing dogfight.

On 9 March 1917 the F.E.8 had its blackest day. At 0845 hours, ten machines took off from 40 Squadron's aerodrome at Treizennes, although one of them, 6426, flown by 2nd Lt L.B. Blaxland, was forced to abandon the patrol with engine trouble. At around 0915 they ran into a patrol of eight Albatros D111 of Jasta 11, led by von Richtofen. Only one British pilot, Lt D.H. de Burgh, in F.E.8 No.5384, emerged from the ensuing dogfight to land back at Treizennes undamaged. Of the others, 2nd Lts L.B. Haselar (A4874) and W.B. Hills (6397) were both shot down by Karl Schaefer. No.6456 was shot down by Kurt Wolff and overturned on landing, its pilot, Lt T. Shepard, thus ending the war a prisoner. Lt W. Morrice returned at 0940 with a damaged engine and a badly jammed gun. His aeroplane, 7636, was so shot about that it was deemed beyond repair and was therefore returned to No.1 Depot at St Omer where it was later struck off charge. 2nd Lt W.H. Cox (6445) landed at Treizennes at 0950 with minor damage, and, feeling unwell, was followed ten minutes later by 2nd Lt H.S. Pell in 6456. 2nd Lt H.C. Todd landed at another airfield with his aileron controls shot away, but managed to fly his machine, 6425, home later the same day after repairs had been made. Perhaps the pluckiest of all was 2nd Lt R.E. Neve whose mount, 6399, was shot down in flames. Wounded, he dived for the ground, jumping clear just before the machine crashed, and was taken to No. 33 casualty clearing station near Bethune. Richtofen was himself shot down that day by a bullet through his fuel tank. He switched the engine off as soon as he smelled petrol, thereby reducing the risk of fire, and landed safely. However, since his sole victory claim for that date was a DH2 it may not have been one of 40 Squadron's F.E.8s that brought him down.

Robert Loraine had left 40 Squadron on 12 February 1917, returning to England to take up command of the 23rd wing, and it was his replacement, Maj L.A. Tilney, who had the onerous duty of writing letters of condolence to the missing pilots' next of kin. A few days later he had the more pleasant task of informing his pilots that their outdated pushers were at last to be replaced with Nieuport 17s, a neat tractor

A 40 Squadron pilot poses for the camera. Although the Lewis gun has an ammunition drum fitted, the spare magazine racks on the cockpit sides are empty. Author's collection

Squadron Use

5 Squadron	7457
29 Squadron	6378; 6380; 6381; 6383; 6385; 7457
40 Squadron	6384; 6388; 6397; 6398; 6399; 6402; 6407; 6410; 6419; 6423; 6425; 6426; 6428; 6445; 6447; 6455; 6456; 6465; 6469; 7595; 7597; 7600; 7604; 7606; 7670; 7622; 7624; 7627; 7629; 7635; 7636; A4871; A4871; A4874; A4875
41 Squadron	6394; 6415; 6416; 6417; 6429; 6431; 6432; 6435; 6437; 6438; 6445; 6447; 6452; 6453; 6454; 6460; 6465; 6470; 6471; 7613; 7615; 7616; 7626; 7630; 7631; 7643; A4870; A4873; A4881; A4885; A4887; A4915; A4925; A4937
68 Squadron	A4895
6 Reserve Sqn	6405
10 Reserve Sqn	6401; 6403; 6406
Air Fighting School (Lympne)	A4944
CFS	6390; 6392

biplane with a 110hp engine and a single machine-gun. Although it too was obsolescent it was a sufficient enough improvement on the F.E.8 that most pilots welcomed the change, Capt de Burgh commenting: 'Much as we liked the old F.E.8 it was at that period hopelessly outclassed by the German aircraft.'

On 12 March the first two Nieuports arrived, and by May the whole squadron had been re-equipped, leaving 41 Squadron to soldier on until July as the only F.E.8 unit on active service until it too received replacement machines, in this case the DH5. This too gave some slight improvement in performance over that of the F.E.8, but had back-staggered wings, with the upper behind the pilot's head rather than in front, as was more usual. This arrangement left many pilots whose experience was other tractor types feeling somewhat exposed, but obviously had no such effect on those used to the F.E.8., which is possibly why the substitution was made.

The F.E.8 thus has the dubious distinction of being the last single-seat pusher fighter to see active service, remaining in use until it became obsolete, then being replaced by machines which were, in reality, little better except that they were tractors, and so gave a cosmetic improvement to the RFC's line-up. The real advance in fighter design, represented by the two-gun Sopwith Camel and the Royal Aircraft Factory's own S.E.5, was already in production and would begin to come into service in mid-1917.

Markings

Production F.E.8s were finished in what was, by 1916, the more or less standard colour scheme for RFC aeroplanes serving on the Western Front. The upper surfaces of the wings and tailplane were finished in P.C.10 (khaki/green) and the undersurfaces were clear doped, giving a straw-coloured finish to the natural linen covering. The nacelle was usually painted P.C.10 overall, although a few had pale undersides to match the wings. National markings were also applied to the then standard scheme, with full chord roundels on the upper surface of the top wing and the underside of the lower wing, close to the tip. Rudder stripes covered the full area of that surface, the fin being P.C.10. The nacelle usually carried a roundel, either in approximately the position of the pilot's knees, or level with his seat.

Serial numbers were most frequently carried on the rudder, but occasionally on the side of the nacelle, behind the cockpit.

Whilst there were no actual squadron markings applied, the principal users of the type, 40 and 41 Squadrons, did mark their aeroplanes in a separate and distinctive manner. Those belonging to the latter unit had large ultramarine numerals, outlined in white, on the nacelle sides and upper centre section to identify individual machines. 40 Squadron's scheme was similar but employed a squarer numerical style, the numbers being borderless and in one pale colour, possibly white.

Production Ends

On 2 April 1917 Brig Gen Brooke-Popham informed the Director of Aeronautical Equipment he could no longer accept further supplies of F.E.8s, even as replacements.

A4875, after it was brought down intact. Author's collection

Production

3689–3690 –	Royal Aircraft Factory (cancelled – intended for RNAS).
6378–6477 –	Darracq Motor Engineering Co. Ltd.
7456–7457 –	Royal Aircraft Factory (prototypes).
7495–7644 –	Vickers Ltd.
A41–A65 –	Royal Aircraft Factory (not built).
A4869–A4944 –	Darracq Motor Engineering Co. Ltd.
A4945–A4987 –	Darracq Motor Engineering Co. Ltd. (not built).
A5491 –	Darracq Motor Engineering Co. Ltd. (not built).
A8894 –	No.2 A.R.D. (construction No.005).

In October 1916, a further order for 120 machines (A4869–A4988) had been placed with the Darracq Co., with deliveries beginning early in the new year. However, since the type was no l onger to be used on the front line production was halted before the batch was completed, A4944 being the last machine produced. On 27 April 1917 No.1 Aeroplane Depot at St Omer began to ship surplus F.E.8s back to England, Nos 6464, 6475, 6476, 7642, A4885, A4908 and A4912 being the first to return.

The F.E.8's withdrawal from the Western Front was not quite the end of its career on active service, however, for a few were assigned to home defence duties, stationed at aerodromes around London with the intention of protecting the civilian population from the Zeppelin threat. There is no record that any F.E.8 ever engaged an enemy airship in combat.

The type also saw service with a number of training units, including No.10 Reserve Squadron at Joyce Green and No. 1 Reserve Squadron, as well as with the Advanced Air Fighting School at Lympne and the Armament Experimental Station at Orfordness.

It is not known whether any F.E.8s survived the war; certainly there were none on the strength of the post-war Royal Air Force, nor are any preserved in museums. However, whilst there are no original examples extant, two reproduction machines do exist in the USA. One is on display in the Museum of Transportation at Owls Head, Maine, and the other at the National Air and Space Museum, Washington, D.C.

Specification – F.E.8

Powerplant:	100hp Gnome Monosoupape nine cylinder rotary
Weights:	Empty 895lb (406kg); loaded 1,346lb (611kg)
Dimensions:	Wingspan 31ft 6in (9.6m); length 23ft 8in (7.2m); height 9ft 2in (2.8m)
Performance:	Speed at sea level 94.5mph (127km/h); at 6,000ft (1,829m) 79mph (108km/h); at 12,000ft (3,658m) 67mph (108km/h); ceiling 15,000ft (4,572m); climb 1 min to 1,000ft (305m); 2 min 10 sec to 2,000ft (609m); 7 min 30 sec to 5,000ft (1,524m); 23 min 40 sec to 10,000ft (3,048m); 37 min 30 sec to 12,000ft (3,658m); endurance 2¾hr

These figures represent a performance average. Actual tests conducted by 40 Squadron during October 1916 revealed that individual machines varied considerably. Climb to 6,000ft (1,829m) ranged from 8 minutes to 12, whilst top speed at that height varied from 70mph (113km/h) to 82mph (132km/h). These variations were due to a number of factors including engine performance and the condition of the fabric, which grew soggy with age as it soaked up castor oil thrown out by the engine.

The reproduction F.E.8, now in the National Air & Space Museum in Washington D.C., which was built and flown by the late Cole Palen in his Rhinebeck Air shows. Author's collection

CHAPTER SIX

The S.E.5

B.S.1 on Farnborough Common. Of all its innovative features, only the single bay bracing would immediately be copied. Others, like the monocoque fuselage, would be ignored for many years.
Author's collection

After the tragic crash of the S.E.1 on 18 August 1911, the canard layout was discontinued, and the S.E. designation was eventually considered to stand, not for Santos, but for Scouting Experimental, replacing 'Bleriot Scout' to describe small, fast, tractor types. Of these only two machines had, by then, been designed, and only the first actually constructed, the other remaining no more than a design concept.

The B.S.1 was designed by Geoffrey de Havilland, assisted by H.P. Folland and S.J. Waters, its basic configuration being achieved by scaling down the rotary-engined B.E.3. Its forward fuselage was built around four longerons which extended only 3ft (.9m) aft of the cockpit, the rear portion being of monocoque construction, and the whole of streamlined circular cross-section. Less streamlined was the sturdy twin-skid undercarriage, which was demanded as much by the unprepared surface of Farnborough Common as by the fashion of the day. Lateral control was by warping and single bay bracing was used, perhaps for the first time anywhere. Power was provided by a 100hp Gnome rotary engine, immediately behind which was a divided tank, holding 22 gallons (100

Specification – B.S.1	
Powerplant:	100hp Gnome
Weights:	Empty not known; loaded 1,232lb (559kg)
Dimensions:	Span 27ft 6in (8.39m); chord 3ft 9½in (1.16m); gap 4ft 7in (1.40m); length 20ft 6in (6.25m); height 8ft 10in (2.69m)
Performance:	Maximum speed 92mph (147km/h); climb 800ft/min (244m/min)

litres) of petrol and 11 (50 litres) of oil. The rear face of this tank was employed as an instrument board: the rev. counter; air speed indicator; altimeter; compass; and watch were directly attached thereto.

Test-flown by de Havilland on 13 March 1913, its performance was spectacular, with a top speed of over 90mph (145km/h) and an initial climb of 800ft (244m) per minute. However, it was immediately apparent that the rudder, directly scaled down from that of the B.E.3, was too small, a situation made worse by the fabric covering to the wheels, which reduced their resistance, but added keel area forward of the centre of gravity. de Havilland therefore designed a larger rudder and put its manufacture in hand, but continued to test-fly the aircraft with the original surface still fitted. However, on 27 March he started a turn whilst flying at about 100ft (30m), stalled and entered a spin, breaking his jaw and losing some teeth in the consequent crash.

Although the aircraft was extensively damaged, authority for its repair, at an estimated cost of £900, was granted by the War Office, and it was rebuilt under the designation S.E.2. As such, it differed little from the B.S.1 except that the tail surfaces were completely revised and the engine was replaced with a Gnome of only 80hp. The new tailplane was semi-circular in plan, with inversely tapered ailerons, triangular dorsal and ventral fins and a larger rudder, of high-aspect ratio, which had its lower edge capped in steel to act as a tail-skid. Completed by October 1913 it was again tested by de Havilland, and found to be only slightly slower in speed and climb than before, the engine's reduced power output being partly compensated for by its lower weight.

Despite O'Gorman's protestation that the aircraft was an experimental type unsuited to service use, the War Office insisted that it was handed over to the RFC, and this was done on 17 January

The S.E.2 in its original form seen on Farnborough Common, 12 October 1913. Crown copyright – DERA

Specification – S.E.2	
Powerplant:	80hp Gnome
Weights:	Empty 720lb (327kg); loaded 1,132lb (513kg)
Dimensions:	Span 27ft 6in (8.39m); chord 3ft 9½in (1.16m); gap 4ft 7in (1.40m); length 20ft 5in (6.23m); height 9ft 3½in (2.83m)
Performance:	Maximum speed 85mph (136km/h); climb not known

The S.E.2 as rebuilt, only its heavy undercarriage marring its prophetically modern appearance. Author's collection

(Below) **The S.E.4, with its original inverted tripod undercarriage, looks exactly what it was designed to be, the fastest aeroplane in the world.** Author's collection

Specification – S.E.2 Rebuilt	
Powerplant:	80hp Gnome
Weights:	Empty not known; loaded 1,200lb (366kg)
Dimensions:	Span 27ft 6in (8.39m); chord 3ft 9½in (1.16m); gap 4ft 7in (1.40m); length 20ft 10in (6.35m); height 9ft 3½in (2.83m)
Performance:	not known

Specification – S.E.4	
Powerplant:	160hp Gnome
Weights:	not known
Dimensions:	Span 27ft 6in (8.39m); chord 3ft 9½in (1.16m); gap 5ft 1in (1.55m); length 21ft 4in (6.51m); height 9ft (2.75m)
Performance:	Maximum speed 135mph (216km/h); climb 1,600ft/min (488m/min)

1914, it being given the serial number 609. However, in early April it was returned to the Factory for repair, thus allowing O'Gorman to develop it further. Its fuselage was replaced with a conventional wire-braced structure, faired to a circular cross-section with formers and stringers. This, Henry Folland's first major design, fulfilled O'Gorman's prediction that it would be lighter than the monocoque which it replaced. The engine cowling was replaced by one of reduced resistance and the bracing wires changed to the Factory's new streamlined 'rafwires'. New tail surfaces and a conventional tail-skid were also fitted. In this form it was officially designated the 'S.E.2 Rebuilt', although the title S.E.2a has subsequently been frequently applied to it. The modifications were not completed until 3 October, by which time not only was the nation at war, but it had already been long superseded as a research vehicle by the even more advanced S.E.4. Therefore, as soon as Frank Goodden had completed some fairly basic test flights, it was returned to the RFC, joining 3 Squadron in France on the 27th.

Design of the next machine in this series, the S.E.3, was abandoned before completion in favour of the S.E.4, which Henry Folland intended should be the fastest aeroplane in the world, every possible attention being paid to reducing resistance and improving performance. The fuselage, like that of the rebuilt S.E.2, was faired to a circular cross section, blending smoothly into the cowling which closely enclosed the fourteen-cylinder, two-row, 160hp Gnome rotary engine. Its four-blade propeller was fitted with a large spinner, leaving only a narrow slot through which cooling air could reach the engine, but dramatically reducing its drag. Single-bay bracing was employed, with swaged 'rafwires' and single 'I' shaped interplane struts, their ends just broad enough to allow attachment to both wing spars. The centre-section struts were made hollow, thereby providing a drag-free route for the aileron cables. Full span ailerons were fitted to all four planes, and could be lowered together to act as landing flaps, or reflexed slightly to further reduce drag at high speeds. The undercarriage comprised an inverted tripod of streamlined struts, with a transverse leaf spring at its apex, the wheels being attached to its ends. The tailplane was identical to that fitted to the rebuilt S.E.2, the gaps between all fixed and movable surfaces being covered with elastic net to reduce drag. In a final effort to reduce resistance still further it was intended that the cockpit should be fitted with a canopy of moulded celluloid, but although this was apparently manufactured it was never used, pilots all disliking the idea immensely.

Completed by 17 June 1914, it was test-flown by Norman Spratt, who found its performance simply staggering, with a top speed of 135mph (217km/h) and a climb of 1,600ft (488m) per minute. However, he also found that the spring undercarriage caused excessive roll, and within a week this was replaced by a more conventional 'vee' strut structure. Problems with engine cooling were overcome by fitting a modified spinner which had a hole at its nose, and an internal fan to provide adequate air flow over the cylinder heads. Problems with the engine's general reliability were not so easily resolved and it was eventually abandoned, being replaced with a single row Gnome of 100hp. Thus powered, the S.E.4's top speed was reduced to a more commonplace 92mph (148km/h), although its landing speed remained high for that time, at 52mph (84km/h).

Taken over by the RFC at the beginning of August, it was given the serial number 628, but never had a chance to see active service for on 12 August it was badly damaged when a wheel collapsed on landing, fortunately without injury to the pilot, and it was written off.

Designed by Henry Folland towards the end of 1914, the S.E.4a was more a development of the rebuilt S.E.2 than of the S.E.4, although it incorporated the multi-function full-span ailerons introduced by the later machine. There was no centre section, its upper wings meeting above the fuselage centre line, and including 3½ degrees of dihedral. The fuselage was again built around a wire-braced structure, the forward portion of each longeron being of steel tube, and the remainder of spruce, with fishplate joints just aft of the cockpit. The fuselage was faired to a circular cross-section and blended neatly into the cowling which enclosed its 80hp Gnome rotary engine, and a dish-shaped spinner covered the propeller boss.

Completed and ready for inspection by 23 June 1915, it was taken up for its first flight two days later. Three further examples were completed by early August, but lacked both the spinner and the streamlining of the prototype, their fuselages being flat-sided except for a small triangular fairing behind the engine cowling. They were handed over to the RFC, and given the serial numbers 6510–12. One

The first S.E.4a, with fully rounded fuselage sides, and with a mounting for a Lewis gun above the upper wing. Author's collection

Henry Philip Folland (1889–1954)

Like many early aeronautical engineers Folland began his career in the automobile industry, serving an apprenticeship with the Lanchester Motor Co., before moving to Daimler as a draughtsman in 1908. Four years later he joined the Royal Aircraft Factory, and rose to become one of its Design Office Section Leaders, taking responsibility for the design of the S.E.5. Following Frank Goodden's fatal crash in January 1917 he resigned, but was persuaded to remain in aircraft design, and so became Chief Designer for the Nieuport and General Aircraft Co., for whom he designed the 'Nighthawk' fighter and 'Goshawk' racer. In 1921 he joined the Gloster Aircraft Co. as Chief Designer, and later as a Director, producing a range of fighters including the 'Grebe', 'Gamecock', 'Gauntlet' and 'Gladiator'.

In 1937 he founded the Company which bore his name, remaining Managing Director until his retirement in 1951. The Folland Aircraft Co. was eventually incorporated into the Hawker Siddeley Group and is perhaps best known for its 'Gnat' light fighter, which for many years was the mount of the Royal Air Force aerobatic display team, the 'Red Arrows'.

Specification – S.E.4a

Powerplant:	80hp Gnome
Weights:	not known
Dimensions:	Span 27ft 6in (8.39m); chord 4ft 2in (1.27m); gap 4ft 9in (1.45m); length 20ft 10½in (6.37m); height 9ft 5in (2.87m)
Performance:	not known

crashed at Hounslow during September, killing its pilot, Capt Blood, while the others presumably went to France as scouts. Although at least one of them was later fitted with a Lewis gun above the upper wing, firing clear of the propeller disc, the lack of an effective interrupter gear seemed, at this time, to leave the fighter role in the hands of the pusher, and no further use was made of the S.E.4a.

H.R.M. Brooke-Popham (1878–1953)

Henry Robert Moore Brooke-Popham appears to have been a born administrator, the perfect Staff Officer: a man who could clearly see what needed doing, and could see that it was done.

He was first commissioned in the Oxford Light Infantry in 1898, and attended the Army Staff College in 1910. After learning to fly at the British & Colonial Aviation Company's school at Brooklands, where on 18 July 1911 he was awarded Royal Aero Club certificate No.108, he transferred to the Air Battalion, and quickly became Commanding Officer of 3 Squadron.

In 1915 he took command of the RFC's third wing, based at St Omer, but the following year he was appointed Quartermaster General, with a brevet rank of Brigadier-General, and it was in this post that he was able to do the greatest good for the Flying Corps, for as QMG he was responsible for provision of equipment to all RFC units, although purchase and procurement remained under War Office control.

Post-war he became the first Commandant of the RAF Staff College and then, after a period as AOC Iraq, the first Air Commandant of the Imperial Staff College. By 1935 he was Inspector General of the RAF, with a rank of Air Chief Marshal and in 1940 became C in C, Far East.

Engine Innovations

As mentioned in the history of the B.E.2, the 150hp Hispano-Suiza engine, the prototype of which first ran in February 1915, represented a quantum leap in engine design. Each bank of four cylinders was cast in a single block, thus creating an engine which had similar overall dimensions to many engines giving only half its power, and which was both lighter and stronger. Bench tests were conducted in Paris, commencing on 21 July, and were intended for the benefit of the French Air Force, but clearly did not escape the notice of Brooke-Popham, then GSO1 at RFC HQ in France, as a British order for an initial batch of fifty engines was placed in August, and negotiations started with a view to building the engine under licence.

As described earlier, the engine was initially seen as a simple means of boosting the performance of the now outclassed B.E.2c, which was then the most numerous aircraft on active service, and the first example, which was received in February 1916, was indeed so installed by the Depot at St Omer. However, there were other ideas too on how best to utilize the advantages of the new engine.

On 28 February 1916 Trenchard revealed a specification which he considered that the next generation of fighters, that is those for 1917, would need to meet. This included a climb to 10,000ft (3,048m) within 15 minutes, a speed of at least 100mph (160km/h) at that height, and a ceiling of 18,000ft (5,486m). Endurance was to be 4 hours, although 3 was acceptable as a minimum, and it says much for the 'state of the art' at the time that Trenchard found it necessary to point out that it must be able to fire ahead.

At Farnborough, Mervyn O'Gorman held a meeting with F.M. Green, his Chief Engineer, John Kenworthy, the Chief Draughtsman, and William Farren from the physics department, to suggest that the Royal Aircraft Factory should design a fighter around the Hispano-Suiza engine. Two rival concepts were initially prepared, one by a team headed by Kenworthy, who had designed the F.E.8 that had recently entered production, and the other apparently arising out of a suggestion made by Frank Goodden, the Factory's chief test pilot, and designed by Henry Folland, who had produced the S.E.4.

Maj F.W. Goodden (1889–1917)

Major Frank Widenham Goodden RFC (Special Reserve) was head of the Experimental Flying Department of the Royal Aircraft Factory from early 1914 until his death on 28 January 1917 when the aeroplane he was testing broke up in the air.

Born in Pembroke, South Wales where his father was a photographer, Goodden took up the then fashionable sport of ballooning in 1910 and, inspired by Alberto Santos-Dumont's dirigible flights around the Eiffel Tower, attempted, unsuccessfully, to make a balloon flight around St Paul's. Next he became mechanic to the airship pioneer E.T. Willows, and on 4 November 1910 accompanied him on his cross-Channel flight. They left Wormwood Scrubs at 3.25p.m. watched by a large crowd which included the Prime Minister, H. Asquith, Winston Churchill and Lloyd George, and finally landed near Douai at 2.00 the following morning.

1911 saw Goodden making exhibition parachute descents from the balloon 'Enchantress' at various outdoor events, and the following year he built and flew a monoplane of his own design. He then moved on to the W.H. Ewen School at Hendon as an exhibition pilot, taking the British record with fourteen successive loops, before joining the Royal Aircraft Factory. By 19 May 1914, he was a captain in the RFC Special Reserve and was one of the pilots chosen to fly in review before the King and Queen when they made an official visit to Farnborough.

As well as carrying out routine testing, he made the first flights of a wide range of Royal Aircraft Factory designs including the F.E.2a, F.E.2d, F.E.4, F.E.8, R.E.8 and S.E.5.

Kenworthy's design was a curious machine which appeared to owe a great deal to the ill-regarded B.E.9, for whilst technically a tractor he had sought to gain the pusher's advantageous field of fire by placing the pilot in a 'pulpit' ahead of the propeller, rather than by employing one of the crude and rather unreliable interrupter gears then available to the allies. A Lewis gun on a swivel mounting was to be employed, although the drawings show this rather too close to the pilot's face for safety. Other aspects of the design, however, were very good, with the fuel tank immediately below the engine so as to concentrate the mass in a small area and so ensure good manoeuvrability. The rear fuselage was of narrow cross-section in order to reduce resistance, and the single bay wings were of unequal span, the upper overhanging the lower by some 5ft (1.5m) on each side.

Folland prepared two schemes, differing only in detail, for a compact single-seat tractor biplane with an estimated empty weight of 1,150lb, of which 500 was allowed for the engine, radiator, and so on and 120 for the gun and ammunition. Folland also chose to ignore the primitive interrupter gears then available, and instead employed a Lewis gun firing through the hollow propeller shaft of a geared engine, an arrangement which was proposed for several other aircraft to be powered by the new engine, and which may have been suggested by the Hispano-Suiza company. The pilot sat high so that the upper wing obscured only the narrowest possible angle of his forward vision, whilst his downward view was to be enhanced by reducing the chord of the lower stub wings to little more than the distance between the two spars.

General arrangement drawings for the rival designs were completed during June and July, and after due consideration it was Folland's design, scheme two, in which the engine was positioned lower in the fuselage, which was chosen for a fully detailed design. So far had the design process progressed from the empiricism of only a few years earlier that Folland's notebooks contain over forty pages of detailed stress calculations for this single scheme. Calculations of the loads upon each metal fitting confirm that even the Main Lift Wiring Plate could satisfactorily be fabricated from mild steel. As the design concept developed into fully detailed drawings, various modifications inevitably took place. The stub wings of the lower centre section were, after all, filled out to a full aerofoil section, with triangular cut-outs in their trailing edges. At the beginning of August the fin and rudder from the now abandoned F.E.10 were adopted instead of the slightly smaller surfaces originally drawn by Folland, although the tail-skid which had previously been attached to the lower edge of the rudder was now

The prototype S.E.5, A4561, with Frank Goodden in the cockpit showing the high seating position and semi-conical windscreen. Author's collection

connected directly to the stern post, the rudder being cut away to accommodate it.

The completed drawings depict a neat, single bay biplane with remarkably clean lines, designed to be simple to manufacture and easy to maintain. All cable runs were routed internally to reduce drag as much as possible, thus the centre-section struts were of steel tubes, with wooden fairings, the interplane struts remaining solid spruce. The wings were of RAF14 section, braced with streamlined 'rafwires', and with an additional flying wire attached to the mid-bay compression rib of the upper wing. Incidence and dihedral angles were both 5 degrees. Ailerons were provided on all four wings, the tips of which were sharply raked. Both upper and lower wings had the same planform, yet the rib spacing differed slightly to allow for the differing loads upon them. The engine was fully cowled, except for the camshaft covers which projected slightly on each side, their drag reduced by small fairings. A car-type radiator, with a curved top, was fitted to the front of the cowling, a hole in its centre providing a path for the propeller shaft. The fuselage frame was a conventional wire braced box-girder, its forward section clad with ply to increase its strength, and with a curved top decking. The longerons were of spruce, and the engine bearers of ash, stiffened by three ply-covered spruce bulkheads. Transverse steel tubes formed attachments for the lower wing spars. The main petrol tank was positioned immediately behind the engine, its top shaped to match the contour of the decking, a wind-driven pump mounted beneath the fuselage maintaining a pressure of 2½ psi. A hand pump was provided for emergency use, as was a 4 gallon (18 litres) gravity tank built into the leading edge of the upper port wing. The undercarriage legs were of steel tube, the front pair having wire bracing across their diagonals, and the one-piece axle was housed in a streamlined fairing, with further teardrop fairings over the shock-cord bindings. There was a large, semi-conical windscreen, and a fairly comprehensive array of instruments: air speed indicator; altimeter; bubble clinometer; compass; rev counter; fuel and oil pressure gauges; and a holder for a watch. A variable incidence tailplane was provided, as was a radiator temperature gauge, although there was no means of temperature control. The petrol gauge was fitted directly to the rear of the tank, thus making it easy to install, although considerably less easy to read. A rotary selector switch allowed the pilot to choose either tank, or to transfer fuel from one to the other. A Very pistol holster and cartridge rack completed the cockpit. As was usual at the time, the pilot was provided with a single broad seat belt. There were no shoulder straps.

The Design is Realized

A contract for three prototypes was issued in September 1916, although it is possible that these were already under construction at that time, the first six production Hispano engines having finally arrived in August. The serial numbers A4561–3 were allotted to these machines on 28 September, and on 5 October the numbers A4845–68 were assigned to the first production batch of twenty-four, which were also to be built by the Royal Aircraft Factory.

The first prototype, A4561, was presented for inspection around noon on 20 November 1916, approval for flight being given at 9.30pm the same day. It was fitted with a direct-drive Hispano-Suiza 8A, serial number 5213/WD10100, driving a two-blade propeller. Short stub exhausts were fitted in the centre of each manifold. No armament was fitted, nor could it be, as the Lewis gun installation designed for it required a geared engine. Although transparent panels were provided in the top decking forward of the cockpit level with the proposed position of the gun's breech, these may have been included merely to allow a little more light on to the instrument panel.

The following day, it was prepared for flight, the radiator and fuel tanks filled, and after lunch it was wheeled out on to the snow-covered grass of Farnborough Common near to the office block, where a number of senior staff were gathering to witness its first flight. Frank Goodden took his seat in the cockpit, the propeller was swung and the engine gave a few coughs, but failed to start. It was swung again, and again, without success. The plugs were removed, heated, and replaced but, despite the best efforts of a number of propeller swingers, the engine still refused to start. Finally, with dusk approaching, A4561 was wheeled back across the road to the sheds. Next morning it was brought out again, and this time the engine started easily, for at first light an auxiliary petrol tap, installed in the fuel pipe from the gravity tank where it passed under the instrument panel had been discovered, and switched on.

Albert Ball

Born 14 August 1896 in Nottingham, a city of which his father was once the mayor, Albert Ball grew up with a keen interest in all things mechanical. On leaving school, at the age of 17, he joined an engineering company but, at the outbreak of war, volunteered as a private in the 2/7th Battalion of the Sherwood Foresters (as the Notts & Derby Regiment was affectionately known). He was quickly made an NCO and on 29 October 1914 received a commission.

Keen to get into action as soon as possible he transferred first to a Cyclist unit and then, having learned to fly at his own expense, to the RFC, receiving his Brevet on 22 January 1916. After a brief spell at Gosport he finally got to France, being posted to 13 Squadron to fly B.E.2cs. His aggression, even in that staid and stable aeroplane, was soon noticed, and on 7 May he was posted to 11 Squadron to fly a Nieuport Scout, scoring his first, unconfirmed victory two weeks later. On 25 June he brought down an enemy observation balloon, an action for which he was awarded the Military Cross. With the introduction of homogeneous fighter squadrons he was transferred to 60 Squadron, where he was given a roving commission and allowed to hunt where he wished.

On 4 October 1916 he was posted to Home Establishment for a rest as an instructor, his score then standing at 30. Whilst in England he attended an investiture at Buckingham Palace, receiving his MC, plus a DSO and bar. A second bar was awarded later.

Unhappy in his new role, he clamoured to be returned to France, finally doing so as a Flight Commander with the newly formed 56 Squadron. Initially unhappy with his S.E.5, A4850, he was given a Nieuport too, and again allowed a roving commission.

On 7 May 1917 he was brought down, allegedly by Lothar Von Richtofen, and crashed behind the lines. He was buried, with full military honours, in the German cemetery at Annoeullin, on 9 May, and awarded a posthumous Victoria Cross the following month. His final score was 44.

Goodden took off at around 10.00a.m. for a flight lasting some 20 minutes and, on landing, announced to the crowd that had gathered to watch 'She's a pixie!'. He took A4561 up again the following day, this time for 25 minutes. Pilot for the machine's third recorded outing was Capt Albert Ball, then Britain's leading fighter pilot, who took off at 12.25p.m. for a flight lasting 10 minutes. Ball's reaction was less enthusiastic than Goodden's had been, for he considered the new machine inferior to both the rotary powered Nieuport (his current mount), and to the projected Austin AFB1, into whose design he had recently had some input.

On 10 December it was flown over to Hounslow, remaining there until 2 January

1917. Its future armament was obviously under consideration, for whilst there it was examined by Capt W.D.S. Sanday of 42 Reserve Squadron, who reported, on 17 December, that the present windscreen would not allow pilots to rectify the jams normally experienced with a Vickers gun, were one to be fitted.

The second prototype, A4562, was ready for inspection exactly one week after the first, although approval for flight was not given until Friday, 1 December. Like the first, it was fitted with a 150hp direct drive engine, and was, initially, unarmed. Its first recorded flight was made the following Monday, with Frank Goodden at the controls, and two days later Lt Roderic Hill of 60 squadron took it up. A performance trial, at a loaded weight of 1,827lb (828kg), found that its maximum speed was 127½mph (205km/h) at 1,000ft (305m) and 116mph (187km/h) at 9,000ft (2,743m). The climb to 5,000ft (1,520m) took 5 seconds under 5 minutes with twice that height being reached in 12 minutes and 25 seconds.

It would appear, however, that A4562 suffered a heavy landing, or perhaps a taxiing accident, for on 21 December it was re-inspected after the undercarriage had been replaced. It had also been fitted with what would be the standard armament for the type, a belt-fed Vickers gun and a Lewis gun, not firing through the propeller shaft as originally intended, but on a Foster mounting above the upper wing, firing clear of the propeller disc. Since this latter fitting was the preferred weapon of Albert Ball, who had made A4561's third flight, it is possible that it had been fitted at his suggestion. The Vickers was offset to port, a depression having been made in the upper surface of the petrol tank in order to accommodate it, with its breech within the cockpit so that jams could be dealt with. It was fitted with a Hyland type 'E' loading handle and synchronized by the newly developed hydraulic Constantinesco gear. Both guns were angled upwards at an angle of 5 degrees, their aiming points converging at a range of 150yd (137m), both Aldis and ring and bead sights being provided, the former on the fuselage centre line and the latter fixed to the cooling jacket of the Vickers gun. A new, armoured seat was also provided, its height adjustable to three different positions.

On 22 December 1916 Goodden took it up for a 15-minute test flight and two days later flew it over to the Depot at St Omer for evaluation. On 26 December it was flown by 2nd Lt F.H.B. Selous of 19 Squadron, then equipped with SPAD VIIs, which were also powered by the Hispano-Suiza engine, and a comparison was made between the two types in which the S.E. came out equal, or ahead in almost every way.

Report on S.E.5 Compared with SPAD in the Air by 2nd Lt F.H.B. Selous

I flew the S.E.5 at St. Omer and noticed the following points:

Control Elevator: The S.E.5 is slightly lighter in the elevator than the SPAD but the machine is harder to keep in a steep dive.
Laterally: There is not any difference between the S.E.5 and the SPAD.
View: The view in all directions is very good and much better than the SPAD, especially forwards and downwards.
Climb and Speed: This cannot be judged accurately without flying the machines together, but the S.E.5 has a much greater range at speed than the SPAD and will fly at 45mph.
General Flying: Although the S.E.5. is stable, it can be manoeuvred quite as well as the SPAD. The S.E.5 can be landed much slower than the SPAD and has a flatter glide.

Brig Gen J.F.A. Higgins, Commander of the RFC's 3rd Brigade, was also present at St Omer during A4562's visit, and on 27 December informed GHQ:

> I inspected the S.E.5 yesterday and saw it flown by Maj Goodden and Lt Selous (No. 19). Lt Hill (No. 60) also flew it. The pilots report it is quick fore and aft but not as quick as either the SPAD or the Nieuport. They report the view as very good. I consider this is correct.
>
> It appears to give 127 or 128mph on the indicator at 500ft. The range of speed is astonishing. I should put it at from 40–125mph.
>
> It appears easy to fly and strong. In my opinion this the best single seater I have seen. The instruments and fittings seem to be suitably placed.

As a result of this in-service evaluation a number of modifications were recommended. These included the provision of inspection covers over the pulleys fitted where the internal control cables changed direction, and the addition of radiator shutters to give some control over engine temperature. A modified windscreen, which would allow improved access to the Vickers gun, was needed, as was a rack in which to store spare drums for the Lewis. The Lewis gun's release lever was to be moved from the spade grip, to the pistol grip and the spade grip removed.

Triggers for both guns were to be fixed to a sliding sleeve fitted around the control column so that their position could be adjusted to suit individual pilots. The pilot's convenience was to be further enhanced by the addition of a small knob to the wheel of the tail trimmer, to make adjustment easier, and by fitting a throttle control to the control column. Provision for a wireless set was also requested and a small locker was formed behind the cockpit into which it might be fitted, although no such installation was made.

On 31 December 1916 Brooke-Popham instructed the Depot to have the modifications completed by 2 January, but although they did their best they lacked the resources to tackle many of them, and on 4 January Lt Selous flew A4562 back to Farnborough for the outstanding works to be completed.

A4561 had also undergone some modifications, the upper centre section being replaced with one having a larger trailing edge cut out. An overwing gravity tank was fitted to this new centre section, the port wing being replaced with a new unit, without the inbuilt tank. Extended sides were fitted to the windscreen and the exhaust manifolds were replaced, the new ones being 'L' shaped with their outlet at the rear.

A4563, the last of the three prototypes, incorporated the centre section and upper port wing removed from A4561 during its modification. The gravity tank had been removed from the wing, and replaced by an overwing tank similar to that now fitted to A4561. It was powered by the first of the 200hp Hispano-Suiza engines, No.7019/WD10111, which had been received from the manufacturers on 28 November 1916. The increase in power had been achieved by a similar increase in engine speed, to 2,000rpm, a 41:24 reduction gear giving a propeller speed of 1,170rpm, which in turn necessitated the use of a slightly larger propeller, although the higher thrust line meant that there was no reduction in ground clearance. The installation of a geared engine would have allowed the use of the originally planned armament, a single Lewis gun firing through a hollow propeller shaft, yet no gun, of any type, was installed.

A4561 with its windscreen sides extended. The exhaust outlets have been repositioned to the rear of the manifold. Author's collection

The third prototype S.E.5, A4563, fitted with a 200hp geared Hispano-Suiza driving a four-blade propeller at 1,170rpm. Note the higher thrust line and unusual head rest. Author's collection

A4563 was presented for inspection in the morning of 12 January 1917 and was approved within a matter of hours, Frank Goodden taking it up for its first brief test flight the same afternoon. Later flights included a 40-minute climb test on 16 January, an engine test the following day, and a 10-minute flight on the 24th to test a Claudel carburettor, which suggests that the original fitting may have been a Zenith Duplex, the alternative standard fitting for that engine.

Despite Albert Ball's hostility to the type, and some reservations regarding the effectiveness of its lateral control, the S.E.5 was clearly a considerable improvement on single seaters then in service, and further production orders were placed. A second batch (A8898–A8947) was ordered from the Royal Aircraft Factory, along with 200 machines (B1–200) from Martinsyde at Brooklands, and a similar number (B501–700) from Vickers at Weybridge. Other orders followed, a total of eight contractors eventually manufacturing the type, with Messrs Vickers using factories at Weybridge and Crayford in order to meet production demands.

A Tragedy

The modifications to A4562 which followed its service evaluation appear to have taken several weeks to complete and it was not until 26 January 1917 that it flew again. Two days later, on Sunday 28th, Frank Goodden took it up again for a further test flight. He took off at 11.00a.m. and 8 minutes later he was flying towards Farnborough from the Cove end of the airfield at around 1,000ft (305m) when the port wing cell began to break up and the aircraft crashed, Goodden receiving injuries which must have been immediately fatal. An inquest held at Cambridge Military Hospital, Aldershot, on 31 January recorded a verdict of Death by Accident.

An enquiry into the cause of the accident, during which A4561 was tested to destruction, took somewhat longer to reach a conclusion. Statements taken from witnesses suggested that the port interplane struts had become detached, allowing the wing cell to collapse, but no cause of this failure was immediately apparent. One theory was that the Constantinesco gear had broken, allowing a component, which could not be found in the wreckage, to fly off and hit the strut. A second suggested that the propeller had disintegrated, and that a piece of it had knocked out the strut.

Lt A.P. Thurston (later Dr Thurston MBE, but at that time on the War Office staff) conducted his own investigation into the cause of the crash. He visited the crash site and collected all the propeller fragments he could find, gathering a total that weighed only 2lb (0.9kg) less than the propeller had done when complete, conclusive proof that it had still been intact when the crash occurred. Next he recovered all the pieces of the wing, and laid them out on top of an outline of the wing chalked on a concrete floor. From this, he found that all the internal bracing wires were intact but that one of the spars had failed in torsion. An examination of A4561 (before its destruction) had revealed signs of incipient failure in the spar of its wings. Thurston therefore concluded that the failure was due to the downward torsion caused by the load reversal which occurred in certain manoeuvres and recommended that the compression ribs should be modified to include a plywood web which would resist this torsion. The drawings were therefore revised accordingly and the modification incorporated into all production aircraft.

Subsequently, William Farren, the physicist involved in the original design of the S.E.5, found that the stress calculations for the overhanging portion of the wings were incorrect. Rather than redesign the entire wing structure, particularly as the type was already in volume production, it was decided that the easiest way to achieve the desired factor of safety was to shorten the rear spar, reducing the overall span by some 15in (38cm), and to revise the rake of the wingtips to allow the original front spar to be retained. The Factory's drawings of the aircraft equipped with the shorter span wings bear the title S.E.5a, clearly suggesting that it was this feature, rather than engine power, which distinguished the two variants. However, the RFC's rigging notes, when eventually issued, were entitled 'S.E.5 – 150hp Hispano-Suiza: S.E.5a–200hp Hispano-Suiza' and since it was these documents rather than the production drawings which received the wider circulation, the latter, incorrect, distinction has become widely accepted.

However, despite new drawings being issued as quickly as possible, it was too late to incorporate the amendment into the initial batch of twenty-five aircraft built by the Royal Aircraft Factory and these were completed with the longer span wings of the prototype, making them the only true S.E.5s. Report and Memorandum No.491, published in April 1917, includes detailed stress calculations for the original S.E.5 (28ft (8.5m) span) wing, and states that the wings would bear 5½ times their normal loading (Folland had actually designed for a factor of safety of six), but the front spar would then fail under shear at a point just inboard of the strut position, exactly as appears to have happened to A4562. Since this loading could be reached when flattening out from a steep dive or at the beginning of a loop, the R&M concluded that a strengthening of the wing at this point (which had already been carried out) would greatly increase the overall strength of the whole wing.

Following the crash of A4562, Henry Folland, who was deeply upset by the death of Frank Goodden, resigned from the Royal Aircraft Factory. However, his talents were too good to waste, and he was soon persuaded to return to aircraft design, joining the Nieuport Company.

Into Service

The first of the Royal Aircraft Factory's production S.E.5s, A4845, was completed by the end of February and presented for inspection early on the morning of 1 March. It appears to have been subjected to a rather more searching examination than that given to A4563 only six weeks before, as approval for flight was not given until 7.50p.m. the following day. It was generally similar to the prototypes, after modification, with the compression ribs suitably strengthened, and it was armed as the ill-fated A4562 had been, with a synchronized Vickers gun and an overwing Lewis. Criticism of the original semi-conical windscreen had been addressed and a new fitting had been devised which was large enough both to allow full access to the breech of the Vickers and to afford the Lewis some protection from the slipstream when it was lowered to change drums.

After test-flying at Farnborough, A4845 was flown to the experimental station at Martlesham Heath for their opinion, which turned out to be less than wholly enthusiastic. Lateral control was considered to be poor, particularly at low speed, and it was suggested that it should be

Specification – S.E.5

Powerplant:	150hp Hispano-Suiza driving a T.28041 propeller
Weights:	Empty 1,280lb (581kg); loaded 1,850lb (839kg)
Dimensions:	Span 27ft 11in (8.51m); chord 5ft (1.53m); gap 4ft 7in (1.40m); wing area 249.8sq ft (23.23sq m); incidence 5 degrees; dihedral 5 degrees; stagger 1ft 6in (0.48m)
	Length 20ft 11in (6.38m); height 9ft 6in (2.90m)
Performance:	Speed at sea level 128mph (205km/h); speed at 10,000ft 114mph (182km/h); climb 14min 15sec to 10,000ft (3,050m); ceiling 17,000ft (5,185m); endurance 2½hr

Specification – S.E.5a

Powerplant:	200hp Wolseley Viper driving a AD662 propeller
Weights:	Empty 1,406lb (638kg); loaded 1,940lb (880kg)
Dimensions:	Span 26ft 7in (8.11m); chord 5ft (1.53m); gap 4ft 7in (1.40m); wing area 245.8sq ft (22.86sq m); incidence 5 degrees; dihedral 5 degrees; stagger 1ft 6in (0.48m)
	Length 20ft 11in (6.38m); height 9ft 6in (2.90m)
Performance:	Speed at sea level 134mph (214km/h); speed at 10,000ft 126mph (202km/h); climb 10min 50sec to 10,000ft (3,050m); ceiling 22,000ft (6,710m); endurance 2¼hr

Pilots' Opinions

'It was a beautiful little aeroplane. A lovely machine to fly, very easily handled, and quite an advance on any machine I'd flown before.'

Maj F.J. Powell, CO, 41 Sqn RFC.

'The last word in fighting scouts ... It could be looped and rolled and dived vertically without breaking up. Altogether it was a first class fighting scout, probably the most successful designed during the war.'

Lt Cecil Lewis, 56 Sqn RFC.

'I liked the machine immensely, as it was very fast after the Sopwith Scout and one could see out of it so thoroughly well.'

Capt J.T.B. McCudden, RFC.

'Many of us felt that it was the best fighter produced by Britain in the First World War. It was certainly one of the most beautiful little aeroplanes ever built.'

Capt W.S.Douglas, RFC.

The first production S.E.5. Its exhaust outlets are here at the front of the manifold. J.M. Bruce/G.S. Leslie Collection

How They Compared				
	Max. Speed	*Ceiling*	*Climb (to 10,000ft)*	*Endurance (sea-level)*
S.E.5 (150hp)	128mph (206km/h)	18,000ft (5,486m)	12min 36sec	2½hr
S.E.5 (200hp)	134mph (216km/h)	22,000ft (6,706m)	10min 50sec	2¼hr
Nieuport 17	103mph (166km/h)	17,500ft (5,334m)	12min 30sec	1½hr
Sopwith Camel	113mph (182km/h)	18,000ft (5,486m)	11min 45sec	2½hr
Albatros DV	116mph (187km/h)	20,500ft (6,248m)	13min 10sec	2hr
Fokker Dr1	103mph (166km/h)	20,000ft (6,096m)	10min 55sec	1½hr
Fokker DVII	117mph (188km/h)	22,500ft (6,706m)	11min 20sec	1½hr

modified to give more movement. The new windscreen proved as unpopular as the original had been, since it interfered with the pilot's view around the long nose when the tail was raised for landing. But despite these criticisms, the S.E.5 was, of course, a considerable advance on those machines, such as the Sopwith Pup and the F.E.8 which were then in service, and must have been welcomed as such.

The remainder of the batch of twenty-four machines was completed during March, with the last, A4868, being delivered on the 30th. Although their airframes were all similar, their engines were not – while most had 150hp Hispano-Suizas manufactured by Société Anonyme des Automobiles Aries, A4851's engine was built by the Hispano-Suiza factory in France, A4868's was made by Wolseley Motors and A4862 had received the engine that had been removed from A4561 before it was tested to destruction.

An early S.E.5, with the 'glasshouse' windscreen. Note the slipstream-driven fuel pump beneath the fuselage. The cylinder heads have small fairings at each end, which later Wolseley 'Viper' engines did not. J.M. Bruce/G.S. Leslie Collection

S.E.5 A8907 showing the high seating position originally employed. To the rear of the cockpit is the small locker introduced to house a wireless set. Although no such installation was ever made, the locker remained. Author's collection

Propellers varied too, some machines being fitted with type T28041, as the prototype had been, others with types T28051 or T28066.

As they were completed, these S.E.5s were sent to 56 Squadron, which was then at London Colney in Hertfordshire, under the command of Maj R.G. Blomfield, with Albert Ball as 'A' Flight Commander. The Squadron was preparing to go overseas for the first time. The first machine was received on 13 March 1917, and two days later A4850 was taken on charge and issued to Ball, whose poor opinion of the type appears to have remained unchanged for the following week he wrote:

> The S.E.5 has turned out to be a dud. Its speed is only about half Nieuport speed [it was in fact at least 10 per cent faster – author], and it is not so fast in getting up. It is a great shame, for everybody thinks they are so good and expects

a lot from them. Well I am making the best of a bad job. If Austin will not buck up and finish a machine for me, I shall have to go out on S.E.5s and do my best. I am getting one ready. I am taking one gun off in order to save weight. Also I am lowering the windscreen to take off resistance. A great many things I am taking off in the hopes that I shall get a little better control and speed. But it is a rotten machine.

removal of the large 'greenhouse' windscreen and the substitution of a small screen taken from an Avro, with the plywood decking ahead of the cockpit suitably amended. The adjustable seat was removed and replaced by a plain board, allowing the pilot to sit lower, with the Aldis sight, which had originally been fitted near to the top of the windscreen, gear suffered numerous teething problems, and to rely instead on the overwing Lewis with which they were already familiar.

At least one other machine, Capt I.H.D. Henderson's A4853, had adopted the Avro windscreen and modified decking by 7 April, when Mr H. Greenly from the Royal Aircraft Factory's drawing office visited London Colney to draw up these alterations

Albert Ball seated in the cockpit of A4850 at London Colney; its 'glasshouse' windscreen has been removed, the lower end of the Foster mounting now being braced by wires. A new centre section, with inbuilt gravity tank, has been fitted. The 'RA' markings on the Rudder and Elevators indicate that the 'dope' used was Raftite, to colour scheme A. Author's collection

Ball's modifications, which were completed by 2 April, included the removal of the Vickers gun, which allowed the fitting of a new petrol tank of slightly larger capacity, and the fitting of a second Lewis gun firing at a downward angle through the cockpit floor. The first modification may have made some kind of sense since his previous plane, the Nieuport, was equipped only with a single Lewis on a Foster mount, but the second made no sense at all since it was impossible to aim the gun. Other modifications included the being similarly lowered. A small head fairing was fitted to the rear decking. The centre section was replaced with one having an enlarged trailing edge cut-out and with a gravity tank built into it, the overwing tank thus being eliminated. Finally, the standard 700 × 100mm (27 × 4in) wheels were replaced with 700 × 75mm (27 × 3in) wheels from a Bristol Scout.

Although Ball appears to have been the only pilot actually to remove the Vickers gun, it would appear that many others chose simply to ignore it, for the Constantinesco before the Squadron left for France. On arrival at Vert Galant aerodrome they were promptly visited by the indefatigable Brooke-Popham, who immediately saw that many of these modifications were clearly advantageous, and the following day issued the following instructions:

1. The following alterations will be made to the S.E.5s of No. 56 squadron:
   (a) The present windscreen will be taken away and a simple 3-ply cowling with an Avro windscreen at the rear will be

substituted, similar to the sample machine I was shown yesterday.

(b) The present adjustable and armoured seat will be taken out and a simple board fitted across. This should be placed somewhat lower than the lowest position of the present seat.

(c) The gun mounting for the Lewis gun must be made to fit better and the slide lengthened by about 2in so that cover from the Avro windscreen is afforded when changing drums. No.2 Aircraft Depot will assist the squadron in making the extensions for the slides.

2. The squadron commander will be given a free hand as regards details of the above alterations provided that all twelve machines of the squadron are the same.

Please note that the Vickers gun is to be left where it is. The design of two Lewis guns in Capt Ball's machine is not approved, but this machine need not be altered back again.

3. Instructions regarding the removal of the gravity tank on the top plane will be given as soon as certain information has been obtained from England.

It would appear that Brooke-Popham then changed his mind about Ball's machine, for the following day it was taken to No.2 Depot at Candas for the standard armament to be refitted. However, no spare petrol tank with the trough for the gun was available and so the Vickers gun was mounted externally, on top of the forward fuselage. A Constantinesco gear was refitted to control the gun, and the 'L' shaped exhaust manifolds were replaced with those from a SPAD, which terminated aft of the cockpit, reducing the chance of the pilot being affected by the exhaust fumes. The lower end of the Foster mount remained secured in position with bracing wires, all other machines having the tubular metal arch straddling the Aldis sight which was first fitted to A4853.

On 14 April Trenchard wrote to the War Office requesting that the provision of new centre sections, with inbuilt gravity and radiator header tanks, should be made as soon as possible as it was beyond the resources of the aircraft depots in France to produce these items within an acceptable time, although a small number were made by No.1 Depot at St Omer. Response was swift, the Royal Aircraft Factory being able to report, on the 19th, that twelve centre sections, incorporating these tanks, were in hand and would be sent over to France as soon as possible. Drawings of the amended centre section were issued to all contractors for the type so that the modification could be incorporated into future production machines. However, it quickly became apparent that the centre sections would need to be further modified, as they proved to be insufficiently strong to absorb the recoil of the Lewis gun, no provision for the fitting of this weapon having been made in the initial design. Damage must have occurred even in test-firing the guns, for on 25 April, Brooke-Popham informed No.2 Aircraft Depot at Candas:

A view through the 'glasshouse' windscreen. Note the gravity fuel tank on the upper centre section. The Aldis sight is missing. Normally two spare ninety-seven-round ammunition drums would be carried in the wooden rack at the top of the instrument panel, in addition to that fitted to the gun (which is also missing in this view). J.M. Bruce/G.S. Leslie Collection

It has been found that the present centre sections are not sufficiently strong enough to stand the blast of the overhead gun. You will, therefore, send these centre sections to your Aeroplane Repair Section immediately they arrive for the following alterations to be made:

a) The central former rib to be removed and a strong rib to be substituted. The flange of this rib is to be quarter-inch ash, with ash flanges of corresponding strength; these ash flanges to be cut down in thickness where they pass over the main spars so that the height of the gun mounting remains the same.

b) Three-ply to be put on as covering over the top of the centre section between the front and rear spars. Fabric to be placed over the three-ply and continued back to the trailing edge.

Details of this modification were communicated to the Royal Aircraft Factory, and revised drawings issued so that the centre sections of future production machines could be similarly strengthened. The amendment was not made retrospective, however, since completed machines could continue to be modified at the depot, and it was not until October 1917 that aircraft left their respective factories with the modified centre section, the first machines thus strengthened being B31 (Martinsyde), B561 (Vickers, Weybridge), B8231 (Austin) and C5301 (Vickers, Crayford).

Meanwhile, on 22 April 1917, 56 Squadron was judged to be ready to fly its first patrols, although pilots were strictly forbidden to cross the lines on their first outing. Ball engaged an Albatros two-seater, but broke off when it dived for home. Early the following day he scored the Squadron's first victory whilst flying a lone patrol in his Nieuport, and later that morning scored the S.E.5's first victory too, when he shot down an Albatros Scout. After several combats, from which he eventually emerged victorious but with his aircraft shot about, Ball's opinion of the S.E.5 began to improve, since the S.E.5 never let him down. By the end of the month the Squadron's score stood at seven enemy aircraft destroyed and five driven down out of control, with the loss of only one of their own pilots, Lt Kay.

Unfortunately, a far greater loss occurred on 7 May when after a day of rainstorms, and with the sky still heavily clouded, 56 Squadron was ordered to fly an evening patrol, eleven aircraft taking off at 5.30p.m. Frustrated by a day of inactivity the enemy were also out in force and a number of combats occurred, as a result of which 56 Squadron got split up, its pilots tired and reaching the end of their fuel, as they made their way home individually. Five aircraft landed safely back at Vert Galant and two landed at other airfields; two pilots, Capt Meintzes, and Lt Leach, were wounded, and two, Capts Albert Ball and Chaworth-Masters, were eventually posted missing. In fact, Chaworth-Masters had been shot down and killed by Ltn Karl Menckoff of *Jasta* 3, whilst Ball had crashed near Annouellin. Credit for bringing down Britain's leading ace was claimed by Lothar Von Richtofen, whom Ball had certainly engaged in combat that evening, but the real cause of the crash in which Albert Ball died may never be known.

The Lewis gun lowered on the Foster mount so that the ammunition drum could be changed. This was never an easy operation in gloves, and in a 120mph (193km/h) slipstream. Author's collection

Unidentified S.E.5a with the four-blade propeller used with the 1,170rpm geared engine. Author's collection

Whatever the circumstances of Ball's death the war had to go on and replacement pilots, including Captains Bowman and Prothero, and replacement aircraft were immediately sent to return the Squadron to full strength.

On 11 June 56 Squadron, which was still the only S.E.5 unit in France, received its first 200hp machine. Remarkably, this was A4563, the third prototype, testing of which had been suspended following the fatal crash of its sister ship, A4562, at the end of January. By 22 May, when it next took to the air, it had been extensively modified to incorporate not only the remedial modifications made as a result of Goodden's crash and those carried out to 56 Squadron's machines, but also one or two which were introduced with the Royal Aircraft Factory's second production batch (A8898–A8947), including the new shorter span wings, and the provision of twin banks of radiator shutters, controlled by the pilot. One non-standard feature was the headrest fairing, which was curved in profile. The engine had been changed, presumably because the one installed initially had long since been used elsewhere, and a four-blade propeller fitted. On 29 May, following test-flying at Farnborough, it had been taken to the recently formed Aeroplane and Armament Experimental Establishment at Martlesham Heath, where it was received far more favourably than the first production S.E.5, the smaller windscreen and radiator shutters receiving due praise. A4563 was equally favourably received by 56 Squadron, with whom it served until 29 September, when, damaged in combat, it was returned to the Depot, where it was repaired and assigned to 84 Squadron. It was eventually struck off charge on 25 February 1918 after suffering irreparable damage when its undercarriage collapsed on take-off.

Production Continues

Further modifications, largely resulting from experience in service, were incorporated in the second batch of aircraft built by the Royal Aircraft Factory, although these initially had the large windscreens and over-wing gravity tanks, which were replaced by the Depot in France before the planes were sent to a squadron. The machines built by other contractors appear to have all incorporated the modifications introduced by 56 Squadron, completion of the earliest examples being somewhat delayed as a result. Concerned that the reduction in aileron area brought about by the revised wing-tip shape would adversely affect the aircraft's already marginal lateral control, the Factory conducted a number of experiments aimed at bringing about the necessary improvement, the most successful of which was to shorten the control cranks by 15 per cent. Tested by Capt Roderic Hill and Lts Armstrong and Noakes, this gave significantly better lateral control than that of the first production machines, although all three pilots still considered there to be scope for further improvement.

Other improvements included the provision of radiator shutters, controlled by the pilot, and the replacement of the slip-stream-driven fuel pump by a mechanical pump. In addition, the undercarriage legs were modified to move the wheels forward by 1½in (3.8cm) to improve stability when landing. The throttle control mounted on the control column, which had proved pointless, was eliminated, and a circular hand grip was fitted to the top of the column, with separate triggers for each gun side by side in its centre, allowing the pilot to fire either or both guns at will.

A8898, the first aircraft from the Factory's second batch, was finished, ready for inspection on 18 April 1917, less than three weeks after completion of the first batch, and was test-flown two days later. It was quickly sent to France, joining 56 Squadron as a replacement aircraft, and was flown by Albert Ball on 1 May. It was fitted with a 150hp Hispano-Suiza engine, licence-built by Wolseley, the majority of the batch having engines from the same source, although that fitted to A8917 was built by the parent company. A8922, the twenty-fifth machine, was completed by 25 May, giving a production rate of almost five aircraft a week, which was better than many contractors could achieve. However, the next example, A8923, was not completed until five days later, this being the first of the batch to be fitted with a 200hp geared engine; around half of the remainder were similarly equipped, their engines being early examples built under licence by Peugeot and Wolseley Motors. Performance, thus powered, was so much improved, as demonstrated by A4563, that it had been decided that this should be the standard engine for all future machines. Clearly, there was no doubt that such engines would be readily available, as many thousands had already been placed on order, not only from the Hispano-Suiza Company itself, but from numerous subcontractors including Brasier,

S.E.5as under construction in the Vickers (Weybridge) factory. Brooklands Museum

Production

S.E.5:
A4561–A4563: A4845–A4845 – Royal Aircraft Factory.

S.E.5a:
A8898–A8947; B4851–4900;C1051–C1150; D7001–D7050; (rebuilds – D7025 on believed cancelled) – Royal Aircraft Factory.
C1751–C1950; E5937–E6036; H674–H733 (cancelled from H711) – Air Navigation Co.
B8231–B8580; C8661–C9310; E5637–5936; F7951–F8200; H5291–H5540. (cancelled) – Austin.
C1751–C1950 – Bleriot.
B1–B200; D3911–D4010; E3154–3253; F5249–F5348; F8321–F8420 (cancelled) – Martinsyde.
C5301–C5450; D301–D450; D8431–D8580; F551–F615 – Vickers, Crayford.
B501–B700; C9486–C9635; D201–D300; D3426–D3575; D5951–D6200; E1251–E1400; E3904–E4103; F5449–F5698; F8946–F9145 – Vickers, Weybridge.
B1001–B1100; (cancelled) – Whitehead.
C6351–C6500; D6851–D7000; F851–F950; F7751–F7800 (cancelled from F7782) – Wolseley.
B733; B848; B875; B891; B6496; B7733; B7735; B7737; B7765; B7770–1; B7786–7; B7796; B7824; B7830–3; B7850; B7870; B7881; B7890–1; B7899; B7901; B7913; B8791; B8932; F4176; F4575; F5910; F5912; F5924; F5956; F6276; F6427;F6431–2; F9568; H7072–4; H7161–6; H7181; H7247–54; H7256–61 – Rebuilds.

S.E.5b:
8947 – Royal Aircraft Factory.

Higher gear ratios turned the propeller faster and allowed the use of a two-blade propeller. Author's collection

Delauney-Bellville, Mayen and Peugeot in France and Wolseley Motors in England. Therefore not only were all future production aircraft intended to have 200hp engines, but, on 10 July 1917, the depots were instructed that any 150hp machines brought in for repair were to be converted to the higher powered engine before being returned to their squadrons.

Although a four-blade propeller (T28096) of coarser pitch, but slightly reduced diameter, was introduced for the geared engine, the higher thrust line brought the tips of the blades into the Lewis gun's line of fire. The solution was for the Foster mounting to be raised by fitting

An S.E.5a with the 'Avro' pattern windscreen. The Aldis sight is missing, although its mounting brackets are still in place. Note the raised Foster mount required to keep the Lewis gun's line of fire above the propeller arc when a geared engine, with a higher thrust line, was fitted. J.M. Bruce/G.S. Leslie Collection

One week's output from the Vickers (Weybridge) factory photographed on the finishing straight at Brooklands for publicity purposes. Brooklands Museum

two streamlined spacer blocks above the centre-section spars and extending its lower mounting by a corresponding amount. This placed the gun's pistol grip out of the reach of pilots of short stature, an *ad hoc* extensions occasionally being fitted to the grip as a result.

The additional weight of the geared engine, together with the slightly higher landing speed created thereby, placed a small but telling increase in the load borne by the undercarriage, and failures became more frequent, their collapse on alighting causing damage to the aircraft varying from simple broken propellers to near write-offs. On 13 July 1917 Maj Blomfield brought this weakness to the attention of the 9th Wing with a request that something be done. As a result, a wholly new undercarriage was designed, in which the forward legs were narrow 'inverted vees' of ash, faired together and having the appearance of a solid tapered strut, the rear legs were also of ash, and the wheel position was moved a further 2in (5cm) forward to improve balance. Officially designated the 'three strut undercarriage', it was usually referred to more simply as the 'wooden undercarriage.'

A 200hp S.E.5a with an unusual steel tube three strut undercarriage and flame dampers. J.M. Bruce/G.S. Leslie Collection

Although the new drawings were completed fairly quickly, as with the strengthened centre section the modification was not made retrospective, and it was not until almost the end of the year that it began to appear on production machines. The first aircraft to have the new undercarriage appears to have been B4897, one of the Royal Aircraft Factory's third batch (B4851–B4900), which completed its AID inspection on 20 November 1917, the remainder of the batch being similarly fitted. Other manufacturers introduced it as follows: Austin, from B8481; Bleriot, from C1825; Martinsyde, from D3911; Vickers (Crayford), from D8431; Vickers (Weybridge), from D5951; and Wolseley, from D6851.

In January 1918 68 Squadron's CO reported favourably on the new wooden undercarriage, and by April it had become the standard fitting for all new aircraft, although Wolseley later developed their own version, with a solid front leg. Unfortunately, America's entry into the war had adversely affected supplies of spruce and ash to other nations, including Britain, and alternatives had to be found. However, the substitution of Red Cypress proved unsuccessful, and in May 1918 steel tube undercarriages had to be temporarily reintroduced for some machines until a more suitable timber could be found. Towards the end of the war, the Royal Aircraft Factory developed a sturdy oleo undercarriage for the S.E.5a, but, perhaps because attention was already being focused on new designs for 1919, it found no favour. A steel tube version of the 'three strut' undercarriage was also developed, but appeared on only a few examples retained at Farnborough post-war.

Engine Problems

By the end of 1917 some 800 S.E.5 and 5as had been produced and five active service squadrons, Nos 40, 41, 56, 60 and 84, were equipped with them, although Nos 40 and 41 had only been re-equipped in November, having previously flown the Royal Aircraft Factory's F.E.8. Two further squadrons, Nos. 24 and 68, were in the process of re-equipping when the year ended, the former unit having received its first S.E.5a on Christmas Day. The reason for this seemingly slow conversion to the new type was simple, in that engine deliveries had failed to match airframe production and by January 1918 some 400 S.E.5as were stockpiled, complete except for their engines.

Delivery of engines built by companies based in France was understandably slow, such firms naturally giving some degree of priority to the needs of their indigenous aircraft industry, and so the War Office looked to Wolseley Motors to meet their immediate needs. Those engines built by the English company were designated the W.4b 'Adder', and differed slightly from the French engines in that they had slightly raised compression ratios and modified gearing. Although Wolseley was familiar with metric measurements and well experienced in engine manufacture, having previously produced Renault-designed engines, early-production 'Adders' performed very poorly on test, one breaking four crankshafts in as many hours' running, and a programme of progressive modification had to be undergone before Wolseley-built engines would perform satisfactorily.

However, some French-built engines fared little better, many of those delivered from Brasier having imperfectly hardened gears which frequently failed at speed. Indeed, so desperate did the situation become that in October 1917 those engines with soft gears were actually installed into aircraft and their pilots instructed not to run them at above 1,750rpm. Even as late as 8 March 1918 Brooke-Popham felt obliged to issue instructions that Brasier-built engines were only to be issued if no other engine with the 24:41 reduction gear ratio was available. However, the situation did generally improve early in 1918 when the first batches of 8,000 200hp engines ordered by the Admiralty the previous summer began to become available. Such resources were now effectively pooled under the control of the recently created Ministry of Munitions, with the dynamic Sir William Weir, as Director General of Aircraft Production, able to distribute them according to need.

The blunt nose contours and lower thrust line of a Wolseley 'Viper'-powered S.E.5a. Note the absence of cylinder head fairings and the wooden, three-strut undercarriage. Author's collection

Unfortunately, it turned out that these engines were by no means all alike. Some had the original 24:41 ratio reduction gear, which gave a propeller speed of 1,170rpm, while others had 21:28, 26:39, 35:59 or 28:37, all giving higher propeller speeds. These higher ratios were much preferred in service, for they allowed the fitting of a two-bladed propeller, thus eliminating much of the adverse torque of the four blade propeller fitted to the 1,170 engine. In the latter case, it was frequently necessary to fit a length of rubber shock cord to the rudder bar in order to relieve the pilot of the need to keep a constant pressure on the rudder bar in order to maintain a straight course.

In view of the considerable difficulties experienced with geared versions of the Hispano-Suiza engine, it was fortuitous that an order should have been placed with Wolseley Motors for a further 400 direct-drive engines. Although it had been intended that these should be the original 150hp version, examples of which had already been manufactured by Wolseley as the 'Python', somehow Wolseley misinterpreted the War Office's requirements and instead set about developing a direct-drive engine which would develop 200hp. This they achieved by an increase both in compression ratio and crankshaft speed, at the same time introducing several detail modifications which included a second oil pump. Thus was born the Wolseley W4a 'Viper', which made its first flight, powering B4862, on 23 August 1917. Two days later it went to Martlesham Heath, equipped with two sets of pistons giving alternative compression ratios of 5.6:1 and 5.3:1, the latter proving to give the best results. As might be expected, the Viper-powered S.E.5a performed at least as well as that powered by the 200hp Hispano-Suiza, and was quickly adopted for production, eventually becoming the most common power unit for the type.

Another engine considered as an alternative to the troubled geared Hispano was the dimensionally similar Sunbeam 'Arab' with B4900, the first S.E.5a powered thereby, being given approval for flight on 24 November 1917. A second example, B4898, was inspected on 2 January 1918 and went to Martlesham Heath on the 25th. Other 'Arab'-powered aircraft included B609, C1111, D7017 and E1366. However, after extensive testing and hampered by some teething troubles, it was not adopted for production S.E.5as, for as a geared engine it could never match the simplicity of the direct-drive Wolseley 'Viper'.

Early 'Viper' installations utilized the same curved top radiator as the Hispano-Suiza, since this had been designed with an ovoid hole in its centre to accommodate the differing thrust lines of the geared and direct-drive engines. However, this radiator had already proved to be far from satisfactory, frequently suffering from leaks, and on 15 September 1917 Brooke-Popham had noted that around 15 per cent of squadron aircraft were out of service at any one time simply due to radiator problems, and requested that something be done. As a result, a number of new radiators were designed, and it appears that several were adopted, for the later Hispano-powered S.E.5as show a distinct lack of commonality in radiator styles.

The radiator installation finally devised for the Wolseley 'Viper' comprised two separate radiator blocks, each with its own set of shutters, joined at the top by a header tank with a distinctive filler cap. This gave the aircraft an apparently squarer nose and necessitated the provision of a slightly deeper lower engine cowling. Yet 'Viper' radiator installations varied too, with different cooling systems being designed by the Southern Area Repair Depot at Farnborough and No.2 Depot at Candas, as well as by the Royal Aircraft Factory itself. On 5 March 1918 Brooke-Popham issued an instruction to the depots that S.E.5as were to be allocated to squadrons according to their radiator type, thus simplifying stores keeping and maintenance.

In a further experiment, B4862, the aircraft in which the Wolseley 'Viper' had been first tested, had its frontal radiator replaced with an underslung unit, which comprised two superimposed 'Viper' radiator blocks mounted transversely beneath the sump cowling, the nose being simply faired over. This installation showed no advantage, either in speed or cooling efficiency, over the original design, which was easier to produce, and so was not adopted. However, it is possible that the experiment was not conducted with a view to production, but merely to test the concept for possible use in other designs, most notably the S.E.5b which was then being developed.

Modified to test the efficiency of the underslung radiator, the nose of this S.E.5a has been neatly, but bluntly, blanked off. The radiator comprised two 'Viper' blocks, complete with their shutters, mounted together. Author's collection

Aircraft fitted with the Hispano-Suiza engine normally had same fairings at each end of the cylinder head where it projected through the fuselage side, which those built with the 'Viper' did not. Those machines which were changed from geared Hispanos to direct-drive 'Vipers' in service frequently retained the raised Foster mount for the overwing Lewis gun, even though the lowered thrust line had rendered it unnecessary, perhaps in case a geared engine should again be fitted in the future, but more probably because it was simpler merely to leave it in place.

Further Development

Even after the S.E.5 had been committed to mass-production, experiment and development of the design continued, not only in experiments using surfaces of differing sizes and shapes. Thus in June 1917, A4864 was fitted with ailerons of higher-aspect ratio whose reduced chord necessitated the introduction of a false rear spar from which to hinge them. These were tested first by Factory pilots, commencing on the 27th, and then by operational pilots from 56 Squadron who were then based near London on home defence duties. 15 July 1917 saw the first flight of A8938 after it had been fitted with an aerodynamically balanced rudder, together with a suitably modified fin, and by 18 September it too had the narrow chord ailerons. By the following week it had also been fitted with new elevators, their chord similarly reduced from 15in (38cm) to 10in (25cm), a modification improvement that in February 1918 the officer commanding the 3rd Brigade wrote to Flying Corps headquarters requesting that all future machines should have the new surfaces, but, for whatever reason, this request was not acted upon and the original 15in (38cm) chord elevators remained the standard fitting on contractor-built aircraft.

Despite this apparent rejection of a seemingly successful design modification, development of the S.E.5a's tail surfaces continued even beyond the end of hostilities. D203, one of a number of machines retained at Farnborough for experimental purposes, was fitted with a balanced rudder in February 1918. It also had the narrow chord ailerons and was flown with reduced dihedral, possibly in order to test the effect

A home defence S.E.5a with modified markings and flame dampers over the exhausts. Author's collection

the hope of improving manoeuvrability, but also as part of the Royal Aircraft Factory's continuing programme of pure aeronautical research. Increasingly aware that manoeuvrability was not necessarily improved simply by increasing the size of the control surfaces, the Factory staff conducted a series of which gave significantly lighter control in pitch. A number of aircraft from the third batch built by the Royal Aircraft Factory were fitted with the narrow chord elevators and sent to France, one of them, B4891, being assigned to Capt J.T.B. McCudden. They were considered such an of a similar modification occasionally carried out on active service in the hope of increasing manoeuvrability. C1063 was similarly rerigged, its dihedral being first reduced to half the normal angle, that is to 2½ degrees, and then to zero, but no advantage was gained thereby.

D203 crashed on 9 March whilst being flown by Maj H. Tizard but was repaired, still with a balanced rudder, and in August was fitted with an experimental undercarriage which incorporated twin axles, hinged on the aircraft's centre line. By 23 October it had been fitted with twin fins, the balanced rudder again being retained; however, as this installation was very short lived it was presumably not successful. A twin rudder installation was also made sometime late in 1919, but was quickly abandoned as its effect upon control was extremely adverse. Experiments with the S.E.5a's rudder continued as late as June 1919, when E5293 was fitted with a low-aspect ratio fin and a rudder whose curved outline gave it a remarkably Teutonic appearance. Inversely tapered elevators were also fitted. Comparative trials demonstrated that the original surfaces remained the most effective of all, and so the shape of those fitted to service aircraft remained unchanged, although a modification was made to the fin structure. It had been found in service that a high-speed dive might cause the leading edge of the fin to distort, bowing out to one side like 'a sail blown out by the wind' and so adversely affecting directional control. The problem was cured by the provision of an additional bracing wire on each side, from the existing attachment fitting on the tailplane spar up to the middle of the leading edge. These wires were fitted at the squadrons, as soon as new aircraft were received from the Depot, and although Martinsyde designed a new fin, with an additional vertical member, for all its later production aircraft from B61 onwards, the wires continued to be fitted.

A further structural modification, introduced early in 1918, also resulted from combat experience, this time of a more tragic nature. A number of aircraft, including B41 and C5334, suffered wing failure in a high-speed dive, the latter claiming the life of Capt F.H.B. Selous, who had prepared the original comparison between the S.E.5 and the SPAD. As a result, it was decided that the wing structure should be strengthened by the elongation of the box rib at the aileron cut-out, the omission of the spindling of the rear spar for 6in (15cm) either side of the box rib, and by a stiffening of the wing ribs aft of the rear spar. These modifications were introduced into production batches commencing with the following machines: B8477 (Austin), C1813 (Bleriot), C6461 (Wolseley), D330 (Vickers, Crayford) and D3501 (Vickers, Weybridge).

E5923 fitted with an experimental low-aspect ratio fin and rudder of remarkably Germanic appearance at Farnborough post-war. J.M. Bruce/G.S. Leslie Collection

A number of experiments were also made to the S.E.5a's armament, the first of which, proposed by 56 Squadron in July 1917, was the provision of twin overwing Lewis guns. It was presumably intended that the Vickers gun should be deleted, and the pilot thus have two weapons of similar type. An experimental installation was made to B4855, although the Vickers was retained, and was tested by 56 Squadron from 25 September 1917. Since at this time the strengthened centre section had yet to be introduced, the structural integrity of this installation must have been questionable, but in any event it was not considered successful and when, on 24 October, the aircraft was returned to No.1 Depot the standard armament was refitted. Later, 41 Squadron attempted to devise a twin Vickers installation, but this too appears to have been unsuccessful.

Another experimental installation, made to B4875 in October 1917 and intended for home defence, involved no less than three Lewis guns. An Eeman mounting was fitted into the cockpit, with triple Lewis guns firing upwards at an angle of 45 degrees, it having been found that this would give the bullets a near flat trajectory for ranges up to 800yd (332m). A new centre section with three slots in a 'Y' formation was fitted, the gravity tank being moved to the root of the starboard wing and transparent panels provided in the fuselage sides just below the upper longerons. The instruments were refitted on whatever surface was left, but reading them cannot have been as difficult as changing ammunition drums must have been, for even though the outer two guns were tilted outboard to improve access to them and the top decking deepened, the cockpit remained extremely cramped. Although testing at A&AEE, Martlesham Heath was scheduled for early December 1917 engine problems kept the aircraft at Farnborough at least until the following February, and there is no record of its ever reaching the testing station. It is possible that the experiment was abandoned because experience had shown that the S.E.5 was not particularly well suited to home defence, if only because its water-cooled engine required a 10-minute warm-up period, which air-cooled engines did not, making hasty take-offs far easier.

The upward angle of the standard armament was also the subject of some experimentation, and the first four machines of the third production batch built by the Royal Aircraft Factory had both their guns set at an angle of 7½ degrees. One of these aircraft, B4853, was issued to the CFS at Upavon in September 1917, the other three going to France where their unusual armament was

S.E.5a C1091 fitted with a variable pitch propeller seen at Farnborough in April 1920. Crown copyright

immediately questioned by RFC Headquarters, but it is not known whether it was modified back to standard.

The Factory's development programme also included what may well have been the first ever variable pitch propeller. The first example, fitted to C1134 in October 1918, was a failure, the blades constantly moving in their sockets, but a second version was more successful and was test-flown fitted to C1148 the following month. C1091 was also fitted with a variable pitch propeller, which it retained at least until April 1920, but it would appear that the whole idea was too far ahead of its time, and the project was eventually discontinued.

85 Squadron's S.E.5as lined up. The white hexagon on the rear fuselage is the Squadron marking, but the aircraft serial numbers have been obliterated by the censor. Author's collection

The S.E.5a in Combat

Notwithstanding any lingering criticism over the effectiveness of its lateral control, the S.E.5a was rightly regarded as a fast, sturdy fighter and a steady gun platform, this latter characteristic allowing its pilots to engage the enemy at longer ranges, with little or no loss of accuracy. It was the mount of many of Britain's greatest aces including Mannock, McCudden, Beauchamp-Proctor as well as Albert Ball, and vies with its contemporary, the Sopwith Camel, for the appellation 'Best Fighter of the War', although in the opinion of one S.E. pilot, the CO of 84 Squadron, there was no comparison:

> ... there is little doubt that the S.E. was the most successful of any of the single seater fighters that we employed during the war.
>
> The S.E.5 retained, in a large measure, its performance at high altitudes, which the Camel did not. And since the S.E.5 was very steady in a fast dive, which nine times out of ten was our way of making our attacks, this was an additional advantage over the Camel.
>
> When we were flying level with them [the enemy] in our S.E.5s and we wanted to get out of range, to clear a jammed gun for instance, all we had to do was to go into a dive.
>
> W.S. Douglas *Years of Combat*

RFC RAF Squadron Service

The S.E.5/5a is known to have been operated by the following units:

Western Front	Nos 1, 24, 29, 30, 32, 37, 39, 40, 41, 47, 50, 56, 60, 61, 64, 68, 74, 84, 89, 92, 94 Squadrons.
Middle East	Nos 17, 63, 72, 111, 145, 150, Squadrons.
Training	Central Flying School, No.1 School of Aerial Fighting, Ayr. No.1 Fighting School, Ayr. No.2 Fighting School, Marske. No.3 Fighting School, Driffield. No.5 Fighting School, Heliopolis. North East Flying Instruction School, Redcar. South East Flying Instruction School, Shoreham. No.1 Observer School, Hythe.

Maj W.S.Douglas (later Air Chief Marshal Lord Douglas of Kirtleside) took 84 Squadron to France in August 1917. Although initially formed in January 1917, it had only recently been brought up to strength and equipped with the S.E.5a, and therefore spent its first few weeks in France in training. However, its first active service patrol, providing escort for a flight of DH4 bombers, was also the occasion of its first combat victory, with Lt E.O. Krohn bringing down an Albatros Scout.

By 1918 single combats were largely a thing of the past. With aircraft formations becoming larger and more numerous, engagements with the enemy became more frequent, although often less conclusive, for this was the time of the 'dog fight', with a mass of machines wheeling and tumbling in the sky, all snapping at each other's tails. One such combat occurred on 2 July 1918 when a flight of five S.E.s from 60 Squadron patrolling near Villers Bretonneux spotted six Pfalz scouts below them, and dived to attack. The S.E.'s leader, Lt A.W. Saunders, concentrated his attack upon the tail-end machine, giving it a long burst with both guns, as a result of which it went down vertically and crashed. Aware now of their attackers, the Pfalz pilots broke formation so suddenly that two of them collided, and they too crashed. The fight then became general, a Hanoveraner two-seater also joining in, but no further victories were scored by either side.

Foreign Service

In addition to the many thousands of S.E.5/5as which served with the RFC and RAF, a small number served with the air services of other nations, principal amongst which was the USA. Following

Combats in the Air.

Squadron: No.85 | Date: 17th June, 1918.

Type and No. of Aeroplane: S.E.5A C1904 | Time:

Locality:

Armament: 1 Vickers & 1 Lewis | Duty: In search of E.A.

Pilot: Major W.A.Bishop VC,DSO, MC. | Height:

Observer: | Result: Destroyed 3; Driven down out of control; Driven down

Remarks on Hostile Aircraft:—Type, armament, speed, etc.

3 crashed

Narrative.

10-25 a.m. STADEN & HOOGLEDE. 18,000 feet.

(i) Between STADEN & HOOGLEDE, 18,000 feet at 10-25 a.m. I turned back a two-seater who was approaching our lines, finally closing to 75 yards. After 20 rounds he burst into flames.

10-50 a.m. SAILLY-SUR-LE-LYS. 4,000 feet.

(ii) Over SAILLY-SUR-LE-LYS 4,000 feet at 10-50 a.m., seeing 1 Albatross I zoomed into the edge of a cloud. Albatross passed cloud & I secured position on tail. After 15 rounds he fell and crashed just South of village.

10-55 a.m. LAVENTIE.(near) 2,000 feet.

(iii) After attacking (ii) I saw a two-seater E.A. quite low, I dived at him from East but he turned and got East of me. After 2nd burst of 20 rounds he fell in a turning dive, then crashed between LAVENTIE and main road.

SE5 -12

W.A. Bishop Major,

Effective though the S.E.5a was in combat, few pilots could claim to have shot down three enemy aircraft in a single mission.

F8085, built by Austin, was one of a batch bought by the USA in October 1918. Post-war it was shipped back to America. Author's collection

(Below) **Eberhart assembled S.E.5a (or S.E.5E) serial AC22-325 photographed in 1926. Its wheels and tyres appear to be non-standard.** Author's collection

(Bottom) **A Wolseley 'Viper'-powered S.E.5a in service with the South African Air Force post-war. It was withdrawn from service in 1930 and is today preserved in the South African Museum of Military History.** Author's collection

her entry into the war, in April 1917 the USA sent a commission to Europe in order to ascertain which of the current, and future, combat aircraft she should manufacture, under licence, to equip her own air service. The S.E.5a was selected, not as a front-line fighter, for it was recognized that by the time facilities for mass-production could be established the design would be approaching obsolescence, but as an advanced trainer. An order for 1,000 machines, to be powered by a 180hp direct-drive version of the Hispano-Suiza built under licence by Wright, was placed with Curtiss. A number of British-built machines were shipped over to the USA, along with the drawings, to act as patterns. The first Curtiss-built machine, SC43153, was completed ready for testing by August 1918, but such was the fickle nature of the American aeroplane production programme, that the contract was then cancelled. Instead, some thirty-five or so S.E.5as were purchased from the RAF in October 1918 and served with the 25th and 141st Aero Squadrons.

During 1922/23 fifty S.E.5as were assembled from spare parts by the Eberhart Steel Co., and these are therefore commonly referred to as the S.E.5E, although their maker's plate bears the designation S.E.5A. They differed from the original design in that their fuselages were plywood covered throughout, and they were powered by the 180hp Wright-built Hispano, usually with a short stub exhaust from each cylinder.

The S.E.5a was also operated by the Australian Flying Corps in France during the war, forming the equipment of 2 Squadron AFC, and post-war the Australian Government received a gift of thirty-five S.E.5as from the British Government, as the foundation of its own Air Force. These machines served with the Central Flying School and No. 1 Flying Training School, both at Point Cook, and with Nos 1, 2 and 3 Squadrons. Some were later fitted with an oleo undercarriage similar to that designed at Farnborough in 1917, the last of them remaining in service until 1927.

Similar gifts were made to the governments of both Canada and South Africa, the latter receiving twenty-two machines as well as the former twelve, including D8472, D8479, D8489, E3172, E3173, F9016, F9114, F9117, F9128, F9136 and F9139.

The S.E.5 also saw service in Poland in 1919/20, with some twenty-four machines flying against the Bolsheviks on the Ukrainian front. The type also made its way to Japan and to Chile, eight machines, C9182–4, C9204, E5814, E5958–9 and E5962, joining that nation's air service in 1919.

Colours and Markings

Production S.E.5/5as were finished in the standard RFC colour scheme of P.C.10 vertical and upper surfaces and clear doped undersides, with the P.C.10 overlapping by approximately 1½ inches (3.8cm). Rudders were striped with the national colours across their whole area, and roundels were carried on the fuselage sides, just aft of the cockpit, and on the wings. Initially, those built by the Royal Aircraft Factory had the wing roundels immediately inboard of the aileron position, thus placing them approximately at mid-span, but from C1051 on these were moved to the, by that time, more normal position of half a diameter inboard of the wing-tip. Complaints that it was difficult to differentiate between the outer blue circle and the surrounding P.C.10 led to the introduction from May 1917 of a narrow white outline around the roundel.

The application of the aircraft serial number varied somewhat in style, according to the custom of the company manufacturing the particular machines. Those built by the Royal Aircraft Factory had the serial painted on the fin in white, the characters being 4in (10cm) high, whilst those produced by Vickers had the characters in black, with an apostrophe between the initial letter and the numerals. Bleriot-built machines used 8in (20cm) high white characters, placing the initial letter on a separate line above the numerals in order to make enough space.

Squadron codes, consisting of stripes or geometric shapes, were usually added in white, frequently over-painting other markings, such as the small 'lift here' notices which marked the fuselage strut positions. Typical codes were the solid white circle of 60 Squadron or the hollow hexagon of 85 Squadron. 92 Squadron had three vertical white bars on the rear fuselage, whilst No.1 used a single vertical stripe ahead of the cockpit, and No.2 Squadron AFC had a white boomerang behind the fuselage roundel.

Many squadrons also applied Flight markings, usually by different coloured wheel discs, occasionally quartered with white; 60 Squadron went further, painting wheel discs, cowlings and fairings, then adding a coloured stripe to the fin. 56 Squadron combined both flight and squadron codes into one marking, a dumb-bell shape painted behind the roundel in red, white or blue.

Letters or numerals distinguished individual machines within each squadron, these usually being painted on the fuselage sides. Any other individual markings were officially discouraged but, given the individualistic nature of many fighter pilots, some painted pet names or other good luck symbols onto their machines. Similarly, head fairings were sometimes removed, or cockpit sides cut down, to suit the whim of individual pilots. At one time Capt McCudden had his S.E. fitted with a large propeller spinner removed from a shot-down LVG, which he claimed added 2mph (3.2km/h) to the machine's top speed.

A few aircraft, including D3511, which was flown by Maj Dallas, CO of 40 Squadron, were finished with an experimental camouflage scheme of irregular shapes of differing colours, which was applied over the original finish, partially covering the aircraft serial number.

Those S.E.5as operated by the USA during the war retained their P.C.10/clear-doped overall finish, but had American national markings applied. Each US squadron also adopted a badge which was then painted onto every machine, but these were far more colourful than the geometric shapes used by the British. For example, that employed by the 25th Aero Squadron, during its brief wartime career with the S.E.5a, depicted an executioner wielding a large axe.

B605, its engine covered to help protect it from the frost, displays the more colourful markings permitted at a UK based training unit. Author's collection

Final Developments

In February or March 1918 a two-seat, dual-control trainer version of the S.E.5a was created by the provision of a second cockpit, forward of the original. This conversion necessitated the removal of all armament in order to save weight and the reduction of the fuel tank capacity to a mere 17 gallons (77 litres) in order to create sufficient space for the second cockpit. The machine was used by the CFS at Upavon, and proved sufficiently useful that in September it was proposed that more machines should be converted, a project which was cancelled with the ending of the war. Similar conversions were carried out, post-war, in both Canada and Australia, the latter eliminating the fuselage petrol tank altogether and substituting two large gravity tanks fitted above the roots of the upper wings.

Early in 1918 the Royal Aircraft Factory produced a further modification to the original S.E.5. design, the sesquiplane S.E.5b. The prototype was created in the usual Farnborough manner, by the conversion of an existing aircraft, in this case A8947, the last of a batch built the previous summer. The nose contours were completely redesigned to reduce drag, the frontal radiator being replaced by an angled underslung radiator, the installation being similar to that tested on B4862 shortly before. The original Aries-built 200hp Hispano-Suiza engine was retained, although with its reduction gear removed to provide a lower thrust line which, together with a large spinner, further improved the streamlining of the nose. A curved head rest, similar to that previously fitted to A4563, was fitted. The tail surfaces, which included narrow chord elevators, were retained unaltered but the wing structure was entirely new, the upper wing being increased both in span and chord and the lower correspondingly reduced. The reduction in chord made the lower wing too thin for RAF 14 aerofoil section, and a new section, RAF22, was employed instead in order to provide spars of adequate depth and strength. The difference in span of the

S.E.5a B18 converted into a two-seat trainer. Few such conversions were made, most pilots having to make the step up from simpler trainers without dual instruction. Brooklands Museum

The S.E.5b, A8947; the radiator could be retracted for gliding. Author's collection

two wings meant that the interplane struts had to be angled outwards in order to meet each spar at the appropriate point. The ailerons were of narrow chord, the upper wing being provided with false rear spars from which to hinge them.

Thus modified, A8947 was submitted for inspection on 4 April 1918, approval being given on the 8th, with its first flight made on the same day. Extensive testing gave rather disappointing results, for although it looked far faster than the production S.E.5a, in practice it was found that the increased induced drag of the upper wing more or less exactly offset any reduction in drag offered by the new nose contours, and despite the new machine's far more racy appearance, overall performance showed no improvement over that of a standard S.E.5a, similarly powered.

By 9 January 1919 A8947 had been refitted with standard wings of equal span and chord, and was then test-flown to provide comparison performance figures. In this form the design has, occasionally, been referred to as the S.E.5c, but this does not appear to have been an official designation. The tests showed that the sesquiplane version had the lowest stalling speed and the best gliding angle, although this could only be obtained if the radiator were to be retracted. The equal span version had the lowest drag, particularly at higher speed, whilst the original frontal radiator, understandably, gave the most efficient cooling. Thus, overall, it would appear that Folland's original design remained superior.

Specification – S.E.5b

Powerplant:	200hp Hispano-Suiza
Weights:	Empty not known; loaded 1,950lb (885kg)
Dimensions:	Upper span 30ft 7in (9.33m); lower span 26ft 6in (8.80m); upper chord 6ft (1.83m); lower chord 4ft 3in (1.30m); gap 4ft 7in (1.40m); wing area 278sq ft (25.85sq m); dihedral 2 degrees 30 minutes
	Length 20ft 10in (6.35m); height 9ft 6in (2.90m)
Performance:	not known

Specification – S.E.5E

Powerplant:	180hp Wright
Weights:	Empty not known; loaded 2,060lb (934kg)
Dimensions:	Span 26ft 7in (8.11m); chord 5ft (1.53m); gap 4ft 7in (1.40m); wing area 245.8sq ft (22.86sq m); incidence 5 degrees; dihedral 5 degrees; stagger 1ft 6in (0.48m)
	Length 20ft 11in (6.38m); height 9ft 6in (2.90m)
Performance:	Speed at sea level 129mph (206km/h); speed at 10,000ft 117mph (187km/h); climb 13min to 10,000ft (3,050m)

G-EBCA (ex F9556) in July 1928, at which time it was powered by an 80hp air-cooled V8 Renault engine.
Author's collection

Post-War

By the time of the Armistice a new generation of fighters, designed around newer and more powerful engines, was already on the way, and had the war continued the S.E.5a would, eventually, have been superseded by the newer designs. It is scarcely surprising therefore that, in the greatly reduced peacetime Royal Air Force, it should have been replaced, largely by the rotary powered Sopwith Snipe, as the principal mount of the few remaining fighter squadrons.

A number were retained at Farnborough as test vehicles long after the war, and these continued to be employed in the development of parachutes, variable pitch propellers, exhaust systems and numerous other programmes, many of which were already in hand when the armistice reduced the urgency for their completion. Five S.E.5as from the RAE (as the Royal Aircraft Factory had become in 1918) took part in the 1923 RAF Pageant, giving a display of formation aerobatics which demonstrated their agility to the full. Their pilots

This much-modified S.E.5a still bears its British Civil Registration G-EBGL on the ventral fin. Its role with the Skywriting Corporation of America must have been purely promotional, as its exhausts have not been modified. Author's collection

were: Ft Lt P.W.S. Bulman, MC, DFC; Ft Lt E.R. Scholefield, AFC; Ft Lt G.S. Oddie, DFC; Flying Officer J.Chick, MC; and Flying Officer H.H. Junor, DFC.

As we have already seen, Imperial Gift S.E.5as formed part of the initial equipment of the air forces of Australia, Canada and South Africa, remaining in service until late in the 1920s. S.E.5as, many of them assembled from spare parts by the Eberhart Steel Company, served with a number of units in the USA until they were eventually replaced by indigenous designs. The type was also active in the war against the Bolsheviks in 1919/20.

With the ending of the war many redundant S.E.5as were simply broken up for scrap, but around fifty found their way onto the civil register, changing ownership for prices of between £5–£50. A number of these were fitted with engines that were simpler to maintain and less thirsty than the Hispano-Suiza around which they had been designed. Thus G-EAZT (ex E6013) and G-EBTK each acquired the air-cooled V8 RAF1a engine; G-EBCA, which was owned at one time by Dr Whithead Reid and which was finally written off in a crash in 1935, had an 80hp Renault, with which its top speed was around 65mph (105km/h); and the comedian Will Hay had an S.E.5a powered by a 120hp V8 'Airdisco' engine, a development of the Renault created by the Aircraft Disposal Company specifically for the civil market.

Some civil S.E.5as which had retained their original engines took part in the 'round the pylon' air races that had been a spectacular part of public flying displays ever since their introduction at Rheims in 1908. For example, the line-up for the 1927 Aerial Derby contained three S.E.5as: G-EBPA; G-EBQM, a Wolseley 'Viper'-powered example then owned by a serving RAF pilot, Flying Officer Allen. H. Wheeler; and G-EBOG which was flown by Dudley Watt, a

G-EBIC with its exhaust modified for skywriting. Today it is preserved at the RAF Museum, Hendon, London. Author's collection

skilful and daring racing pilot whom the press frequently referred to as 'Dangerous Dan'. G-EBOG was later fitted with a 300hp Hispano and modified specifically for racing, then being known as the DW1.

In July 1921 the universities of Oxford and Cambridge, whose annual boat race has long been one of London's major sporting spectacles, transferred their traditional rivalry into the air and staged the University Air Race at Hendon. The victor was W.S. Wilcox of Caius College, Cambridge, flying S.E.5a G-EAXU (ex F5333), the other finishers being, in order: G-EAXT (F5258); G-EAXV (F5253); G-EAXX (F5257); and G-EAXQ (F5249).

However, perhaps the S.E.5a's greatest post-war role was in aerial advertising. 'Skywriting', as it became known, was the brainchild of Maj John Clifford ('Jack') Savage, who first conceived the idea before the war. Whilst watching a display of aerobatics he thought it would be good idea if the aircraft's path could be marked out in some way. He therefore began to develop the technique of deliberately making smoke, taking out a number of patents not only on devices for generating the smoke, but also on a method of stopping it instantly so as not to leave untidy ends to the smoke trail. His first aircraft appears to have been the S.E.5a F9022 which he bought from the Aircraft Disposal Company at Hendon in February 1920, and which entered the civil register as G-EATE. This was modified for skywriting by extending the engine exhaust pipes to a single outlet behind the tail, the rudder being divided to accommodate them. Chemicals were introduced into the exhausts from a tank in the rear fuselage, and the exhaust pipes wrapped with asbestos insulation in order to keep the gases hot.

In 1922 Savage began the aerial advertising campaign by writing the word 'VIM' in huge letters of white smoke. Other advertisers included CASTROL, PERSIL and the DAILY MAIL. The letters were written flat, a sharp kick on the rudder being required to form the corners of such letters as 'P' or 'D'. From the pilot's perspective the letters were also upside-down and backwards, and as the success of the operation required more pilots Savage trained them in the technique by riding bicycles around the tarmac.

Towards the end of 1922 Savage turned his attention to America, and on 28 November wrote 'HELLO USA' in the sky over New York. The next day he wrote the phone number of his hotel, and as a result received over 7,000 calls, his first contract being to advertise 'Lucky Strike'. Thus was born 'The Skywriting Corporation of America', with a fleet of modified S.E.5as. An attempt was also made to introduce the service in Europe, Savage taking five S.E.s to Germany, where, as commercial aircraft, they were obliged to acquire German civil registrations.

Almost as soon as the smoke letters first appeared, a campaign started to have the skywriting stopped. Although legislation to stop the sky being used as an advertising hoarding was first mooted in the mid-1920s, it did not enter the statute books until 1958, by which time Savage's skywriters were long gone, for after a while the novelty of the smoke letters wore off, and people simply stopped looking up at them. The American corporation was wound up in 1927, its eight S.E.5as being sold off, whilst the British company, Skywriting Ltd, survived until early in 1930, when it too was wound up.

Three of Jack Savage's skywriting S.E.5as exist to this day: G-EBIA, G-EBIB and G-EBIC. The first of these, after masquerading as 'D7000' and then 'F703' is now restored to what is believed to have been its original service serial number, F904, and is preserved by the Shuttleworth Collection in Bedfordshire, appearing regularly in flying displays.

Preserved Examples

Original Aircraft:

F904	Shuttleworth Collection, Old Warden Aerodrome, nr Biggleswade, Bedfordshire – airworthy.
F938	RAF Museum, Hendon, London – static.
G-EBIB	Science Museum, Kensington, London (possibly ex-F937 or F939) – static.
A2–4	Australian War Memorial, GPO Box 345, Canberra, Australia (ex-C1916).
320	Museum of Military History, PO Box 52090, Saxonwold, Transvaal, South Africa (possibly ex-F7781 or 7783) – static.
AS22–325	USAF Museum, Wright Patterson AFB, Dayton, Ohio, USA (Eberhart-built) – static.
'B4863'	Currently Letcher and Associates Mojave CA. Converted back to SE5E configuration as it was when flown by Lindburgh.(Eberhart built – converted to S.E.5a configuration) – believed airworthy.

Reproductions

At the time of writing (mid-1998) at least three full-scale reproductions are believed to be extant in the UK with several more in the USA, and further examples are currently under construction. Known locations are:

Princes Mead shopping centre, Farnborough, Hampshire.
Yorkshire Air Museum, Elvington, nr York.
Brooklands Museum, Brooklands, Surrey.
Fort Rucker Army Aviation Museum, Alabama, USA.
Champlin Fighter Museum, Mesa, Arizona, USA.
Air-Sea-Space Museum, USS *Intrepid*, New York City, USA.
Owls Head Transportation Museum, Maine, USA.
Memorial Flight Association, Dugny, Paris, on loan from and built by John Tetley, Selby, York. To fly with Hispano 200hp. (Reduced scale examples are both too numerous, and too mobile, to be recorded in a publication of this nature.)

F904, beautifully preserved by the Shuttleworth Collection at Old Warden, Bedfordshire, where it still takes to the sky. Author's collection

A collection of 85 per cent scale 'S.E.5s' photographed at the 'Aerodrome 92' flying display at Lake Guntersville, Alabama. Author's collection

G-EBIC, which was sold to Mr R.G. Nash in 1937, was acquired by the Royal Aeronautical Society in 1956, joined the Royal Air Force museum collection in 1963, and, now magnificently restored to its original identity, F938, is on public display at Hendon.

In 1937 Maj Savage presented the third of the trio to the Science Museum in Kensington, where it was converted back to it wartime configuration. However, it has now been restored to its appearance during its period of greatest fame, as the Savage Skywriting flagship, G-EBIB.

Today there are, once again, several S.E.5as on the British civil register, and many more are registered in the USA. However, these are not original aircraft, but scale reproductions powered by air-cooled engines of around 65hp, and are largely home-built by pilots who cannot resist the desire to own, and fly, one of the greatest fighters of all time.

CHAPTER SEVEN

Conclusion

Following the Inquiry, chaired by Sir Richard Burbidge, into the management of the Factory in mid-1916 (*see* Chapter Two), a number of changes occurred, some in accordance with the Inquiry's recommendations, and others as a result of those changes. Although it was generally accepted that aeroplane design should be allowed to start, where an unfulfilled role was clearly apparent. At the same time, greater use was made of the Farnborough workshops as a manufacturing establishment and contracts were accepted for volume production not only of the indigenous S.E.5, but also of some private designs, including the Handley Page 0/400. accordance with the Burbidge Committee's recommendations. The increase in production brought about a similar increase in the demand for raw materials, the transport of which Fowler simplified by extending the Factory's internal railway system to meet the London & South Western Railway main line at Farnborough station, a project

The pusher F.E.9 was clearly obsolete even before it was built. Author's collection

discontinued and the Factory's attention directed solely at research and development work, this was, inevitably, a gradual process, with existing projects such as the S.E.5 being allowed to be brought to fruition. Some new projects were also

Mervyn O'Gorman's contract was not renewed, and on 21 September 1916 he was replaced as Superintendent by Henry W. Fowler, formerly Chief Mechanical Engineer with the Midland Railway, who oversaw the reorganization of the Factory in in which his former occupation must have been of great assistance. Fowler's tenure in office was comparatively brief, for his talent for organization was again recognized, and during 1917 he became Assistant Director of Aircraft Production at the Ministry of

Munitions, in addition to his duties at Farnborough. However, in March 1918 he took up the latter position full-time, the new Royal Aircraft Factory Superintendent being W. Sidney Smith, formerly Chief Inspector of Factories.

O'Gorman later joined the Aircraft Manufacturing Company at Hendon, once again working alongside Geoffrey de Havilland, under Holt Thomas. Many other Royal Aircraft Factory staff left too, some out of a sense of loyalty to O'Gorman, who had first recruited them into aeronautical work, some following a desire to continue with new design work, and others simply because the Burbidge Committee's report had made them aware of how relatively poorly they were paid when compared with people holding equivalent positions in industry.

S.W. Hiscocks joined O'Gorman at Airco, where he became Works Manager. Henry Folland, who had resigned from his post at Farnborough following the tragic death of Frank Goodden, had been persuaded to accept the position of Chief Designer with the Nieuport and General Aircraft Company. He was joined there by L. Hall, who had hitherto been manager of the Royal Aircraft Factory's Mechanical Engineering Department and by several former draughtsmen and designers, as well as by S.Heckstall-Smith, formerly the Factory's Assistant Superintendent.

In January 1917 F.M. Green, formerly the Factory's Chief Engineer, took up a similar position with the Siddeley-Deasey Company at Coventry, being joined there by J. Lloyd who had been partially responsible for the design of the R.E.8. John Kenworthy, Chief Draughtsman and designer of the F.E.8, left too, becoming Chief Designer for Austin Motors' aeroplane division. William Farren, whose research had been instrumental in the redesign of the S.E.5's wing-tip, eventually left too, although he was to return, as Director, during the Second World War.

The Factory's engine department also suffered badly from this migration of staff, with J.E. Ellor, the supercharger expert, joining Rolls-Royce, J.S.Irving becoming Chief Engineer at Sunbeam, G.S. Wilkinson moving to Napier, and S.D. Heron joining Green at Siddeley-Deasey. Heron appears to have taken with him the initial drawings of the RAF8, a 300hp, fourteen-cylinder, two-row, air-cooled radial engine, which Green had been granted permission to develop, and which formed the basis for the design of what later became the highly successful Armstrong-Siddeley 'Jaguar' engine. Heron, however, resigned in mid-1917 when J.D. Siddeley sought to interfere with his work, and the design was ultimately completed by S.M. Vaile.

This continuation of ideas that had been developed at the Royal Aircraft Factory in designs produced by private companies was fairly widespread in aeroplane design as well as in engines, and this too appears to have had the blessing of those in authority. One obvious example was the Siddeley-Deasey RT1, whose development from the R.E.8 has already been described (*see* Chapter Three). This employed the fuselage and tail surfaces, but with new two-bay mainplanes of equal span, the upper being considerably broader than the lower. Three prototypes were built, the first, B6625, having a Hispano-Suiza engine in a cowling reminiscent of that of the S.E.5, the second being powered by an RAF4a, and the third by a Hispano with an underslung radiator. Although it received a favourable report when it was tested in December 1917, it was not adopted for production, possibly because it did not represent a sufficient improvement over the machine it was intended to replace.

Another Siddeley-Deasey design with its roots in the work of the Royal Aircraft Factory was the SR2 fighter, the Siddeley Siskin. Based upon a design concept which might otherwise have been developed as the S.E.7, powered by the RAF8, the Siskin was completed ready for testing by July 1919. One example flew in the 1920 RAF pageant, but had to make an embarrassingly public forced landing due to the failure of its ABC 'Dragonfly' engine. The type later entered RAF service powered by the Armstrong-Siddeley 'Jaguar', developed from the RAF8 which was the Siskin's original intended powerplant.

Henry Folland's Nieuport BN1 was another sturdy looking little fighter with obvious connections to its designer's previous work. Powered by the Bentley BR2 230hp rotary engine, it had the general appearance of the S.E.4, and included a ventral fin and tail-skid assembly clearly 'borrowed' from the S.E.5. It was not adopted for production, that honour going instead to the similarly powered Sopwith Snipe, but formed the basis of Folland's next design, the Nieuport Nighthawk. This again used the S.E.5 ventral fin and tail-skid, and in addition was designed around components and fittings already in production for the S.E.5/5a. However, in common with many aircraft of that period it was powered by the disastrous ABC 'Dragonfly', and so was never able to fulfil its obvious promise.

The design staff who remained at Farnborough after the departure of O'Gorman seemed, for a while, to lose direction and a number of designs produced at this time appear to have warranted much of the criticism that detractors had constantly made of the Royal Aircraft Factory and its products. The F.E.9, designed towards the end of 1916 as a replacement for the F.E.2 series, was another two-seat pusher, powered by the 200hp Hispano-Suiza engine, and with the nacelle close to the upper wing so that the observer could defend the machine's tail without resorting to the acrobatics necessary in the F.E.2. This was all very admirable when the machine was conceived, but although the pusher concept was almost immediately rendered obsolete by the introduction of the gun synchronization gear, the design was completed and work begun on the manufacture of a batch of twenty-four. The first of these was completed in April 1917, and was test-flown by Roderic Hill, who found the controls ineffective. Service trials in June confirmed his opinion, and the project was scrapped. However, the Factory, perhaps rightly in view of its designated role of research and development, regarded the machine's poor handling as something of a challenge, and the three examples which had by then been completed were retained at Farnborough for experiment, numerous different forms of fin, rudder and elevator being tested thereon.

Despite its, by now, proven obsolescence, the Factory seems to have been remarkably reluctant to abandon the pusher concept and from the F.E.9 was developed the N.E.1, or Night-flying Experimental. Like the F.E.9, it was powered by the 200hp Hispano-Suiza engine and utilized a number of F.E.9 components, including the tailbooms, rudder and tailskid. The first prototype, B3971, made its maiden flight on 8 September 1917, and began service trials at Martlesham Heath on 6 November. Although the big pusher had a number of interesting and innovative features, including, initially, a searchlight built into its nose, these were insufficient to save it from a less than enthusiastic report, for it really offered few advantages over the F.E.2b/d that it was presumably intended to replace. Six prototypes were completed and used for numerous experiments in air defence and bomb dropping, but no production orders were placed.

The last aircraft to be designed by the Royal Aircraft Factory, the A.E.3, was also the only one to be given an official name, becoming the Farnborough Ram under a system of nomenclature introduced by the Royal Air Force during 1918. Intended primarily for ground attack, the A.E.3 was a development of the N.E.1, but with an armoured nacelle to afford the crew some protection from the inevitable retaliatory ground fire. Three prototypes, B8781–B8783, were built, the first two powered by the Sunbeam 'Arab', and the third by the Bentley BR2, but, yet again, no production orders were placed for the type, those responsible for equipping the Royal Air Force clearly preferring more conventional designs. Other designs, although possessing greater promise, were similarly unsuccessful in their bid to enter production, for good as they may have been, other designs proved better.

Contemporary with the N.E.1 was the Royal Aircraft Factory's only flying boat design, the C.E.1, which was conceived in February 1917 in answer to the growing threat to sea-borne supplies from enemy submarines. The C.E.1 was a two-seat biplane with a wooden hull having a single step, and was, almost inevitably, a pusher, its tailbooms meeting at the elevator spar in what was, by then, standard 'Factory practice'. Although two prototypes were built, and tested both at Hamble and the Isle of Grain, no production orders were placed for the type, the twin-engined Felixstowe F.2 flying boat being judged superior.

Similarly, the T.E.1 of early 1917 was to have been a two-seat fighter based upon a scaled-up S.E.5. It showed some considerable promise but, although three prototypes were ordered and construction started with some urgency, the project was cancelled before they could be completed, partly because the machine's intended powerplant, the 200hp Hispano-Suiza, was already in short supply, and partly because its intended role was, by then, already filled by the superb Bristol F2b 'Fighter'.

The Royal Aircraft Factory also collaborated in the production of the gigantic Tarrant Tabor, fabricating all of its metal fittings and providing facilities for its assembly in the Airship Shed. A huge triplane, its centre wing spanning over 130ft (40m), the Tabor was intended to bomb Berlin from bases in England. Its builders, W.G. Tarrant & Co. Ltd of Byfleet, were specialists in the construction of timber buildings, who, after mass-producing wooden components for other aircraft manufacturers, decided it was time to build a complete aeroplane of their own. The Tabor's original design called for four engines mounted in tandem (tractor/pusher) pairs in the lower interplane gap, but none of sufficient power were available and the design was modified to accept six

The intriguing, but unsuccessful N.E.1. Its wide track undercarriage was designed to facilitate landing at night. Author's collection

C.E.1, N97, at the Isle of Grain. The hull incorporated a 'step' (here concealed by the launch trolley) and a water rudder. P.H.T. Green Collection

The huge Tarrant Tabor at the western end of the Factory site prior to its fatally unsuccessful take-off attempt. Author's collection

napier 'Lions', each of 450hp, the additional two being fitted, as tractors, above the centre wing. Although started in mid-1918, construction of the only prototype, F1765, was not completed until May 1919. Despite advice to the contrary from the Farnborough staff, Tarrant believed that it would prove tail-heavy in flight and added half a ton of lead ballast to the nose before the first take-off attempt. This, combined with the high thrust line of the upper engines, caused it to nose over on its first take-off run, with both pilots, Capts F.G. Dunn and P.T. Rawlings, being killed. A sad end to the last service aircraft built at the Royal Aircraft Factory's site.

However, the field of endeavour in which the Royal Aircraft Factory continued to excel was that of applied research, its staff ever-ready to investigate whatever aeronautical queries might be brought to their attention. Not only did the Royal Flying Corps, and later the Royal Air Force, look to Farnborough for solutions to its problems, so too did private industry, aircraft designers such as Henry Folland, who had previously worked at the Royal Aircraft Factory, being especially conscious of the wide range of facilities contained therein. Thus, in addition to designing new bombs and bombsights, aircraft compasses and pigmented 'dopes' for differing theatres of war, the Farnborough staff carried out research into the optimum shape for interplane struts, and investigated the reduction in propeller efficiency which would occur in a tandem tractor/pusher installation such as that proposed for the Handley Page V/1500 or the ill-fated Tarrant Tabor.

A great deal of work was also done on the development of a parachute suitable for use in aeroplanes, that in general use by balloon observers, the static line 'Guardian Angel' being too bulky to be easily stowed in the cockpits of the day. Several types were tested, trial descents being made with each, and, although the test programme had not been completed when the war ended, research continued, albeit with reduced urgency, parachutes being first issued to RAF pilots in 1922.

When the ABC 'Dragonfly' engine, which was intended to power many of the aircraft being developed to replace those in service in 1918, proved seriously flawed, it was to Farnborough that the industry turned for a solution. Designed to give 340hp, and to weigh 600lb (272kg), production 'Dragonflies' weighed around 660lb, (300kg) yet could achieve only 295hp. More serious was the cylinder head cooling, or rather the lack of it, for during bench testing it was not uncommon for the cylinder heads to begin to glow dull red! This problem was overcome by the design of a completely new cylinder head, the RAF21TD, which was founded on the sound engineering practice laid down by Gibson and Heron before they left Farnborough to join private industry, rather than on the revolutionary ideas of the 'Dragonfly's' original designer, Harold Bradshaw. Unfortunately, the engine had been designed to run precisely at the critical torsional vibration frequency of the crankshaft, and with the cooling problems resolved, it became clear that after a few hours' running the engines began to break up. New pistons and a modified crankshaft did a little to alleviate the problem, and the only real solution was to completely redesign the engine. Fortunately, the Armistice removed the need for this particular engine, and production was cancelled. However, it had brought to Farnborough's attention the problem of torsional vibration, into which research was begun by a team headed by B.C. Carter, with a view to ensuring that future engine design might take this into account.

The formation, on 1 April 1918, of the Royal Air Force inevitably led to confusion over the meaning of the initials R.A.F., and so in June 1918 the Factory, adopting a suggestion first made by Mervyn O'Gorman some two years earlier, changed its name to the Royal Aircraft Establishment. This name was far more in keeping with its true role, for it had never really been an aircraft *factory*; indeed, during its entire 10-year lifespan, less than 600 complete aeroplanes had been built there.

The coming of peace, and the reduction in size of the armed forces, saw a similar reduction in the staffing levels at Farnborough. From a peak of over 5,000 during 1916–18, by mid-1920 the number of employees had been cut to 1,380, this not inconsiderable workforce continuing the programme of research and development which continues, in the relocated DERA, to this day. The Factory site, vacated in favour of newer premises on the other side of the airfield, is the subject of an impressive proposal for an aeronautical museum, preserving for ever the work of the Royal Aircraft Factory and the RAE.

Farnborough Air Sciences Trust

Formed in November 1993, the Farnborough Air Sciences Trust is a registered charity dedicated to preserving the main Factory site from demolition, and to creating an Air and Space Sciences Centre. Included in their proposals are the original Workshop buildings, the plinth of the 140ft radius whirling arm which was built in 1913 to test propellers, and the portable airship shed as well as many, more modern, RAE buildings including several wind tunnels. This site will house a major aeronautical museum, conference centre and library.

Details of the FAST Association, which supports these proposals, are obtainable from John Binge, 11 Coleford Bridge Rd, Mytchett, Camberley, GU16 6DH.

Index